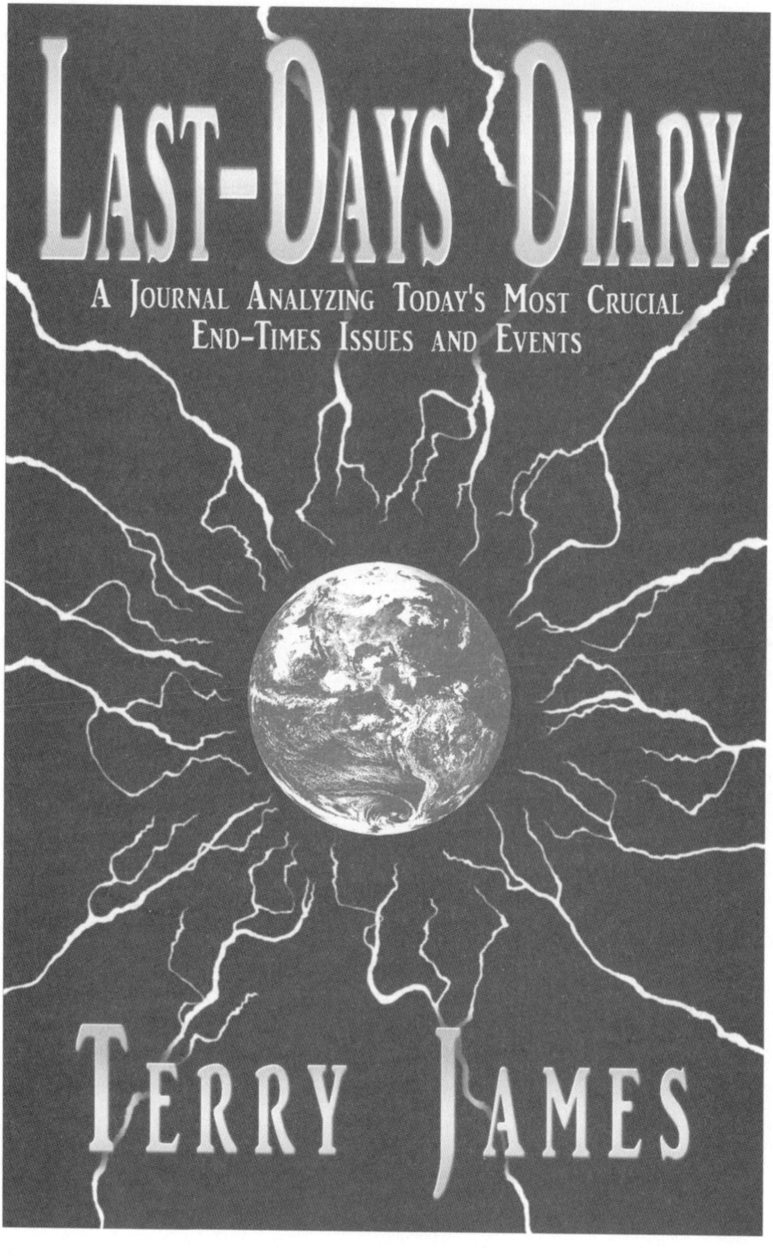

DEFENDER
CRANE

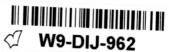

Last-Days Diary
A Journal Analyzing Today's Most Crucial End-Times Issues and Events

Defender
Crane, Missouri 65633
 Published 2012
Printed in the United States of America.
ISBN: 9780984825622

A CIP catalog record of this book is available from the Library of Congress.

Cover illustration and design by Shim Franklin.

All Scripture references are taken from the Authorized King James Version.

Acknowledgments

To Margaret, the love of my life and best friend—my greatest thanks for all good things of life we've enjoyed together.

My gratitude to Todd Strandberg—my family-close friend and partner, and founder of www.raptureready.com, the most highly visited Bible prophecy website on the Internet—for giving me the opportunity to write to such an extensive audience. And to that audience, I give my thanks for their interest in making our "Nearing Midnight" updates among the most widely read columns in America and the world.

To our editor, Angie Peters, the very best there is in our opinion, my love and thanks for her work on this book.

My thanks and love to Dana Neel, whose research expertise and assistance are indispensible.

Dr. Larry Spargimino's foreword for this book is deeply appreciated, as are his continued generosity and many kindnesses over the years of our close friendship.

To my Lord and Savior, Jesus Christ, my greatest love and devotion, although words are inadequate to express all He means to me.

Contents

Foreword

Dr. Larry Spargimino

Everyone has a desire to know the future. Some will even pay big bucks to get an inside tip on what's next. Astrological charts and horoscopes, along with prognostications from a variety of self-proclaimed prophets, are coming down the pike with increasing regularity. But in a real sense, tomorrow is already here, unfolding in current events that amazingly line up with the prophecies of the Bible.

Undoubtedly, the burgeoning of demonic activity and developments in Israel and the Middle East, along with technological marvels that only a few years ago were considered science fiction, make it clear that planet earth and its inhabitants will have a sudden meeting with the events and people chronicled in the Bible. They are casting a shadow from the future into the present.

Last-Days Diary labels itself as "a journal analyzing today's most crucial end-times issues and events." It is a wake-up call for those who are carnally at ease. This compelling volume reports news items for particular days in recent history. The reader gets an overwhelming sense of the reality of the unfolding of Bible prophecy. It is fact, not fiction. It is a hard-hitting book that will thrill those who have been studying prophecy for many years. It will also instruct and warm the hearts of those who avidly want to know more about one of the most intriguing proofs that the Bible is God's Word—prophecy.

Author Terry James is a well-known author. He has worked as a co-author with other prophecy experts, and has also served as a general editor of numerous books on Bible prophecy. His ability to connect Bible prophecy with current events is known the world over. A good example is the entry of March 8, 2010, "Big Brotherism":

> My friend has told me...that cameras train on his home from right across the street, atop a telephone-type pole. It is just a matter of time until all of England is under a surveillance system much more sophisticated and intrusive than our 1940s author, George Orwell, could have imagined. All of Europe is soon to follow suit, and we can see more than cursory evidence that America is coming into Big Brotherism's orbit of control.

May God use this book to keep the flame of prophetic hope burning brightly, and to help us to never forget the command of Scripture regarding the real focus of preparedness:

> We know that when he shall appear, we shall be like him; for we shall see him as he is. And every man that hath this hope in him purifieth himself, even as he is pure.
> (1 John 3:2–3)

Preface

Planet earth's news and entertainment media were for months ablaze with incendiary anticipation of the Mayan calendar doomsday predictions. Most everyone has become aware of the tremendous amount of ink, cyberspace, and documentary film devoted to the Mayans and all that is wrapped up in the fears that they were indeed onto something with regard to the end of the world as we know it.

Thunderous pronouncements come from constant media mantra-meanderings about the end of days as foretold by the Mayan calendar hundreds of years ago. Is this generation looking the end of the world squarely in the face?

Suddenly it is as if those of the news and entertainment world have forgotten that prophecy is, at best, fodder for fun-poking, and now believe they have credible soothsaying that is filled with foreboding. They often snicker at Bible prophecy and those who bring it into public discourse; they aren't snickering at the foretellings left us by the long-since extinct Mayans. Something of catastrophic nature, they are fearfully conjecturing, might be about to change life forever on the big blue marble.

Jesus—God the Son and the second person of the Trinity, thus the greatest of all prophets—spoke of the consummation of human history. He said the following about the end times and the signs that would be prevalent at the time of His return:

> So likewise ye, when ye shall see all these things, know that it is near, even at the doors.
>
> Verily I say unto you, This generation shall not pass, till all these things be fulfilled.
>
> Heaven and earth shall pass away, but my words shall not pass away.
>
> But of that day and hour knoweth no man, no, not the angels of heaven, but my Father only.
>
> (Matthew 24:33–36)

This is the very thing this book is all about. It is an attempt to carefully analyze and document month-by-month, week-by-week, day-by-day, hour-by-hour, and even, in some cases, minute-by-minute unfolding issues and events involving prophecies that Jesus and the prophets of the Bible said will precede Christ's Second Coming.

These incremental dissections of the news that traverses our monitor screens unveil just how near we are to the Tribulation hour. Since we are observably so near the time when Daniel's seventieth week will begin to hammer this fallen sphere with God's judgment and wrath, the student of Bible prophecy can know how much closer Christ's sudden intervention is in the Rapture of His church—all born-again believers (John 3:3).

It is true that we cannot know the day or the hour. But Christ has commanded those who claim Him as our Lord to be alert to the times and seasons. We are told we can know when He is near, even at the door.

My prayerful desire is that the progression of issues and the march of events examined and presented in this volume will ignite in the reader the passion to get the word out: Jesus is coming! Perhaps He is coming this very day!

Jesus tells us today, through His Olivet Discourse exhortation of nearly two thousand years ago: "And what I say unto you I say unto all, Watch" (Mark 13:37). Again the Lord directs our attention skyward when He says: "And when these things begin to come to pass, then look up, and lift up your heads; for your redemption draweth nigh" (Luke 21:28).

Last-Days Diary
January 2010

A Cry for Peace and Safety

January 4, 2010
Peace—The Mantra for 2010

Peace is more than the absence of war in which blood is shed while weapons destroy and death tallies take their toll. Peace is contentment, with prospects for a future free of worry that conflict will disrupt tranquility. There is neither contentment nor tranquility upon this fallen sphere.

Conflict is everywhere one looks. Unsettling issues assault the eyes and ears—the senses—of the world community. Anxieties and perplexities inundate societies and cultures, nations, and continents. The voices of humanity cry "Peace! Peace!" when there is no peace. As much as I would like to bring tidings of great joy—having just celebrated the birth of Christ—I cannot do so from the perspective of what is going on here on earth. The year 2010 just ahead looks bleak for a world of inhabitants who, by and large, reject the only One who can bring peace. The rejection portends the ascent of evil that is prophetically scheduled to grow worse, according to the apostle Paul, who said that "evil men and seducers shall wax worse and worse, deceiving, and being deceived" (2 Timothy 3:13).

JANUARY 2010

While seducers are on the scene in this generation at every level of human interaction, deadly conflict lurks just around the geopolitical corner in the region of planet earth foretold to be the host geographical area of man's most horrific war. The Prince of Persia foments rage against God's chosen nation, inciting the likes of Iran's Islamic leadership to create weapons that can destroy Israel, thus hoping to derail God's prophetic plan to install the King of all kings upon the throne of David. Alliances form that make the wary student of Bible prophecy know that the prophet Ezekiel's Gog-Magog coalition is coming together. One day the "evil thought" of Ezekiel 38:10 will come to a Russian leader's mind. All hell will break loose in the most volatile region on earth.

Politicians in America and in other nations lie to their publics, promising resolution to civil and economic strife and perplexities that have no chance of improvement, based upon those leaderships' self-serving motives and intentions. They seduce the publics they are supposed to serve, and instead rule with deluding words that flow from the mind of the great deceiver himself—the father of lies.

Religious leaders—even supposed Christian leaders—move their flocks in directions away from, not toward, the God of Heaven and His prescription for living a peaceful life on this ever-darkening planet. Indeed, the seducers of religiosity grow worse and worse, and the gospel light dims for America as it has been dimming for so long in Europe, out of which the American republic burst under God's great providence.

Still, the delusion that man-made peace can prevail over this sin-blackened world persists. The cry for peace and safety is already ratcheting up in the region prophesied to host the worst and final war of the age—Armageddon. That cry for peace and safety predicted to characterize the end of the age is front and center in today's headlines.

> The United States is drafting two letters of guarantee for Israel and the Palestinians to serve as a basis for the relaunch of stalled Middle East peace talks, Arab and Western diplomats in Cairo said.
>
> "U.S. special envoy George Mitchell will present two draft letters of guarantee, one for Israel and one to the Palestinian Authority during his next visit to the region," one Arab diplomat told the news agency Agence France-Presse.
>
> "The United States are hoping that the two letters will serve as a basis for the relaunch of Israeli-Palestinian negotiations but we don't know if they will satisfy the Palestinians who want a complete freeze of settlement activity before talks resume," the diplomat said.[1]

But, the cry for peace isn't working—not yet, anyway. One day the "prince that shall come" (Daniel 9:26) will confirm such a covenant of peace that will temporarily induce euphoria for a fearful world. But the present Israeli prime minister isn't fooled into thinking such a covenant is at hand.

> "There's no more time for excuses. It's time for action," [he said].... The prime minister expressed his hope that some progress would be made in the Israeli-Palestinian peace process in the coming weeks. The PA, he added, "is running low on excuses."

> [Benjamin] Netanyahu also said that Israel's most important challenge is Iran's attempt to get nuclear weapons.[2]

All of this gloom for the new year is depressing, you say. What a downer to begin 2010! The hope in all of this is glorious beyond imagination, however. It is the "blessed hope" of Titus 2:13 who remains in complete control. For the student of Bible prophecy, whose Lord is the King of kings, all of the foreboding for this world that is passing away means that Christ's return to make all things right on planet earth must be near indeed. The Prince of Peace is about to intervene dramatically into the disastrous affairs of man.

January 11, 2010
Brit Hume's Strong Stance

It was heartening last week to see long-time newsman Brit Hume witness to viewers the power of Jesus Christ. The journalist, now-retired television news anchor for *Fox News* who still serves as opinion commentator on occasion, spoke to a question about the troubled golf star Tiger Woods. When asked what advice he might have for Woods, a man beset by problems stemming from moral failings (by his own admission), Hume said his advice would be to turn to Christianity, because therein is offered forgiveness and reconciliation. Hume threw in that Woods had some linkage to Buddhism, although he, Hume, didn't know to what extent Woods was a practicing Buddhist. Hume intimated that there isn't forgiveness in that religion, but that there is forgiveness, after repentance, in Jesus Christ. That, Hume said, is who Tiger Woods needs.

Here are some of Hume's exact words of advice:

> The extent to which he can recover, it seems to me to depend on his faith. He's said to be a Buddhist; I don't think that faith offers the kind of forgiveness and redemption that is offered by the Christian faith. So, my message to Tiger would be, "Tiger, turn to the Christian faith and you can make a total recovery and be a great example to the world."[3]

To be frank, it was a shock—not because we found out in that revealing moment that Brit Hume is a believer, but that he would be so forthcoming when the question was put directly to him. Also, I was surprised that the others in the panel on *Fox News Sunday* and the host—whom I believe was Chris Wallace; I don't remember—didn't take exception. Hume's was an extremely politically incorrect thing to say. It seemed to me that the question was almost set up for presenting Hume's thoughts on the matter.

I do, as a matter of fact, believe it was set up—but, not by Wallace or Hume. I believe the God of the universe set up the situation. It was a defining moment in television history, in my view.

This is indeed an evil day. Television in general is at the center of presenting that evil to viewers in America and the world. TV news reports on the evil often seem to exude delight in and exaggeration of the evil for purposes of audience ratings.

So, it was with an "Amen!" that I greeted Mr. Hume's strong stance. He didn't equivocate. He just laid it right out there. "Jesus Christ is the answer to all of the problems of all of mankind" was the message viewers should take from that amazing, Holy Spirit-given moment of truth for this evil day.

Fox News and Brit Hume received accolades for the message, but as expected, the vitriol flew from the blogosphere and beyond. Hume was on *The O'Reilly Factor* Monday evening to again comment on the matter. The show's host, Bill O'Reilly, asked the journalist about the accusations that he was proselytizing. Hume said:

> Tiger Woods is somebody I've always rooted for....
>
> Now we know that the content of his character was not what we thought it was. He is paying a frightful price for these revelations. My sense is that he has basically lost his family....
>
> And my sense about Tiger is that he needs something that Christianity, especially, provides and gives and offers. And that is redemption.[4]

O'Reilly went on to indicate that while *Fox News* had received many positive comments, the anger was even more forthcoming. O'Reilly asked Hume why he thought the mention of Christianity can so anger people. The TV journalist said that it's a mystery why there should be such anger to Jesus Christ and His message.

I wanted to shout at the screen, "John 15:18–22! That's why the hatred!"

> If the world hate you, ye know that it hated me before it hated you.
>
> If ye were of the world, the world would love its own; but because ye are not of the world, but I have chosen you out of the world, therefore the world hateth you.

> Remember the word that I said unto you, The servant is not greater than his lord. If they have persecuted me, they will also persecute you; if they have kept my saying, they will keep yours also.
>
> But all these things will they do unto you for my name's sake, because they know not him that sent me.
>
> If I had not come and spoken unto them, they had not had sin; but now they have no cloak for their sin.
>
> He that hateth me hateth my Father also.
>
> If I had not done among them the works which none other man did, they had not had sin; but now have they both seen and hated both me and my Father.
>
> But this cometh to pass, that the word might be fulfilled that is written in their law, They hated me without a cause. (John 15:18–25)

Brit Hume is likely not well versed in readily being able to give Bible answers to questions like the one posed by Bill O'Reilly. Nonetheless, he—even if unknowingly—lived, in those few minutes on the two programs, before a hostile world the exhortation of Paul the apostle:

> Wherefore, take unto you the whole armor of God, that ye may be able to withstand in the evil day, and having done all, to stand. (Ephesians 6:13)

In prefacing the Hume interview with praise for the journalist, O'Reilly said that Hume is a Washington D.C. insider who is quite popular with his fellow "insiders." One must wonder whether that is still true after his stand for Jesus Christ. One thing is for sure, Brit Hume's stand for Christ is popular in the golden halls of the heavenly throne room.

January 18, 2010
Israel Betrayed by U.S.? Part 1

Israel today stands in the bull's eye of rage. This is true in the case of being targeted by the Jewish state's perennial antagonists, the Arab and Persian Islamist enemies. It is true in the case of the entire international community, whose constituent nations see Israel as the congestive blockage to regional and world peace. But it is the growing antagonism by United States presidential administration operatives that is most disconcerting while this beleaguered planet wobbles toward a time of unprecedented trouble.

As a matter of fact, that coming time of unparalleled strife that will bring all nations to Armageddon is termed "the time of Jacob's trouble" by Jeremiah the prophet (Jeremiah 30:7).

And, it is Jacob's trouble—the prophesied end-of-days dastardly treatment of Israel by the nations of earth—that will cause the God of Heaven to bring them to Armageddon. This is what the prophet Joel foretells:

> I will also gather all nations, and will bring them down into the valley of Jehoshaphat, and will plead with them there for my people and for my heritage, Israel, whom they have scattered among the nations, and parted my land. (Joel 3:2)

This will be the gathering of the nations of earth predicted in the book of Revelation:

> For they are the spirits of devils, working miracles, that go forth unto the kings of the earth and of the whole world, to gather them to the battle of that great day of God Almighty....
>
> And he gathered them together into a place called in the Hebrew tongue Armageddon. (Revelation 16:14, 16)

This will be the culmination of mankind's dealing treacherously with God's chosen people, the Jews. The promise made to Abraham by the Lord includes severe repercussions for anyone who would curse the progeny of Abraham, Isaac, and Jacob:

> And I will bless them that bless thee, and curse him that curseth thee: and in thee shall all families of the earth be blessed. (Genesis 12:3)

God's declaration is most dramatically validated by looking at twentieth-century history. Adolf Hitler and the Nazi regime made hatred of and genocide against the Jew their focus of the unalloyed evil they spewed. The ashes of the Führer and of his Nazi colleagues are scattered in ignominious disgrace across the landscape that Josef Goebbels and the Nazi propagandists arrogantly boasted would be *über alles*—the all-powerful homeland for their thousand-year Reich.

Any consideration in research of Germany's history involving the last two years of World War II and the years immediately following that most terrible of earth's conflicts to that point must acknowledge that it was as if the very wrath of God was upon the nation. Such documentation includes black-and-white film footage of German men and women forced by Allied Commander General Dwight D. Eisenhower to walk by the skeletal remains of thousands of Jewish corpses—thus, Eisenhower stated, so that the German people and the world would never forget the Holocaust. Its aftermath would forever be recorded.

Yet today, even mainstream news journalists are observably fuzzy-minded in consideration of the genocide that took perhaps 6 million Jewish lives as well as the lives of other peoples. They show their loss of memory by not jumping full force down the throats of diabolists like Iranian dictator Mahmoud Ahmadinejad, who regurgitates the lie that the Holocaust is a fable conjured by the Jews of the world. Rarely is there a repudiation of such blatant lies coming from the would-be destroyers of the Jewish state and the Jewish people.

Tragically, the refusal to educate generations subsequent to the time of World War II on the truth about the insane treatment of the house of Israel is leading to a future time of even greater atrocities, thus judgment, according to God's prophetic Word. The God of Heaven will react violently, according to Bible prophecy—more violently, even, than He reacted to the death-dealing of the Nazi demoniacs:

> The burden of the word of the LORD for Israel, saith the LORD, who stretcheth forth the heavens, and layeth the foundation of the earth, and formeth the spirit of man within him.
>
> Behold, I will make Jerusalem a cup of trembling unto all the peoples round about, when they shall be in the siege both against Judah and against Jerusalem.

> And in that day will I make Jerusalem a burdensome stone for all peoples; all that burden themselves with it shall be cut in pieces, though all the people of the earth be gathered together against it....
>
> And it shall come to pass, in that day, that I will seek to destroy all the nations that come against Jerusalem. (Zechariah 12:1–3, 9).

We come to the question posed by this article's title: "Israel Betrayed by U.S.?" The words are in the form of a question because like so much of this American administration's dealings, the "transparency" presidential candidate Barack Obama and then President Obama promised is not forthcoming. Obama's intended dealing with Israel is wrapped in an impenetrable fog of political doublespeak. Here is a news brief to begin pointing out the administration's not-so-transparent thinking regarding the U.S./Israeli relationship for the future:

> U.S. President Barack Obama's special Middle East envoy, George Mitchell, threatened late last week to withhold financial aid to Israel if the Jewish state does not accept demanded concessions to get the stalled peace process back on track.[5]

Next week, we will look into whether America, the nation almost certainly brought into existence to stand with His chosen people during Israel's rebirth into modernity, is leading the way into setting up the worldwide anti-Israel marginalization prophesied by Zechariah.

Terry James

JANUARY 2010

January 25, 2010
Israel Betrayed by U.S.? Part 2

Refusal of the current American presidential administration to acknowledge that God has any say one way or the other in the affairs of man, much less any business meddling in the conduct of the American State Department's dealing with Israel and its antagonists, is a foregone conclusion. After all, Mr. Obama has himself stated that America is not a Christian nation.

I must say that I agree with the president on that one point. The United States was never a "Christian" nation, in the sense that America turned en masse to total commitment to following Jesus Christ. That has never happened. However, this country, since its earliest stages of planning by the Founding Fathers, has had woven into its national documents of inception Judeo-Christian principles of God's prescription for conducting life and government.

Based upon that easily provable truth—because all one has to do is to cursorily scan the founding documents to understand biblical influence—it's easy to know that America is a nation under providential watchfulness, to say the very least. God, in starkly plain language, spoke through prophetic omniscience to what will happen when anyone, be it individual or corporate, deals treacherously with His chosen people. Therefore, for anyone—including the president of the United States or any other member of the government of this nation—to ignore what is said about interacting with Israel in the Bible, from which the Founding Fathers so obviously gleaned the wisdom to form this nation, is foolhardy.

I realize that stating that governmental leaders don't recognize God in their governing isn't a profound revelation, because all of humanistic government ignores the Creator of all things. I just wanted to get the fact stated as to the real crux of the problem regarding the lack of lasting peace in the Middle East and the world. The administration and the State Department, it is obvious, give God's Word on the matter of Israel no weight whatsoever in considering policy toward the Jewish state. They forge ahead, setting timelines for producing a two-state solution to the "Palestinian problem" as they see it.

Mideast envoy George Mitchell recently stated that he saw the problem of Israel's making peace with Palestinian leadership as something that must be done within two years. The former Senate majority leader, chosen by President Obama to deal with the differences between the Palestinian Authority and Israeli leadership, made it clear how he—thus, how the Obama administration—views the hold-up to peace in the region.

In an interview with acclaimed broadcaster and interviewer Charlie Rose just prior to Mitchell's departure for Israel, Mitchell was asked what leverage the U.S. has to get Israel to comply with Arab and international demands. He answered, "Under American law, the United States can withhold support on loan guarantees to Israel."[6]

Although a senior State Department *faux pas* fireman, speaking with anonymity, said that Mitchell's remarks were not meant as threats to Israel if compliance with American and international concession demands were not met, Israeli leadership wasn't buying. Israeli Finance Minister Yuval Steinitz bluntly let it be known that Obama, Mitchell, and the U.S. State Department could keep their money. He said that Israel wouldn't be needing loan guarantees because Israel wouldn't be borrowing. The Jewish state, he said, had already raised enough money for foreseeable needs.

JANUARY 2010

All of the back-pedaling the Obama administration can do cannot obfuscate the truth. It is trying to hide its disdain for Israel's perceived obstinacy in preventing this president from having a clear pathway to establishing the desired two-state configuration.

U.S. Secretary of State Hillary Clinton recently praised Israel's decision to unilaterally make a gesture of goodwill toward the Palestinians by implementing a partial freeze on establishing new settlements. However, Israel is always met with intransigence when dealing with the Palestinian Authority, as with most all among the Islamic community. The Israeli leadership is growing weary of the one-sided abusiveness, and of the pressures from the American and international leaders who insist Israel is the problem in disrupting the "Roadmap to Peace."

Israeli Prime Minister Benjamin Netanyahu, in expressing his feelings on the matter, said, "It is the Palestinian Authority that needs to change its ways—certainly not the Israeli government."[7]

Israel's decision to go ahead with settlements then brought immediate, not-so-veiled threats by envoy Mitchell. There is no doubt that the former senator's tone and remarks reflect the mindset of the president and those around him. They see the Jewish state as the holdup to Obama getting glory from making the perpetually elusive peace the international community seeks.

Has Israel been betrayed by the U.S.? It seems for now that substantial influence within the U.S. Congress is saying, "No."

> Visiting senior U.S. senators told their Israeli hosts on Sunday that they disapprove of the Obama administra-

tion's attempt to pressure Israel by threatening to withhold aid, and vowed they would never let that happen.

Senator John McCain told a Jerusalem press conference that he expects Obama to explicitly announce that his administration is not planning to alter America's policy regarding financial aid to Israel.

Senator Joe Lieberman promised that even if Obama did try to use U.S. financial aid as leverage, Congress would never approve such a measure.

McCain and Lieberman were also joined by senators John Thune and John Barrasso.[8]

If America joins the rest of earth's nations in the gathering against Israel, as prophesied in Zechariah12:1–3, her betrayal will mean America's doom. All nations who come against the Jewish state, God says, will be cut into pieces. Israel, on the other hand, will remain no matter what, the God of Heaven declares in the strongest possible terminology:

> Thus saith the LORD, who giveth the sun for a light by day, and the ordinances of the moon and of the stars for a light by night, who divideth the sea when its waves roar; The LORD of hosts is his name:
>
> If those ordinances depart from before me, saith the LORD, then the seed of Israel also shall cease from being a nation before me forever. (Jeremiah 31:35–36)

FEBRUARY 2010

Antichrist's Launching Pad

February 1, 2010
Antichrist's Launching Pad

Jesus said in His Olivet Discourse, as recorded in the Gospel according to Luke, that "distress of nations, with perplexity" would be "upon the earth" (Luke 21:25). Moving forward into 2010, it becomes increasingly obvious that peace in the Middle East is foremost on the minds of the leaders of the major world powers. Distress over the possibility, even the probability, that nuclear conflict might eventuate in the region causes perplexity of the most portentous sort.

Absence of peace in the world, and particularly in the region surrounding modern Israel, creates at this late moment in the fleeting age a vacuum into which the prophesied end-of-days leader will one day vault to power. Antichrist will climb a platform of peace upon which to launch his most terrible campaign of conquest. We get some idea of this supernaturally imbued man's spectacular rise and reign through the Old Testament prophet Daniel:

> And in the latter time of their kingdom, when the transgressors are come to the full, a king of fierce countenance, and understanding dark sentences, shall stand up.

> And his power shall be mighty, but not by his own power; and he shall destroy wonderfully, and shall prosper, and practice, and shall destroy the mighty and the holy people.
>
> And through his policy also he shall cause craft to prosper in his hand; and he shall magnify himself in his heart, and by peace shall destroy many. (Daniel 8:23–25a)

It is a strange, deadly peace that is prophesied to serve as launching pad for the "beast," as he is termed in Revelation 13. Paul, the apostle and prophet, gave dire warning about that esoteric peace that will pervade in the days approaching the time of the end:

> For when they shall say, Peace and safety; then sudden destruction cometh upon them, as travail upon a woman with child; and they shall not escape. (1 Thessalonians 5:3)

Paul foretold that this murderous peace will come immediately following the "thief-in-the-night" break-in upon an unsuspecting world of earth's inhabitants. (Read 1 Thessalonians 5:1–7.) This refers to the resurrection and translation of the saints of the Age of Grace—the Rapture. The apostle, as he did in speaking of the Rapture in 1 Corinthians 15:51–55 and 1 Thessalonians 4:13–18, used personal pronouns to indicate exactly the people about whom he was prophesying. Concerning those alive at that future time, Paul used "we," "us," and "our" to indicate Church-Age saints and "they," "them," and "those" to indicate the lost—the unbelievers—who will be left behind when the stupendous event—the Rapture—takes place.

February 2010

There will be a cry for peace and safety leading up to this time of world-rending intervention by Christ, and an even more urgent demand for peace and safety following that calamitous event. I infer from my study in the matter that the left-behind people who say "peace and safety" seem to be saying also that "now we have peace and safety." I'm convinced that this is the peace perpetrated upon planet earth by the "king of fierce countenance" (Daniel 8:23) who "by peace shall destroy many" (Daniel 8:25).

Today, leaders of the planet's most powerful governments consistently fret over the boiling pot the so-called Holy Land presents in threatening to again bring the nations into world war. Other potential conflicts, like that presented by the exchange of fire between North and South Korean forces the past week, are cause for concern. But it is the building potential for all-out war between Israel and its Islamic antagonists that has the premiere diplomatic powers that be in "distress" and "perplexity."

Particularly, it is the building potential violence between the Jewish state and a soon-to-be nuclear Iran that brings forth the cry for peace and safety. European Union leaders, for example, are frustrated over the peace that eludes all efforts, finding Iran's leadership exasperating.

> European Union foreign ministers on Monday [January 25] left a Brussels meeting without a clear picture as to what should be the bloc's next move regarding Iranian noncompliance with international demands regarding its nuclear programme.…
>
> The EU is becoming increasingly frustrated with Iranian intransigence.… "We have been in talks for six

> years," [France's Europe minister, Pierre Lellouche] said, adding: "All the West's proposals have been rejected."
>
> Mr. Lellouche warned that Iran's enrichment of uranium was now at the "threshold of militarisation." The Security Council permanent five—China, France, Russia, the [United Kingdom] and the U.S.—and Germany have already met once in 2010 to consider further sanctions, but without reaching agreement....
>
> World powers are concerned at the possibility that Iran's nuclear energy programme is secretly aimed at developing weapons in violation of the Non-Proliferation Treaty.[9]

EU leadership, as well as all other leaderships, have solid ground for concern that the volatility could boil over at any time and ignite conflagration in the region. Iran's supreme leader, Ayatollah Ali Khamenei, declared this week that Islamic nations will one day watch the destruction of its most hated enemy, Israel. He is quoted on his website as saying:

> Surely, the day will come when the nations of the region will witness the destruction of the Zionist regime...when the destruction happens will depend on how the Islamic nations approach the issue.[10]

Concerns about Iran's nuclear development and the nations' diplomatic elite's frustration over not knowing what to do about the threat might remind the student of Bible prophecy of another predicted situation. The current angst over Iran's threat evokes thoughts of an apparent note of diplomatic protest that will be issued during a future Iranian (Persian) military action against Israel.

> Sheba, and Dedan, and the merchants of Tarshish, with all its young lions, shall say unto thee, Art thou come to take a spoil? Hast thou gathered thy company to take a prey, to carry away silver and gold, to take away cattle and goods, to take a great spoil? (Ezekiel 38:13)

The powers of the West, and even Saudi and others in the Middle East, will send a weak note of diplomatic protest. There will still, apparently, be an inability to deal with the Iranian (and the accompanying coalition of nations') threat to world peace. The indecisiveness and the cry for peace and safety will ultimately bring the beast to power. He will have the answers to foment the deadly peace people want. It will be such peace that will serve as Antichrist's launching pad to absolute power.

February 8, 2010
Rome, EU, and Israel Linkage Bears Watching

It is, in my view, more than interesting that Rome and the European Union seek to bring Israel into their orbit on a formal basis. This is especially fascinating considering that the world of nations in general is more and more marginalizing Israel because of the Jewish state's perceived guilt in the matter of being the chief obstacle to Mideast peace.

The prime minister of Italy—at the heart of which sits Rome, whose people destroyed the Jewish temple and Jerusalem in AD

70, and out of which the "prince that shall come" is prophesied to emerge—is courting Israel's government, as is reported within the following news excerpt:

> JERUSALEM—Italian Prime Minister Silvio Berlusconi said Monday he hopes to bring Israel into the European Union, at the start of a three-day visit to the Jewish state....
>
> Under Berlusconi's leadership, Italy has become one of Israel's strongest allies in Europe. Berlusconi's efforts to strengthen ties with Israel followed decades of a pro-Arab tilt by previous Italian governments....
>
> Speaking on arrival in Israel, Berlusconi told [Israeli Prime Minister Benjamin] Netanyahu that "my greatest desire, as long as I am a protagonist in politics, is to bring Israel into membership of the European Union."[11]

The fascination ratchets up when one considers the collateral dynamics making the linkage Berlusconi seeks understandable.

Europe, for the most part, is at the mercy of Russia and others to their east for keeping oil and natural gas flowing their way. In that regard, the EU is truly vulnerable to pressures from those regions that sometimes act less than civilized by middle European standards. EU leadership would desperately like to have a source of natural gas, for example, that would assure at least a modicum of independence from Russia and the natural-gas-producing nations in its orbit over which Russia can exert hegemony.

Another interesting news item perhaps further illustrates the point of Israel's growing attractiveness to Berlusconi and his EU colleagues.

> The Canadian Bontan Oil and Gas Company, which has been exploring for natural gas off the coast of Israel, announced Tuesday that it had found prospective resources of up to 6 trillion cubic feet...of natural gas in Mira and Sarah Prospects off the country's coast. As defined on the company's website, prospective resources are "those quantities of petroleum estimated, as of a given date, to be potentially recoverable from undiscovered accumulations by application of future development projects." The two finds could be worth upwards of U.S. $6 billion.[12]

Some students of Bible prophecy have long speculated about the possibility of vast quantities of oil and gas perhaps one day being discovered in the small geographical area covered by modern Israel. There seem to be some indications due to recent exploration that the possibility exists. It seems that the Italian prime minister and others from the region out of which Antichrist is foretold to come might be thinking along the same lines.

Certainly, there is to be something that puts hooks in the jaws of Gog, the leader of the coalition of Ezekiel 38 and 39. The Western powers, as well as the Saudis and others of the region surrounding Israel, it seems, will send a diplomatic note of protest to the Russian leader, asking if he is coming to take "great spoil" from the area occupied by God's chosen people.

The attack, of course, will be satanically inspired, but it is logical to at least ponder whether it will be oil and natural gas that might be the geophysical "hook" that causes Gog and his Persian and other partners to think the "evil thought" foretold by Ezekiel. Israel's being brought into the EU realm by the leaders of the region prophesied to produce Antichrist would certainly be a spectacular stage-setting ingredient to the prophetic puzzle. The beast would, when coming to power, have legitimate claim to all that is Israel's, from the earthly perspective, if Israel were a member of the EU—and if, as many of us suspect, the EU is indeed the nucleus of Antichrist's future kingdom.

According to Daniel the prophet, Antichrist will at least for a time cause great industrial productivity that promises security. This will all quickly turn to hell on earth, of course, as Antichrist's luciferian rage and God's wrathful judgment begins. Antichrist will need, most likely, control of the oil and gas sources in order to "cause craft to prosper" (Daniel 8:25).

The attempts of the leadership of the EU to bring Israel into its sphere of influence by making it a member is a matter to watch.

February 15, 2010
EU: Partly Strong, Partly Weak

It seems to me that this generation stands on God's prophetic timeline very near the time Daniel the Old Testament prophet described, as recorded in the following:

> And the fourth kingdom shall be strong as iron, forasmuch as iron breaketh in pieces and subdueth all things; and, as iron that breaketh all these, shall it break in pieces and bruise.
>
> And whereas thou sawest the feet and toes, part of potters' clay and part of iron, the kingdom shall be divided; but there shall be in it of the strength of the iron, forasmuch as thou sawest the iron mixed with miry clay.

> And as the toes of the feet were part of iron and part of clay, so the kingdom shall be partly strong and partly broken.
>
> And whereas thou sawest iron mixed with miry clay, they shall mingle themselves with the seed of men; but they shall not cleave one to another, even as iron is not mixed with clay. (Daniel 2:40–43)

Daniel was given by God both the vision that Babylonian King Nebuchadnezzar had one troubling night and its interpretation. The dream was of a huge, metallic, man image. The image, Daniel interpreted, was of four world powers and a final, fifth world power, which would come on the scene at the very end of human history just before God judged earth's rebellious governments. Then, the prophecy indicates, a new regime—headed by God Himself—will rule and reign:

> And in the days of these kings shall the God of heaven set up a kingdom, which shall never be destroyed; and the kingdom shall not be left to other people, but it shall break in pieces and consume all these kingdoms, and it shall stand for ever. (Daniel 2:44)

Daniel prophesied that the fifth world power will come out of the fourth. We know the order of world empires from history. The first Daniel interpreted was Babylon, the second would be the Medo-Persian, the third would be the Greek Empire, and the fourth would be the Roman Empire, represented in Nebuchadnezzar's dream by the legs of iron. The fifth empire—the final empire, and the only one that is yet to come into being as fulfilled prophecy—is represented by the feet and toes of that metallic monstrosity.

To my understanding, the five world empires given to Daniel in metallic representations—i.e., gold for the head, silver for the breast and arms, brass or bronze for the belly and thighs, and iron for the legs, feet, and toes—are indicative of money and the power to rule over the earth's inhabitants. Metals have almost always been at the center of any economy throughout history. And when the metals represent the power to mold and construct weaponry and war machinery—spears, bullets, bombs, tanks, planes, and ships, etc.—the power of the metal and the economies of the world powers become understandable. Money is power, and power is control. These are inextricably linked.

The fifth world power will come from the Roman Empire, which disintegrated but is reforming, we who observe prophecy from the pretribulational view believe. We believe that the European Union is almost certainly the nucleus out of which this last Gentile power is emerging. This is the area of central Europe in particular. Rome is the very heart of that nucleus.

Daniel also prophesied about the last world empire's leader who would leap to center stage at just the right moment in Satan's plans to bring him to power:

> And after threescore and two weeks shall Messiah be cut off, but not for himself; and the people of the prince that shall come shall destroy the city and the sanctuary, and the end of it shall be with a flood, and unto the end of the war desolations are determined.
>
> And he shall confirm the covenant with many for one week; and in the midst of the week he shall cause the

> sacrifice and the oblation to cease, and for the overspreading of abominations he shall make it desolate, even until the consummation, and that determined shall be poured upon the desolate. (Daniel 9:26–27)

Antichrist, the "beast," as this vicious future tyrant is termed, will come to power and rule ruthlessly. His power will emanate from economics—the ability to call all to worship him through a mark and numbering system that will control buying and selling. (Read Revelation 13:16–18 to understand this 666 system of absolute control.)

We are witnessing economic rearrangements at present like no other generation has seen. Even the United States—as anyone with any sense of what's been going on in the news will attest—is being forced into a mold of one-world economic order. It is all leading toward the mark and numbering system that will give Antichrist his power. (Read Revelation 17:12–13 to learn of the ten economic power blocs that will develop, then give power and authority to the beast—Antichrist, the ruler of the fifth and final world empire.)

Europe today is in dynamic upheaval, struggling to stand on the feet and toes that will give the eventual Antichrist system its balance, its equilibrium. But just as Daniel foretold, the feet and toes are not made of purely a metal of strength. The EU is made partly of the governmental strength that was the ancient Roman Empire, but also is constructed of weakness intrinsic within the governments of contemporary times. This makes the whole structure that is the final form of all worldly economic-governmental power subject to crashing to final collapse. This is exactly what Daniel foresaw as given earlier in Daniel 2:44.

Last-Days Diary

February 2010

A story this past week gives an excellent example of the struggle the reviving Roman Empire is unwittingly engaged in to construct that final world rule Satan seeks:

> Strasbourg, France—With the European Union's single currency in the grip of the worst crisis in its history, the bloc's new president is expected to use the growing alarm over debt levels to argue for a new form of "economic government" in Europe.
>
> The leaders [meet] on Thursday at a summit meeting in Brussels, now certain to be dominated by worries about deficit and debt levels in Greece. [EU Commission President Herman] Van Rompuy's proposal could take main responsibility for stewardship of economic coordination out of the hands of the twenty-seven nations' finance ministers, elevating it to the level of heads of government. The plan could also reduce the role of the European Commission, the bloc's executive arm.
>
> According to a draft of one of two documents circulated before the meeting, Mr. Van Rompuy (pronounced rom-PWEE) will argue that "recent developments in the euro area highlight the urgent need to strengthen our economic governance.... Whether it is called coordination of policies or economic government," it adds, "only the European Council is capable of delivering and sustaining a common European strategy for more growth and more jobs.... Recommendations for the euro area as a whole and its member states should be strengthened, with a stronger focus on competitiveness and macroeconomic imbalances," the draft says. "This would be in line with

the importance of economic spillover effects in the monetary union and the challenges the euro area is facing."[13]

Paul the apostle wrote of the economic reality that drives the world toward God's judgment and wrath:

> But they that will be rich fall into temptation and a snare, and into many foolish and hurtful lusts, which drown men in destruction and perdition. For the love of money is the root of all evil. (1 Timothy 6:9–10a).

Certainly, the truth of God's Word frames what is happening at this time in history, and where it all is heading as the rulers of this fallen sphere grasp for the wealth of this world and strive to cast off the bonds of governance God wisely placed upon the would-be masters of planet earth.

> Go to now, ye rich men, weep and howl for your miseries that shall come upon you.
>
> Your riches are corrupted and your garments are moth-eaten.
>
> Your gold and silver are cankered; and the rust of them shall be a witness against you, and shall eat your flesh as it were fire. Ye have heaped treasure together for the last days.
>
> Behold, the hire of the labourers who have reaped down your fields, which is of you kept back by fraud, crieth; and the cries of them who have reaped are entered into the ears of the Lord of Sabaoth.

> Ye have lived in pleasure on the earth, and been wanton; ye have nourished your hearts, as in a day of slaughter.
>
> Ye have condemned and killed the just; and he doth not resist you. (James 5:1–6)

We are in the end-of-the-age era of the toes of Nebuchadnezzar's night vision.

February 22
More Stage-Setting for Gog-Magog

An interesting development, although at cursory glance it seems of little importance, brings thoughts of what might come to be. Even the most innocuous of events in these times of stage-setting for fulfillment of Bible prophecy in the Middle East warrant a closer look.

When a Saudi prince says that sanctions on a feared fellow Islamic state enemy, Iran, aren't working, so something stronger should be done, the declaration makes one wonder why this statement is made for public consumption. Iran is indeed Saudi's enemy. Many within Islam have long wanted the Saudi royal family dethroned and replaced with their own dictatorships. Iran is the strongest of the Islamic states, both in military strength and in desire to dominate that Middle Eastern world. Fulfilling such Iranian desires would necessitate the overthrow of Saudi royalty, so the Saudis are taking notice. Those facts alone should stand by themselves to point to the dangers presented by Mideast volatility.

However, being observers of these things from the perspective of Bible prophecy, we look deeper to find meaning. This is especially important to do since so many stage-setting issues and events now line up on the biblically prophetic horizon.

Therefore, it was with observer's antenna raised that I homed in with fascination upon the few words of one of the Saudi spokesmen in a news item. The report said that the spokesman for Saudi Arabia expressed doubt that further sanctions against the Iranian regime's determination to continue with its nuclear development program would do any good.

Now, we might expect an Islamic brother to say this on behalf of another Islamic brother. All Islamic states—as history has proven—so hate Israel that they would want the Western powers to back off of imposing sanctions that bring pressure to bear upon fellow Israel haters.

At first glance, this statement seems designed to alleviate such pressure on the Iranians. But, the Saudi spokesman wants to forget the sanctions so that greater, not lesser, pressure be brought to bear on Iran and its developing nuclear threat. Not only does he want greater pressure, but pressure of the more immediate sort.

> Prince Saud al-Faisal told a news conference in the Saudi capital that the threat posed by Iran's nuclear ambitions demands a more immediate solution than sanctions. He described sanctions as a long-term solution, and he said the threat is more pressing.
>
> The Saudi foreign minister spoke this past Monday in a joint appearance with U.S. Secretary of State Hillary Clinton.
>
> "Sanctions are a long-term solution," al-Faisal said. Then, speaking of Iran and its nuclear program, he said, "But we see the issue in the shorter term because we are

closer to the threat." He said further, "We need immediate resolution rather than gradual resolution."[14]

The news story concluded that the U.S. delegation who shared the press conference with al-Faisal was confused by the Saudi minister's words. U.S. officials traveling with Clinton said privately they were uncertain what al-Faisal meant, since the Saudi government has been explicit in its support of sanctions against Iran. They said he appeared to be suggesting that sanctions may not be effective and that other action could be required.[15]

It seems to me that Saudi royalty genuinely does fear the likes of Iranian dictator Mahmoud Ahmadinejad and the ruling clerics of that biblically prophetic Persian nation. One should not believe for a moment, however, that Secretary Clinton and the U.S. delegation is confused as to what the Saudi kingdom's spokesman means with regard to wanting to move beyond sanctions that aren't working and straight to stronger actions.

The story gave a clue as to what is really meant behind all of the Saudi's words of concern. This is what my antenna picked up—in a brief, obscure part of the story that recorded the Saudi minister saying that "efforts supported by the U.S. to rid the Middle East of nuclear weapons must apply to Israel."[16]

All of Islam, especially militant Islam, hates Israel and its presence in that land—more than they fear each other. And this is where my paranoia, as detractors of my opinion might call it (but better put, my cynicism), leaps to the forefront of analyzing this almost-hidden mention that al-Faisal wants Israel's nuclear capability neutered.

Make no mistake: All the Islamic states of the region would climb on board Israel's being forced or cajoled into surrendering its suspected nuclear capability. The very hint by America's number-one Islamic ally in the region suggesting that Israel be forced to give up its nukes is significant, in my view. Such an ingredient will almost assuredly one day be part of a centerpiece of making the false, deadly peace of Isaiah 28:15 and 18 and Daniel 9:26–27.

Israel will at some point become a people at rest, apparently trusting and depending upon others rather than the Israeli Defense Force to protect the nation. Certainly, they won't be trusting God to defend them. At such a time, the Gog-Magog coalition will attack full force. Look for ever-increasing calls for a nuclear-free Middle East region, as part of stage setting for Ezekiel 38–39 to be fulfilled.

Last-Days Diary

MARCH 2010

Last-Days Lies and Deception

March 1, 2010
The Lie

There is coming, according to God's Word and the apostle Paul, a particular deception that will ensnare the world of people who oppose the Creator of all things. When thinking on 2 Thessalonians 2 about the lie Paul mentions, it seems to me there can be but one sort of lie that Satan would be so determined to foist upon humanity left behind after the Rapture of the church. Here is the prophecy:

> Even him whose coming is after the working of Satan with all power and signs and lying wonders,
>
> And with all deceivableness of unrighteousness in them that perish, because they received not the love of the truth, that they might be saved.
>
> And for this cause God shall send them strong delusion, that they should believe a lie,
>
> That they all might be damned who believed not the truth, but had pleasure in unrighteousness.
>
> (2 Thessalonians 2:9–12)

MARCH 2010

Lucifer, the fallen one, has always sought to separate man from the Lord and His governance. Satan was successful in accomplishing his goal when, in the Garden of Eden, Eve fell victim to the serpent's seduction and then Adam willfully joined her, thus believing Satan rather than the Lord.

God then promised the supernatural seed through mankind that would eventually produce a Savior who would ultimately destroy the serpent and overcome his great lie that separated God and man. Jesus is that seed, the Redeemer of mankind. He said He is "the way, the truth, and the life; no man cometh unto the Father, but by me" (John 14:6).

Jesus is the only way to forgiveness of sin, which separates man from God. This is what is meant by the first Scripture I and many other children learned in Sunday school:

> For God so loved the world, that he gave his only begotten Son, that whosoever believeth in him should not perish, but have everlasting life. (John 3:16)

Paul foretold in the 2 Thessalonians 2 account that the lie the Antichrist regime will impose upon those left behind on earth after the church is taken to be with Christ forever will involve the refusal to believe the truth. They will reject God's way to redemption. They will deny that Jesus Christ—the Truth—is the way to salvation.

The lie, then, will be wrapped up in a grand deception that Christ didn't truly come—in Jewish flesh—to die for the sin of man. This, after all, is the spirit of Antichrist about which John warned:

> Beloved, believe not every spirit, but try the spirits whether they are of God; because many false prophets are gone out into the world.
>
> By this know ye the Spirit of God: Every spirit that confesseth that Jesus Christ is come in the flesh is of God;
>
> And every spirit that confesseth not that Jesus Christ is come in the flesh is not of God; and this is that spirit of antichrist, of which ye have heard that it should come, and even now already is it in the world. (1 John 4:1–3)

That spirit-of-Antichrist lie was intrinsic within Hitler's Nazi regime. The Jews were painted as Christ-killers and the scourge of mankind, not as the chosen people through whom God brought His Only Begotten Son into the world to seek and save lost mankind. That future führer—the satanically empowered son of perdition—will likely mesmerize the post-Rapture world with a lie that denies Jesus Christ ever came to be the sacrifice for mankind. As a matter of fact, Bible prophecy paints him as the one who comes in place of the real Christ. He will claim to be the Savior. He will sit in the temple of God on Moriah in Jerusalem, declaring himself to be God! (See 2 Thessalonians 2:4 and Matthew 24:15.)

I believe the groundwork is being laid today for the lie that will doom much of the world's population after the Rapture. The lie will have to be part of a fearful crisis of some sort. The disappearance of millions will certainly provide a crisis that will have the attention of the world. Any leader who can answer the question of what on earth has happened will get instant attention and adulation.

As mentioned above, the earth is being prepared, I'm convinced, for just such an answer as Antichrist will concoct. A recent news story gives more than an inkling of the groundwork being laid for that lie, I believe:

> It has been the subject of movies for decades—but what would REALLY happen if aliens visited earth? This may sound like a topic for conspiracy theorists or mad UFO obsessives, yet this week, science's finest minds gathered in London to debate that very question.... The conference, The Detection of Extraterrestrial Life and the Consequences for Science and Society, was held at the highbrow Royal Society HQ in central London....
>
> It is often said the discovery of other civilizations would shatter world religions. Delegates were not so sure. Professor Ted Peters, a theologian, briefed the meeting on some survey results that suggested that rather than undermine religious beliefs—whatever the faith—it would strengthen them, by making God's creation seem even bigger and more wonderful.
>
> Not everyone agreed. British physicist Paul Davies thought Christians would have a problem, given the central belief that Jesus died to save us. If we discover other civilizations, it would raise the awkward question: Why just us?[17]

The lie of 2 Thessalonians 2 could well bring into its orbit and make totally believable: 1) universalism—the deception that all people are God's children, and there are many ways to salvation; and 2) the notion that Jesus Christ couldn't have been the

Savior, or else He would have to die on other worlds for those inhabitants and for others in other universes.

With the way psychologically and demonically paved for there to be a massive UFO invasion during the Tribulation, millions looking for explanation of why their world is upside down will undoubtedly readily believe such a lie—the one telling them that the ETs who have just removed millions of rebels from earth have now come to rescue the world from oblivion.

I believe the prophecy that tells of this very event might well be found in the following description given in God's Word:

> And he doeth great wonders, so that he maketh fire come down from heaven on the earth in the sight of men,
>
> And deceiveth them that dwell on the earth by the means of those miracles which he had power to do in the sight of the beast, saying to them that dwell on the earth, that they should make an image to the beast, which had the wound by a sword, and did live. (Revelation 13:13–14)

Our world is filled today with great deception. Lies come from many governmental leaders, media sources, and even from many people in the pulpits of America. It is incumbent upon each who names the name of Christ to be discerning in these closing days of the Church Age. Lost souls hang in the eternal balance.

March 8, 2010
Big Brotherism

Marxism, communism, Nazism, fascism—these evoke thoughts of tyrants and dictatorships. Well, Marxism and communism might be wishful utopianism to some within political ideology circles in these days of movement toward socialism. But for the most part, thoughts of these isms generate study-related memories of the likes of Stalin, Mao, Hitler, Mussolini, and other such humanity-destroying beasts.

The matters involved within the recollection include revolution, war, torture, gulag, genocide—any and all systems of governing that should be avoided at all costs. Fear and apprehension over dictatorships were the very reason the United States Constitution was written. Specifically, the Bill of Rights, the first ten amendments to that Constitution, spells out the rights of each citizen that government cannot usurp. These rights are, the shapers of the Constitution meticulously wrote, "inalienable." That is, these are rights given by God, thus cannot be taken away by men—and/or women—in government.

Another ism has developed that threatens the inalienable rights of man. Its ominous construction continues at a torrid pace and will ultimately be worse than any of the aforementioned isms. As a matter of fact, it will be all of those tyrannical nightmares rolled up into one system of utter decimation. George Orwell and Aldous Huxley, authors of well-known novels, played upon fear of such governments in their futuristic books, *1984* and *Brave New World*. The swiftness of movement of recent developments makes their works of fiction look ever more prophetic.

Orwell used London and Britain in 1984 as the genesis of a world of ruthless control. "Big Brother is watching you" is a phrase the author used with portentous effect. It continues to be used by those who warn of the exponentially encroaching surveillance technologies. Again, Orwell's vision was almost prophetic in the biblical sense.

Last-Days Diary

MARCH 2010

A friend who is a well-known journalist in Great Britain recently e-mailed me with the following troubling, though fascinating, information:

> I was putting together some slides for one of my presentations yesterday and discovered that Britain has 1.5 times as many surveillance cameras as China! We now have cameras that talk to people, bossing them around in the streets! They are being installed in twenty cities. They are also getting listening devices. Some places also have face-monitoring systems so they can scan for people the authorities are interested in.
>
> The average Briton is now filmed about three hundred times per day! We also have camera cars patrolling the streets, filming whatever takes their fancy and harassing motorists.
>
> We are years ahead of America in plans to put GPS systems in cars, etc. They also want even more speed cameras, speed-averaging cameras—you name it. All of them are being linked into one enormous grid. The records of journeys are logged and kept. As you drive down the main highways, your number plates are scanned every few miles. Our son and I spent a day in the control room where all this information is monitored—an astonishing operation, with screens showing all the main roads. The EU is now planning to store all e-mails, log every web page visited, every phone call, etc., which Britain has done for years.

My friend has told me—has told the world—that cameras train on his home from right across the street, atop a telephone-type pole. It is just a matter of time until all of England is under a surveillance system much more sophisticated and intrusive than our 1940s author, Orwell, could have imagined. All of Europe is sure to follow suit, and we can see more than cursory evidence that America is coming into Big Brotherism's orbit of control.

The whole world is on track for super-sophisticated tracking. And a familiar name pops through the inky blackness of cyberspace to make this a readily observable fact. The familiar name is Google.

> Who in the world knows as much about you and your private thoughts as Google? That's the question Katherine Albrecht, radio talk-show host and spokeswoman for Startpage, a search engine that protects user privacy, is posing to American Internet surfers.
>
> "It would blow people's minds if they knew how much information the big search engines have on the American public," she told WND [World Net Daily]. "In fact, their dossiers are so detailed they would probably be the envy of the KGB."[18]

Albrecht detailed how Google and other search engines gather and maintain dossiers on everyone who uses the service. The information is released to governments—for example, to America's Department of Homeland Security—when such information is requested. It seems the Bill of Rights is cast aside without a constitutional amendment of any sort even being considered. Such ability to collect data on victims was merely the dreams of such people as those in Stalin's secret service and Hitler's Gestapo.

Albrecht said Americans unwittingly share their most private thoughts with search engines, serving up snippets of deeply personal information about their lives, habits, troubles, health concerns, preferences, and political leanings.

> "We're essentially telling them our entire life stories—stuff you wouldn't even tell your mother—because [we] are in a private room with a computer," she said.[19]

Big Brotherism, of course—in our view at Rapture Ready—is another way of defining the ideology that is heading up the drive toward establishment of the regime of Antichrist found in Revelation 13:16–18. With government's groping for control in ways that totally disregard the wishes of U.S. citizenry, more often than not throwing constitutional safeguards to the winds of political expediency, the ideology becomes ever more manifest through our daily headlines.

All of this shows how very near this generation must be to the Tribulation hour—thus, that much closer to Christ calling His church to be with Him (John 14:1–3; 1 Thessalonians 4:16–17).

March 15, 2010
Prophetic Ponderings on the Ides of March

Thinking on the portentous date this commentary is posted, my ponderings gravitated naturally toward Julius Caesar's fate. The Roman dictator was, of course, assassinated by those closest to him on March 15, 44 BC, after having been forewarned, according to Shakespeare's literary treatment of the story, to "beware the Ides of March."

March 2010

Remembering Caesar and the reasons for his murder made me think of God's prophetic Word on the future Caesar of the revived Roman Empire. He will be planet earth's final tyrant—the Antichrist. We have considered in these columns many times the movement toward his biblically predicted ascension to power. That movement continues in many areas of today's world, both in major developments and in those less conspicuous.

Rapture Ready consistently presents news and commentary about the onrushing geopolitical flood of major issues and events—most of which, we are convinced, involve Antichrist's ultimately assuming power. We monitor, for example, the European Union reconfiguring to become the nucleus of the revived Roman Empire out of which will develop the ten-toe kingdom of Daniel 2 and Revelation 17:12–13; the global socioeconomic pressures forcing all nations into a "New World Order" that the future tyrant will one day control with an iron fist; and Israel's being pressured by the nations of the world to make a false peace with its blood-vowed enemies, some of whom openly proclaim they want the Jewish state erased from the earth.

When we move from such major issues, we dissect news at the next tier down. We examine the infrastructure of the major prophecies for news of developments we sense might make Antichrist's regime possible. For example, we explore technological developments, such as analyzed in my most preceding commentary, "Big Brotherism," about the surveillance machinery that threatens liberty at many levels.

So, in that vein, when considering the Ides of March, tyrants, and the approaching time of Antichrist, the focus of this week's commentary leaped at me. The serious intention by two well-known senators, one a Democrat and one a Republican, to bring into federal law a major step toward increasing government's intrusive control over "we the people" grabbed my attention.

The legislative move, of course, is portrayed as something to solve a problem and benefit the American people. It is being considered in the name of solving the illegal alien problem.

> Lawmakers working to craft a new comprehensive immigration bill have settled on a way to prevent employers from hiring illegal immigrants: a national biometric identification card all American workers would eventually be required to obtain.
>
> Under the potentially controversial plan still taking shape in the Senate, all legal U.S. workers, including citizens and immigrants, would be issued an ID card with embedded information, such as fingerprints, to tie the card to the worker....
>
> The uphill effort to pass a bill is being led by Sens. Chuck Schumer (D., N.Y.) and Lindsey Graham (R., S.C.), who plan to meet with President Barack Obama as soon as this week to update him on their work....
>
> The biggest objections to the biometric cards may come from privacy advocates, who fear they would become de facto national ID cards that enable the government to track citizens.[20]

Even the left-wing organization usually in favor of ever-expanding government (at least as concerns more social programs), the American Civil Liberties Union (ACLU), sees the dangers of such intrusion by the Federal government. Chris Calabrese, legislative counsel for the ACLU, weighed in:

> "It is fundamentally a massive invasion of people's privacy," [he said]. "We're not only talking about fingerprinting every American [and] treating ordinary Americans like criminals in order to work. We're also talking about a card that would quickly spread from work to voting to travel to pretty much every aspect of American life that requires identification."[21]

He is right. Proposal of such a card brings forth the ominous feeling that somewhere down the line we as Americans might be hearing the words often heard in movies about Hitler's Germany: "Show me your papers." His warning of things to come echoes within the spiritually attuned senses. It's not unlike Julius Caesar being told, "Beware the Ides of March."

March 22, 2010
President Pokes God in the Eye

I thought about writing on something other than this news item that almost certainly involves Bible prophecy. Many, no doubt, will make this the focus of their commentaries this week, thus further consideration might just be duplication. But it is too profound a matter not to address.

Jerusalem—the city about which Jesus prophesied while sitting atop the Mount of Olives giving the many signs that would signal the end of the age and His Second Advent—is directly in the news bull's eye with this story. Jerusalem is the most important city on the planet, in God's holy eyes. And it is in this regard that this news item takes on such gravity, particularly for the United States of America.

The Scripture to consider is this:

> For thus saith the LORD of hosts: After the glory hath he sent me unto the nations which spoiled you; for he that toucheth you toucheth the apple of his eye.
>
> For, behold, I will shake mine hand upon them, and they shall be a spoil to their servants; and ye shall know that the LORD of hosts hath sent me. (Zechariah 2:8–9)

This is a chilling pronouncement on anyone who would cause Jerusalem to come under any control other than the Lord God of Heaven. Just previous to these verses, Jerusalem is measured by God Himself. There is no doubt: Jerusalem is His, and it is for His people alone—the house of Israel.

The news story in question—the one that no doubt will be analyzed and dissected by those who study Bible prophecy from a literal perspective—is excerpted here:

> A widely predicted crisis between Israel and the United States upon Benjamin Netanyahu taking office as prime minister finally erupted this weekend. U.S. President Barack Obama did not hold back in condemning the humiliation caused to Joe Biden with the Israeli announcement of 1,600 new housing units in East Jerusalem during what was supposed to be the vice president's friendly visit to Israel. Instead of accepting Netanyahu's partial apology and letting bygones be bygones, Obama issued a stern warning to the Israeli prime minister and is now demanding that he take "specific actions" to show he is "committed" to the U.S.-Israel relationship and to the peace process itself.[22]

MARCH 2010

U.S. Secretary of State Hillary Clinton relayed a message to the Israeli prime minister in a lengthy phone conversation, during which Netanyahu scarcely got in a word edgewise. And the castigation of the Israeli leader continued from those within the U.S. presidential administration. It is clear that the Obama administration has been waiting for just the right moment to manufacture a crisis in the matter of Israel constructing housing in east Jerusalem. The leverage the American government can bring against Netanyahu and the Israeli government is obvious.

There is no one, in terms of national entities, to stand with Israel against the threat from Iran other than the United States. America alone supplies fuel and spare parts for Israel's air force, as well as the warning signals for any missiles that might be headed Israel's way. So, Prime Minister Netanyahu is confronted by a dilemma: Either go along with the American presidential administration and accept whatever Mr. Obama dictates to appease Israel's enemies or suffer loss of American support regarding Iran. He is expected by the world powers that be to embrace whatever the international community—led by Barack Obama—thinks might be good for the "Roadmap to Peace."

Mainstream U.S. and world news media seemingly always come down *against* Israel's right to determine the disposition of Jerusalem and solidly *for* the Palestinians' right to east Jerusalem as a future Palestinian state's capital.

Always, the news is written in a way that is against Netanyahu and Israel. Most frequently, the stories are framed as derogatory opinion pieces rather than written in the style of true news journalism. An example is the following excerpt from a report about the current America/Israel "crisis" from an AP reporter:

> Israel does not stand to benefit from antagonizing its most important ally, but Netanyahu has historically taken a hard line against territorial concessions to the Palestinians, and a curb on east Jerusalem construction would threaten to fracture his hawkish coalition.[23]

So, the American president, the international community of leaders, and the world news media continue to try to force Israel into their own mold for world peace, which they obviously believe must begin at Jerusalem. They aren't far wrong in that opinion. The peace of Jerusalem is something for which God's people are told to pray:

> Pray for the peace of Jerusalem; they shall prosper that love thee. (Psalms 122:6)

However, the "peace" that will eventuate from the humanistic efforts will be one that will destroy many (Daniel 8:25). It will be peace made "with death, and with hell" (Isaiah 28:15).

All nations that consort to bring this false peace against God's holy city will suffer the fate of being cut in pieces by the God of Abraham, Isaac, and Jacob (Zechariah 12:1–3). Every one of them will be brought to account at Armageddon for trying to deal treacherously with God's chosen nation and people (Joel 3:2). Mr. Prime Minister, it is Israel's God—the only God that exists—to whom you should bow, and upon whom you can depend for Israel's ultimate defense.

No matter if it's prelates, potentates, or presidents, any nation whose leaders poke their fingers in God's eye by dealing harshly with Jerusalem will be brought to account when the Prince of Peace sits on His throne atop Mt. Zion in Jerusalem.

March 2010

When the Son of man shall come in his glory, and all the holy angels with him, then shall he sit upon the throne of his glory.

And before him shall be gathered all nations; and he shall separate them one from another, as a shepherd divideth his sheep from the goats.

And he shall set the sheep on his right hand, but the goats on the left....

Then shall he say also unto them on the left hand, Depart from me, ye cursed, into everlasting fire, prepared for the devil and his angels....

And these shall go away into everlasting punishment. (Matthew 25:31–33, 41, 46a)

March 29, 2010
The Devil's Dementia Goes Viral

Do you ever see news reports and say to yourself: "The world has gone crazy!" or something to that effect? Certainly, this seems to be a world going—or already gone—mad. The observation is worthy of in-depth investigation.

Looking in any direction across the landscape of human interaction produces undeniable evidence: This is a planet of people whose sanity is under assault by an unseen force. It is the same sin sickness that infected the first recorded rebel, Lucifer the fallen one, who is so delusional that he thinks he can still defeat the God of Heaven. Thus, I give the malady the designation the "devil's dementia." Indeed, it has gone viral upon planet earth.

The supernaturally inflicted dementia has brought much of humanity to the point that mankind's thinking has become reprobate.

The word "reprobate" is defined as: morally depraved, unprincipled, or bad. Reprobate thinking is rejected by God and beyond hope of salvation (apart from redemption found only in Jesus Christ). It is the kind of thinking with which Satan, the devil, now incessantly assaults God's creation called man. Mankind is thus fatally infected, his mind only on evil continually, just as prophesied.

Jesus said it would be like in the days of Noah at the time of His Second Coming (Luke 17:26–27). When we check those days, we find the following:

> And God saw that the wickedness of man was great in the earth, and that every imagination of the thoughts of his heart was only evil continually. (Genesis 6:5)

Let us consider the spreading dementia that afflicts our nation and the world at this late hour in history. Analyzing the arenas of human endeavor and the upside-down thinking that pervades will quite possibly further give us a sense of where this generation stands on God's prophetic timeline.

Religious Dementia

Religion, rather than acting as a comforting abode for the spirit as it is purported to do, more often inflames passions and ignites wars than soothes the savage beast within man. The most volatile religion of our time has at its very heart the demand that genocide be perpetrated upon God's chosen people. Jihad is the term for "holy war" that inspires much of Islam. It is sheer insanity that demands that parents strap bombs to their sons and daughters to blow up others—this in the name of bringing into being peace on earth!

March 2010

Christianity today more and more spotlights the madness of the hour. Many who say they are Christians have turned from the very reason for Christianity's name—Jesus Christ and His death, burial, and resurrection as sacrifice so men, women, and children can be redeemed from sin. False teachers and preachers divert the minds and hearts of people to fables. It is an inward turning toward self-centeredness and away from reaching out to the lost of the world as Christ commissioned His followers to do.

In the name of Christ, Catholicism harbors a seemingly endless number of priests who are pedophiles who prey on the innocent children who are supposed to be under their watch. This is reprobate thinking and an assault on God—perversion of the worst sort.

The devil's dementia is working within the church today, through the wolves in sheep's clothing, as condemned by Scripture:

> Now as Jannes and Jambres withstood Moses, so do these also resist the truth: men of corrupt minds, reprobate concerning the faith. (2 Timothy 3:8)

> They profess that they know God; but in works they deny him, being abominable, and disobedient, and unto every good work reprobate. (Titus 1:16)

Socioeconomic Dementia

All one has to do to understand what is going on in bringing down the United States is to cogitate on the thoughts recently uttered by one of America's avowed enemies:

Fidel Castro, Cuba's former president, wrote in an essay that passage of the American healthcare overhaul is "a miracle" and a major victory for Barack Obama's presidency, but called it "really incredible" that the U.S. took more than two centuries from its founding to approve health benefits for all.[24]

The American government and the present administration demonstrate beyond any doubt the dementia that affects U.S. leadership. These "leaders" demand that Americans learn to live within their means, yet the politicians run up tabs of trillions of dollars in the drive to convert the nation to European-style socialism at best—and to a Marxist state at worst. The big tax-and-spenders have strapped and continue to strap future generations with debt that can never be repaid. Only God's staying hand has prevented the complete implosion of the U.S. and world economies to this point.

It is madness, but if viewed through spiritually attuned senses, it's madness that can be understood as defiantly following the reprobate thinking that opposes the God of Heaven. With a considerable majority of U.S. citizenry opposing the massive spending spree, the majority party ignores the people's wishes. Instead it ties to its insane fiscal scheme taxpayer-funded abortions and other anti-God legislation, which enables atrocities such as public schools outlawing Bibles in classrooms while distributing condoms and birth control pills to students.

The madness spreads and metastasizes. *Fox News* reported Thursday, March 25, 2010, that a mother was devastated that her fifteen-year-old daughter was transported to an abortion facility by a public school in Seattle, Washington, for an abortion. This was done because the mother had signed a consent form she thought was for the child's medical safety, in case there was a medical emergency while she was at school. The school powers that be interpreted the consent form as meaning they had the right to abort the child's baby. That the girl was pregnant is troubling enough, but the government-funded school taking such godless action demonstrates a reprobate mindset that would have in earlier generations been unfathomable.

Fox News reported the same day that a phenomenon known as the "flash mob" has come into being, whereby young people assemble on an Internet gathering site, organize, then physically take to the streets to vandalize and destroy merchandise within stores and damage other places. The report disclosed that an activity known as "catch and wretch" is the recreational activity of a growing number of children as young as nine years old. They pick out a victim (sometimes the elderly), as would a pack of wolves, then they beat the victim and do other dastardly things. Lawlessness is the result of the devil's dementia, of which Antichrist will one day be the chief proponent.

Geopolitical Dementia

Nowhere is the upside-down thinking that is the devil's dementia more evident, from the biblically prophetic perspective, than in the arena of geopolitics. Again, on *Fox and Friends* on Friday, March 26, 2010, I heard contributor Geraldo Rivera accuse Israel and Prime Minister Benjamin Netanyahu of being the cause of Middle East tensions. He implied that they were the roadblock to peace in the region because they consistently perpetrated acts against the impoverished Palestinian people.

Rivera had just returned from the region, and, in my view, painted Netanyahu as a tyrant, whose Likud party wanted only to stir the boiling pot that is the Middle East, and was an obstacle to peace. He praised the Obama administration as the sane influence and said the Israeli government should be pressured to give in to the two-state solution and the division of Jerusalem.

The devil's dementia—the reprobate woolly-mindedness—couldn't be more exposed than through Rivera's diatribe. Despite the fact that Israel's enemies, since its reestablishment as a nation in 1948, have been blood-vowed to wipe the Jewish state from off the earth, Rivera and his ilk still spew with a straight face that Israel is the troublemaker.

The history is plain for anyone with a sound mind to understand. Gamal Abdel Nasser, the Egyptian tyrant, attacked Israel with a huge coalition of Arab states in 1956, and again in 1967. Anwar Sadat, Egypt's leader, accompanied by another huge contingent of Arab states, assaulted Israel on Yom Kippur in 1973. The objective in all the wars initiated by the anti-Israel forces was to wipe the nation off the map. The Arab enemies of Israel still hold to the eradication of Israel as their focus of hatred. Iran's Mahmoud Ahmadinejad has at every opportunity declared that he wants to scour the Jewish state from the earth; he even wants to bring on Armageddon so the twelfth imam can emerge from the ashes to institute Allah's glorious reign upon earth.

And the world's diplomats and media call Israel the culprit! The devil's dementia has gone viral, and Jesus Christ is the only cure.

April 2010

The End-of-Days Dragon Arises

April 5, 2010

A Dragon by Any Other Name

About four years ago, a film crew from South Korea's public broadcasting system came to my home to interview me on things to do with Bible prophecy. I remember them as quiet and very polite. We interviewed for about three hours, and I recall that most of my thoughts during that time were along the lines of: "How can these be the same basic people as their brothers and sisters of North Korea?"

The incongruity of these smiling, gentle journalists and film crew members as juxtaposed against my perception of Kim Jong-Il and the people of the "Axis of Evil" couldn't have been more dramatic. The North Korean dictator was saber rattling then, as he continues to do periodically today. His antics are mixed with the occasional, hands-in-the-air claim that he planned nothing dastardly. These from South Korea were just the opposite: good guys who even left for my wife a beautifully crafted porcelain dish as their appreciation for our hospitality.

Considering that the peoples of both north and south of the thirty-eighth parallel on the Korean peninsula are so close racially and in geographic proximity, why does one group move freely and peaceably about the world (even visiting my home) while the other group harbors thoughts of igniting nuclear war for the sake of enabling a tin-horn tyrant?

Bible prophecy leaps to the forefront of the thoughts. The north is under the influence, indeed, of the evil one. George W. Bush had it right, whether it was the term inspired by the president's own brain or those of his speech writers. The leaders of the North Korean regime have demonstrated consistently that it is under luciferian influence, as are other diabolists with whom they are in league.

Enter the chief diabolist state of the Asiatic evil empire that Bible prophecy foretells will one day rage into the occidental world:

> Saying to the sixth angel who had the trumpet, Loose the four angels who are bound in the great river, Euphrates.
>
> And the four angels were loosed, which were prepared for an hour, and a day, and a month, and a year, to slay the third part of men.
>
> And the number of the army of the horsemen were two hundred thousand thousand; and I heard the number of them. (Revelation 9:14–16)

The pact-making for that ultimate assault at Armageddon is front and center in the news:

> BEIJING—China is ready to work with the Democratic People's Republic of Korea (DPRK) to deepen bilateral exchanges and cooperation, so as to bolster the development of the relations between the two countries and militaries....

> The DPRK unswervingly follows a policy of constantly reinforcing the friendship of cooperation with China, An [Yonggi] said, adding the military foreign affairs department of the DPRK will work with its Chinese counterpart to contribute to the development of bilateral military ties. An is scheduled to wrap up his visit to China on April 3.[25]

China is touted today as the emerging industrial entity that will eventually overtake the U.S. as the economic superpower of the world. The woolly minded predict in some quarters that China's newfound economic clout will ultimately make it a responsible world citizen. However, God's Word almost certainly refers to the great Chinese behemoth when foretelling a massive force that could be spawned by no other nation-state.

> And the sixth angel poured out his vial upon the great river, Euphrates; and its water was dried up, that the way of the kings of the east might be prepared.
>
> And I saw three unclean spirits, like frogs, come out of the mouth of the dragon, and out of the mouth of the beast, and out of the mouth of the false prophet.
>
> For they are the spirits of devils, working miracles, that go forth unto the kings of the earth and of the whole world, to gather them to the battle of that great day of God Almighty. (Revelation 16:12–14)

It is more than ironic that China, put forward by some "progressives" as a budding good neighbor because of its need to foster goodwill within the global economic community, has for eons been depicted as a dragon. Shakespeare wrote, "A rose by any other name would smell as sweet." Call this brutal regime—like that of North Korea, over whom it exerts hegemony—a good neighbor, a budding industrial giant, or whatever...but Bible prophecy seems to be forewarning that a dragon by any other name smells just as dangerous.

April 12, 2010
Why Obama's Healthcare Is Wrong

A friend of Rapture Ready who has written to say he agrees with our view on most things says he must take exception with our opinion on the matter of the healthcare legislation recently signed by President Barack Obama.

I haven't addressed to any great extent in this forum what I indeed consider a program that moves America down a dangerous road. The loss of individual freedoms will be the result, to say the very least—but there are deeper considerations I want to address here.

The following is part of our friend's expression of concern regarding our opposition to this, what I see as a great debacle the American people will one day regret profoundly:

> I respectfully take issue with Rapture Ready's stance on healthcare reform. Perhaps the health bill will [be] repealed by Republicans, and you'll probably see that as a godly action, but lack of insurance leads to early death for many. If biblical social justice means that elderly widows get Medicare, it also should mean that orphans and the children of the poor get insurance that the rest of us have.

> For insurance to work, the healthy must have it as well as regulating insurers so they cannot deny it or cancel it when it's needed.

The key words in this friend's objection to our view are "biblical social justice." There is simply nothing biblical about this grab for power and control by a government inebriated on the dollars it can print and spend almost by presidential fiat. If it truly were a biblically correct—rather than a politically correct—effort, I would have no problem with it.

Now to look more deeply into the reason Christians shouldn't support this or any such grab for control that ultimately will enslave.

Human governance, we must remember, is not God's idea. It is man's idea to do things apart from the Creator. We see this from history given us in the Bible—and that's the only history that counts in God's dealing with us.

Adam's first decision to disobey God and instead accept Lucifer's way was rebellion against God's governance, and it came to a crisis point when the whole world became filled with violence and was corrupted in every other way, producing total anarchy. The Flood provided a new beginning.

Then came the crisis on the Plain of Shinar with Nimrod and the tower of Babel. Again, God dealt with the crisis, and the whole humanistic government was destroyed and the people scattered. Peleg and the peoples of earth were geographically redistributed, and all of the rest.

Israel was the next example. The chosen of God—the Jewish people—wanted human government, not God's reign, over them. The Lord let them have Saul. That is because He is a God who gave mankind volition. He wants His creation to love Him unconditionally; He doesn't want robots engineered to adore Him.

Humanistic government is again building to a supreme crisis point. It has always built to crises points. Every civilization, empire, etc., has come apart, dissolved, or been destroyed because of the rebellion and determination to live apart from God.

This time, it is building like the Vesuvius of all rebellions. America is the apex nation of all nations, and is the head of this gargantuan boil that is filling with explosive corruption that will one day blow. All nations of the world are tied inextricably to the U.S.—the most materially blessed of all nations to have come to power upon the planet's surface.

All of this corruption constitutes the Babylonian system, which Daniel and John prophesied in presenting the strange beast that comes up out of the sea in Revelation 1 and lumbers about in Daniel 7.

America is bound to Israel in a supernatural way, and it is all tied together by the incessant call for peace—not God's peace and the Prince of Peace, but humanistic peace. The result is going to be exactly as God gives it in Psalms 2, then the "kings of the earth" will achieve the "peace" they desire, as given in Isaiah 28:15 and 18.

Man will get his humanistic government; the ultimately "evolved" man will be earth's master for a brief time, during which God will let man have his desire to do what is right in his own eyes.

This current bubble of humanistic effort to build utopia, which supposedly can be achieved through a drive for humanistic socialism (that's the only kind of socialism there is), will explode when the Rapture occurs and the top is knocked off the boil.

Only God's staying hand has kept things from imploding—economic collapse, etc.

So, I am against manmade efforts to micromanage our lives. Such efforts comprise the grist for tyranny. You see where it's going. It is nothing more or less than a luciferian grab for power—a voracious lust for control by Lucifer's human agents and agencies.

God gave man, through the Bible, the formula for living life the way He intended. His Word says in effect that we should let those who won't work, not eat (see 2 Thessalonians 3:10 and 12). He gave us the way to take care of the widows, the orphans, the infirm, and even the legitimately indigent. This is to be done through the largesse of God's people, those who fully accept His way of governance. The Lord Jesus Christ is that only way. Man long ago decided to dispense with God's prescription in dealing with matters of societal interaction. Burdensome, enslaving government seeks power through promising deliverance from social ills it can never produce. What it will produce, however, we can see in Bible prophecy's description of humanistic government's final attempt to usurp the throne of God. (Read Revelation 13:16–18.)

April 19, 2010
Jews, Christians Seen as Major World Problem

Prophetic truth emerged during the past week as developing news with Israel and America at its center. An undercurrent of growing dislike for those who hold to biblical literalness at the same time continues to flow and spread within circles of government. But more about that in due course.

Last-Days Diary
April 2010

The prophet Zechariah's ancient prediction that Israel and Jerusalem will be a heavy stone of burden that will, in effect, rupture nations of the world that try to lift them out of the place where God has set them seems on the brink of fulfillment. One news report correctly assesses that no other city on the planet but Jerusalem would make world news headlines for wrangling over whether and where housing construction will take place. What possible difference could such decisions reached within a small city government anywhere else in the world make to international leaderships at the highest levels?

Yet God's words through Zechariah seem front and center while consternation among the nations grows:

> And in that day will I make Jerusalem a burdensome stone for all peoples; all that burden themselves with it shall be cut in pieces, though all the people of the earth be gathered together against it. (Zechariah 12:3)

The news story I mention sums up, in specific terms, Jerusalem's unique position among cities this way:

> News items that would not make it past the local editor's desk in a neighborhood weekly become international news headlines when they concern Jerusalem—and this week it happened twice again. Army Radio reported that the Jerusalem Municipality is planning to approve the construction of a synagogue and other public buildings in the Gilo neighborhood, and the item was quickly picked up by AFP.com [Agence France-Presse], Yahoo.com, and other world media sites.

> In addition, it is also being widely reported that after braving budgetary obstacles, the municipality plans to resume its policy of razing selected illegal structures.
>
> Both of these normative city government activities are an affront to U.S. President Barack Obama, who has been publicly pressuring Israel—specifically, Prime Minister [Benjamin] Netanyahu—to cease both of these activities. In fact, officials in the U.S. administration have even suggested that Obama publicly announce American support for a new Palestinian state in…all or most of eastern Jerusalem. Obama is reportedly "waiting for the right time" to do so.[26]

Anger toward the Jewish state by the man who currently holds what is usually considered the most powerful office in the world is finally causing great concern among the liberal Jewish leaders in the United States—and particularly from a former mayor of New York City, who traditionally has been a blazing proponent for most all Democrat Party ideology.

Edward M. Koch, one of the best-known Jewish leaders in America for many years, and a liberal Democrat who served as mayor of New York City, wrote recently that he is distraught over President Obama's hateful treatment of Israeli President Benjamin Netanyahu, while embracing Afghanistan's President Hamid Karzai, who has threatened to join with the Taliban if America doesn't stop making demands on him.

> I weep today because my president, Barack Obama, in a few weeks has changed the relationship between the U.S. and Israel from that of closest of allies to one in which

there is an absence of trust on both sides. The contrast between how the president and his administration deals with Israel and how it has decided to deal with the Karzai administration in Afghanistan is striking....

[Israel] our closest ally—the one with the special relationship with the U.S.—has been demeaned and slandered, held responsible by the administration for our problems in Afghanistan and Iraq and elsewhere in the Middle East. The plan I suspect is to so weaken the resolve of the Jewish state and its leaders that it will be much easier to impose on Israel an American plan to resolve the Israeli-Palestinian conflict, leaving Israel's needs for security and defensible borders in the lurch.[27]

Now, to get back to the earlier mentioned undercurrent of growing dislike for those who hold to biblical literalness: Troubling developments are afoot in this nation. It seems the only intolerance that is allowed is intolerance of anyone who puts forth the message of God's Word from the perspective that the Bible is to be taken literally.

There is an insidious lumping-together being perpetrated by those who demand that we all be tolerant, but hold themselves to no such restriction. Jews who believe Israel has the God-given right to exist, with Jerusalem as its capital, are not to be tolerated. Christians who believe that the Bible is the literal Word of God, that Jesus is the only way to redemption, and that He is coming back during a war called Armageddon are not to be tolerated. These two groups are in the process of being marginalized by the would-be masters of this nation and the world.

Chuck Baldwin, a pastor and columnist whose articles

sometimes appear in the "Newest Articles" section of www.raptureready.com, made the recent observation that a United States Army officer responsible for disseminating information in an official capacity attacks those military officers who consider biblical prophecy to be taken as literal.

Baldwin gave the officer's words:

> First, millennial thought and its policy implications may create strategic transparency that affords adversaries an advantage in decision-making. Second, an understanding of American millennial thinking may provide adversaries with the means to manipulate American policy and subsequent action. Third, the enemy may exploit American millennialism to increase the fragility of and even disrupt coalitions. Fourth, adversaries may exploit American millennialism to demoralize or TERRORIZE joint forces and the American people. By recognizing these potential vulnerabilities, military leaders and planners may TAKE ACTION NOW to mitigate the effects.[28]

Baldwin wrote that Stuckert, when using the term "millennial thought," means eschatological doctrine—thinking that involves the Second Coming of Jesus Christ. Baldwin infers—and I agree—that Stuckert is saying that a literal interpretation of the Bible in this sense is dangerous and that action should be taken against those who believe this way.

Baldwin writes:

> This is...a report written by an active duty Army major [who is now stationed in Afghanistan, I am told] for one

of America's war colleges. Before analyzing this report, here are some questions to ponder. Whose brainchild was this report? Did the major select the topic himself or did a superior assign it to him? To whom exactly was the report distributed? How was the report used? What are the interconnections between this report and the MIAC [Missouri Information Analysis Center] and Department of Homeland Security reports that draw similar conclusions? And perhaps the biggest question is, What does this report portend for government action in the future?[29]

Jesus' words ring true in these closing days of this Age of Grace:

> If the world hate you, ye know that it hated me before it hated you.
>
> If ye were of the world, the world would love its own: but because ye are not of the world, but I have chosen you out of the world, therefore the world hateth you.
>
> Remember the word that I said unto you, The servant is not greater than his lord. If they have persecuted me, they will also persecute you; if they have kept my saying, they will keep yours also.
>
> But all these things will they do unto you for my name's sake, because they know not him that sent me.
>
> If I had not come and spoken unto them, they had not had sin; but now they have no cloak for their sin.
>
> He that hateth me hateth my Father also.
>
> (John 15:18–23)

Terry James

APRIL 2010

April 26, 2010
End-Times Stage-Setting in View

It becomes increasingly difficult each week to determine which Bible prophecy indicator to examine in this column because so many signals of possible prophetic import beckon—no matter which way on the geopolitical, socioeconomic, geophysical, or religious world horizon one looks.

So, because of length limitations, I've chosen only two items of likely prophetic significance for this update. Had we no such limits, the number of news items of possible prophetic relevance would be overwhelming, the stage-setting for Bible prophecy fulfillment is so prolific.

The first of the items that stir prophetic ponderings is the nation Turkey and its "willingness" to involve itself in diplomacy between the West and Iran's development of its nuclear program. Turkey's foreign minister, Ahmet Davutoglu, after holding talks with his Iranian counterpart, Manouchehr Mottaki, indicated that Iran says Turkey is welcome to mediate to some extent the Western and Iranian governments' standoff with regard to Iran's nuclear technology development.

Western governments object to the Iranian nuclear program because they fear the purpose of the program is to produce nuclear weapons, not to produce electrical energy. The objection is logical because Iran has oil riches that would provide petroleum-based electric power for that nation for many decades into the future.

Iran's President Mahmoud Ahmadinejad has taken practically every speaking opportunity to state that he intends to wipe Israel off the map. Israel is growing impatient with Western attempts to deal gingerly with the Iranian regime. Sanctions in order to make Iran be more forthcoming in proving its nuclear efforts are peaceful haven't proved effective, and at any rate, are most often never fully implemented. It becomes increasingly evident to the Jewish state's top leadership that a military solution might well be the only solution to the threat to their security.

Turkey is currently a member of the United Nations Security Council. It supports Iran's right to pursue peaceful nuclear development. But Turkey, at the same time, is officially against all nuclear weapons development. There will come a time when Turkish leadership will have to either side with the Western concerns—thus with Israel—or with Iran, if the Iranians refuse to provide absolute proof its intentions are peaceful nuclear usage.

Togarmah is the name for the ancient territory now primarily occupied by Turkey. The people of Togarmah are prophesied to join the Persians (primarily present-day Iran) in the Gog-Magog attack of Ezekiel chapters 38–39. Recently, the government of Turkey has changed dramatically from an administration friendly to the West and Israel to one openly hostile in its rhetoric to the Jewish state.

This is partially true because Turkey depends on Iran to supply much of its natural gas for energy. However, the Islamic ties are an increasingly powerful influence that binds together these prophetically intertwined peoples.

The rapid movement of Turkey lately from the Western sphere of influence into the Eastern—particularly into the radical Islamic camp—calls for increased watchfulness.

The second of the stage-setting developments for fulfilling Bible prophecy I would like to look at is the internal pressure building within the European Union.

APRIL 2010

The following excerpt encapsulates to some extent the powerful dynamics that are in the process of rearranging things for the reviving Roman Empire of Bible prophecy:

> A Citigroup note to clients has warned that the eurozone is likely to fall apart unless the European Union's member states fuse both on the fiscal and political level. "Europe needs to stand up and decide if it is going to be a 'United States of Europe' or a 'patchwork quilt' of independent states," reads a note by Tom Fitzpatrick, chief technical analyst at Citigroup in New York.... Investors are warning of threats to the European currency even if the Greek crisis is resolved.... In February this year, hedge fund wizard George Soros also warned the eurozone was bound to break up without fiscal union.[30]

There is great concern building over the euro's continuing downward slide. For example, it has declined 6.1 percent against the U.S. dollar in recent days. The instability and fluctuations are causing the monetary powers that be, particularly in the Western economies, to seek a single currency, ultimately. The EU is the developing model around which many believe the future one-world integration of all things fiscal must be built.

Antichrist, the biblically prophesied final world dictator that is to take power before Christ's return, will come out of the area of Western Europe, according to Daniel 9:26–27. His power will be derived largely from world economic power represented by the ten kings and ten kingdoms of Revelation 17:12–13.

The control of all buying and selling through a numbering-and-mark system is foretold in Revelation 13:16–18, indicating, most biblical eschatologists believe, a supercomputer system of keeping track of all transactions. Certainly, most all of the ingredients for the biblical end-times formula are in focus today. Therefore, the stupendous, twinkling-of-an-eye moment of Christ's call to His church must be near.

Terry James

May 2010

Violence and the End of the Age

May 3, 2010

Violence: An End-Times Volcano

While Iceland spews its lava, abrasive gases, and ash and the Santiaguito volcano in Guatemala belches massive amounts of the same, a volcano of another sort seems to signal prophecy spoken by the greatest of all prophets. Human violence—as dangerous if not more so than that of the geophysical kind—is erupting.

The war on terror declared by President George W. Bush following the September 11, 2001, attacks on New York City and Washington D.C. put the spotlight on human violence spawned by Islamic fanatics. Rumors of war in the Middle East and elsewhere continue to occupy the fears of the world diplomatic community. North Korea's flashing its nuclear threat...Iran's not-so-veiled striving to achieve status as a nuclear power player—all attest to the violence around this fallen sphere.

Mankind has always been violent—since the Fall in the Garden of Eden that soon brought Cain to kill Abel. However, building violence bubbles from the very core of the cesspool of societal abscess. This violence has developed because of man's moving ever farther away from God. It is happening on a global scale, whether considering rage in Greece because of economic upheaval or atrocities by Muslim terrorists perpetrating genocide in Afghanistan and other places. But, it is the violence boiling in American city streets that I would like to consider for the moment.

Gang violence has become so deadly in Chicago that authorities want the military used to deal with the escalating dangers posed to the general public.

> CHICAGO—Two lawmakers who believe violence has become so rampant in Chicago that the Illinois National Guard must be called in to help made a public plea to Gov. Pat Quinn to deploy troops. A recent surge in violent crime, including a night last week that saw seven people killed and eighteen wounded—mostly by gunfire—prompted the request from Chicago Democratic Reps. John Fritchey and LaShawn Ford. They were joined by Willie Williams, whose son was shot and killed in 2006. Chicago has had 113 homicide victims so far this year, Fritchey said. "As we speak, National Guard members are working side-by-side with our troops to fight a war halfway around the world," he said during a news conference in downtown Chicago. "The unfortunate reality is that we have another war that is just as deadly that is taking place right in our backyard."[31]

Growing violence within our nation genuinely threatens stability to the point that the U.S. military is considered necessary to deal with the problem. Yet the mainstream media tries to make Americans believe that the peaceful, patriotic Tea ("Taxed

Enough Already") Party efforts to urge lawmakers toward fiscal sanity is the real public enemy number one. Journalists broadcast and print incessantly that Tea Party members are dangerous and disruptive to the national tranquility.

Reprobate (upside-down) thinking characterizes our lawmakers and their sycophantic news and entertainment media propagandists. Left-leaning political ideology, rather than reason and constitutional law, rules the day. Violence spawned by the lawlessness that is determined to force those who work to produce income to give to a welfare culture full of people who can but won't work rages in our streets and grows by the day.

Dr. Randall Price, an expert on recent Ararat expeditions who has been personally involved in some of them, believes the findings announced this past week about locating Noah's Ark are not legitimate. However, perhaps the very fact that great interest has been created in the possibility that the Ark might have been found at the thirteen-thousand-foot level of Mt. Ararat might be a wake-up call the Lord of Heaven wants the world to hear. That this generation is in the time Jesus said would be like the days of Noah at the time of His Second Coming just might be that message.

Jesus said:

> And as it was in the days of Noah, so shall it be also in the days of the Son of man.
>
> They did eat, they drank, they married wives, they were given in marriage, until the day that Noah entered into the ark, and the flood came, and destroyed them all. (Luke 17:26–27)

When we look at how it was in the days of Noah, we immediately discover the matter that made the Lord have to destroy all people upon the earth with the exception of Noah and his seven family members:

> The earth also was corrupt before God, and the earth was filled with violence....
>
> And God said unto Noah, The end of all flesh is come before me; for the earth is filled with violence through them; and, behold, I will destroy them with the earth. (Genesis 6:11, 13)

Volcano-like violence rumbles in the hearts of mankind. Most all signals of the Tribulation and Christ's return to rule and reign on planet earth are manifest in the headlines of our time. Christ's shout, "Come up here!" (Revelation 4:1), can happen at any moment!

May 10, 2010
America's Only Real Defense

I received a phone call from my friend Chris in New York City the other night and there was incredulity in his distinctive brogue. A subway train conductor, he was flabbergasted over the number of police personnel combing the subway and other places in the great city on the Hudson.

When a New Yorker who sees as much as a subway conductor sees every day gets excited over something, it is best to pay attention. The intensive concern of the authorities was, he and I surmised, over the attempted bombing in Times Square. Rather than easing as the present moved farther from the moment of the discovery of the loaded vehicle, the anxiety and effort to find...we don't know what...is increasing everywhere my friend looks.

A suspect has been arrested for the Saturday, May 1, bombing attempt. His name is Faisal Shahzad, apparently a naturalized U.S. citizen of Pakistani origin. He has, authorities believe, had significant help from terrorists in Pakistan.

> U.S. Attorney General Eric Holder said Mr. Shahzad was detained at John F. Kennedy Airport in New York on Monday as he attempted to board a flight to Dubai. Mr. Holder said it was clear the bomb had been intended to kill Americans.[32]

Since the time of my friend's phone call, made well after the suspect had been taken into custody, the search—for whatever reasons—seems to have intensified. It is said that the bomb found in the car in Times Square was made from fertilizer, fireworks, petrol, and propane gas tanks. It could have, the experts say, caused a significant fireball, though it was crudely constructed. The fact that it was capable of detonation but didn't go off inspired thoughts that brought me to write this commentary.

Why have such attempts to explode terrorist-planted bombs failed in the United States—when the terrorists have been highly successful in exploding their murderous devices in most other areas of the world, including the nations of the West? And why has this level of terrorism not worked here since the attacks on New York and Washington D.C. on September 11, 2001?

True—there have recently been deadly shootings by those who fit the profile of Mideast terrorists in Arkansas and Texas, as well as foiled plots, such as a planned murderous rampage in Virginia. But the hate-filled desire of the radical Islamics in Pakistan, Afghanistan, and other points eastward have not materialized.

We have heard for years that the terrorists will set off nuclear devices in large cities across America and that suitcase atomic bombs are just waiting to be detonated upon orders—from somewhere—to destroy New York, Chicago, Los Angeles, and other huge metropolitan centers. Thankfully, none of these horrendous explosions has happened.

America has the most easily accessible public and government places in the world. And Homeland Security Secretary Janet Napolitano, as well as U.S. Attorney General Eric Holder and most network and cable news pundits, have acknowledged that in the case of the Times Square bombing attempt, it was just good fortune that the explosive didn't ignite. They all say that it was good luck and alert citizenry that saved the day in New York last Saturday.

The federal officials patted each other on the backs for apprehending the suspect, even though he almost got off the runway at JFK before the plane was recalled. But they use the words "very fortunate" and "good luck" to describe the bomb's failed detonation.

Many terroristic plans have been foiled, and those responsible for national security admit that the foiled plans might just be the proverbial tip of the iceberg in consideration of the number of terroristic plots that are ongoing in this nation. Homeland Security officials readily admit that there is no way to keep track of every possible terrorist plot against this, the most hated nation by the Islamist fanatics (second only to Israel).

So it can't just be "good fortune" or "luck" that has spared us truly horrific attacks since the 9/11/01 assaults.

Certainly we who believe that God is in control of all things know that it is God, not "good fortune," who has for some reason spared the U.S. in these deadly attacks. On the other hand, absolutely no other nation is more deserving of God's great protective hand being removed. The light and truth that have been shed on America likely make our people the most responsible for living under the Lord's guidance rather than deliberately pulling in the opposite direction, as we have done in so many ways. It is a strange thing to contemplate. It's like the calm before one of our Arkansas tornadoes. You just sense that the atmosphere is ripe for a coming storm.

The Lord—not Homeland Security, the decreasingly effective U.S. military, or our growingly intrusive yet increasingly incompetent federal government—is our only defense. It is He who, for His own reasons, has prevented those who hate America and Israel from doing their most dastardly worst.

But judgment awaits and is building. It is past time for God's people—the born again—to follow the prescription the Lord gave Israel, as recorded in 2 Chronicles 7:14:

> If my people, who are called by my name, shall humble themselves, and pray, and seek my face, and turn from their wicked ways, then will I hear from heaven, and will forgive their sin, and will heal their land.

Like the psalmist, it is time for those who name the name of Christ to say:

> The LORD is my rock, and my fortress, and my deliverer; my God, my strength, in whom I will trust; my buckler, and the horn of my salvation, and my high tower.

Last-Days Diary

MAY 2010

I will call upon the LORD, who is worthy to be praised; so shall I be saved from mine enemies. (Psalms 18:2–3)

May 17, 2010
The 666 Crisis

Troubling issues and events churn within our hourly news. Powerful monetary exigencies, in particular, command the headlines. Total world financial collapse continues to be perhaps the most serious danger just ahead. Yet, each building economic crisis seems to be absorbed by the previous while the world financial markets adjust to avoid what many fiscal experts believe to be the inevitable.

It's as if a supernatural roadblock is keeping the world from collapse—an otherworldly bubble insulating against implosion. The international economic end should have come, according to all reasoning, months—even years—ago.

Greece is now the head of the European Union's festering economic sore that many fear could be terminal. With the euro sliding precipitously against the dollar and other currencies, the problems within the EU—and by extension the rest of the Western economies—are exacerbated for that developing colossus that many who study Bible prophecy believe is the heart out of which will come Antichrist and his regime of absolute control.

The EU wizards of finance are on the case, trying to stop the descent into disaster.

> LONDON—The euro fell on Tuesday as the relief effects of an emergency aid package to prevent the spread of a European debt crisis dissipated and focus switched

> back to structural problems plaguing the euro zone. European Union finance ministers, central bankers and the International Monetary Fund hammered out an emergency package of loan guarantees to euro zone members over the weekend to try and sure up sentiment in its bond markets and the euro.... The "shock and awe" plan initially boosted sentiment, allowing the euro to surge to near $1.31 on Monday, rebounding from a 14-month trough of $1.2510 hit on trading platform EBS [Electronic Broking Services] last week when investors had feared a sovereign credit crisis could spread from Greece to other euro zone countries.... Investors doubt whether the Greek government will be able to carry out the austerity measures required to restructure its public finances. Other states such as Portugal and Spain also have budgetary concerns.[33]

It isn't too much of a stretch to consider that because the desired unity of European nations is built around a once-ballyhooed but now-failing currency, we might be witnessing the construction of the feet and toes of the metallic man-image Daniel the prophet interpreted for Babylonian King Nebuchadnezzar concerning the king's vision. The euro isn't working; the EU nations, put in simplistic terms, don't trust each other. Here's what Daniel was given to prophesy about the very end of the history of world kingdoms:

> And whereas thou sawest the feet and toes, part of potters' clay and part of iron, the kingdom shall be divided; but there shall be in it of the strength of the iron, forasmuch as thou sawest the iron mixed with miry clay.

May 2010

> And as the toes of the feet were part of iron and part of clay, so the kingdom shall be partly strong, and partly broken.
>
> And whereas thou sawest iron mixed with miry clay, they shall mingle themselves with the seed of men; but they shall not cleave one to another, even as iron is not mixed with clay. (Daniel 2:41–43)

The United States is still the center of world power so far as the Western world is concerned. America's president, whose mercurial efforts to change U.S. economic structure in every possible way—catastrophically, in my opinion—is directly intervening in Europe's monetary manipulations. Mr. Obama's extensive talks by phone with French President Nicolas Sarkozy and German Chancellor Angela Merkel are believed to be perhaps the primary catalysts behind the €750 billion bailout agreed over the weekend by the eurozone leaders.

The gigantic, multi-trillion-dollar Band-Aids that the American administration, aided and abetted by a strangely acquiescent Congress, has pasted over the gaping economic wound from which the U.S. is suffering hasn't worked. Yet, the Europeans seem anxious to follow Obama's failed regimen of treatment. This could be because the already-bankrupt American taxpayers will be expected to contribute mightily to the EU bailout.

The American president recently said in his "New Foundations" speech that he wants prosperity—not fueled by reckless debt, but by skilled, productive workers. He wants sustained growth, not economic stagnation. Yet the policies he now twists the arms of European leaders to adopt continue to prove destructive to prosperity. His calamitous policies continue to be fueled by, in effect, reckless debt—nonexistent money that takes America ever deeper into an abyss of deficits.

The American and EU economies are in such a state of chaos and decline that they must find a way to bring about controls that will prevent complete collapse. Collapse is nonetheless inevitable unless draconian measures are taken.

President Obama's chief of staff, Rahm Emanuel, once told a *Wall Street Journal* conference of top corporate chief executives: "You never want a serious crisis to go to waste." It will take such a crisis—one of unprecedented magnitude—to cause all leaders to institute those draconian measures necessary to control all buying and selling under one system of economy.

That crisis is coming. It will be the dagger that pierces the bubble provided by God's staying hand of judgment upon this fallen world. The Rapture will, I'm convinced, produce the crisis that will clear the path for 666 (Revelation 13:16–18).

May 24, 2010
Greece, Thailand, America, and the Rapture

Greece and Thailand face mobs of addicted citizenries that have been put on rations. Having for years been the wards of government-engendered employment and socialistic largesse, the people of those nations are enraged by the realities of painful withdrawal.

Greece has been required by the European Union to put into effect severe austerity measures in order to qualify for a massive bailout. Without the almost-trillion-dollar infusion, Greece would become insolvent, a thing the EU and Western democracies cannot allow to happen.

Last-Days Diary

MAY 2010

It was a weekend rich in symbolism. Sunday, May 9, was Europe Day, the sixtieth anniversary of the moment when France, Germany, and the other war-shattered European states declared they would pool their resources in a supranational community. The message—"from crisis comes opportunity"—was not lost on today's generation of European leaders. With Greece seemingly on the brink of insolvency and markets pounding other vulnerable euro members like Portugal and Spain, the continued viability of the single currency—the European Union's most emblematic project—is under threat. So in the early hours of Monday morning, after weeks of indecision, Europe's leaders met the challenge by setting up a colossal €750 billion ($950 billion) crisis fund.[34]

The International Monetary Fund/eurozone bailout stipulated that the Greek government drastically cut its huge deficit of 13.6 percent of the nation's gross domestic product (GDP). Jay Bryson, global economist at Wells Fargo Securities, said that Europe's monetary crisis won't ease "until money starts to flow" to Greece from the EU/IMF. He said the crisis will probably linger for a time even with such measures.

The Greek national government has had to do away with a large number of jobs that were linked directly to public services and bureaucratic positions. Ever-increasing government controls destroyed incentives for creating private-sector employment. Demands by Greek citizenry (mostly government employees' unions) that they could retire with full benefits as early as age forty-five in some cases, age fifty-three on average, and massive expenditures on public social services drove deficit spending to calamitous levels.

Austerity implementation and its effects on Greek society have been profound. Rioting in the streets has brought things to the crisis level, and has drawn a harsh response from police and the military. The EU/IMF infusion of a trillion dollars is only a stop-gap effort to prevent total implosion of Greek society, thus possibly the EU itself. When the people have been given their fix to assuage the pain of weaning off the government spigot—what then?

Thailand is perhaps even bloodier than Greece in the government-versus-the unions clashes. Thailand's workers have become accustomed to a bureaucratic handout society. Its "fledgling democracy is now all but dead, bloodied and battered on the streets of Bangkok. How did this happen?"[35]

The question, posed by *ABC News,* frames the situation precisely. America's heretofore relatively stable ally in Southeast Asia is in the process of meltdown because of economic crisis. The government is in disarray due to conflict primarily brought on by handing out more money to the populace than can be sustained, in order to gain political advantage.

Riots fill the streets of Bangkok. A continuing battle rages between the forces of a brutal, unresponsive government (that seems for the moment to be winning the day) and the "red shirts"—organized workers against what they perceive as government discontinuing the policies of universal health care, infrastructure investment, local economic stimulus, and agricultural debt relief. The workers had come to expect all of those policies as guaranteed rights.

The fact is, Thailand is mischaracterized in being called a "fledgling democracy." Like Greece, the masses are addicted to getting socialistic largesse for their votes. The government, used to being in favor because of, in effect, buying votes with a Thai version of pork-barrel spending, is reacting as many socialistic governments do when opposed. Many believe Greece and Thailand are well down the road of the same path America is taking.

Jesus said that it would be like it was in the days of Noah and in the days of Lot at the time God's judgment and wrath begins to fall (Luke 17:26–29). One of the characteristics the apostle Paul gave in his "perilous times" prophecies (2 Timothy 3) is that people will be "incontinent." This means they will lack self-control. A further meaning is that they will be incorrigibly susceptible to violently craving fixes for their addictions.

A major addiction I perceive as becoming pandemic at this late hour of human history is the craving for pay without work by growing numbers of people in America and within the Western economies. Socialism might be considered the virus that infects the masses who demand that the few pay for the many to enjoy the comforts of life.

Noah endured mocking and threats by listless, vile masses as he prepared the ark while preaching the message that his fellow men should repent. Lot, in Sodom, endured the vexation caused by the incontinent (sex-addicted) people who demanded that they be served night and day. Jesus said it will be like that at the time He will catastrophically intervene in the affairs of mankind at the end of the age. People will be prone to addictions without control—"incontinent."

That "perilous times" characteristic of end-times man seems to be infecting this generation in many areas, and especially in matters of economy. The distress it is causing the nations, which are in perplexity as to how to fix the problems involved, will one day cause a tyrant of unprecedented power and authority to call for a one-world monetary system. I'm more and more convinced that the computer solution he will concoct will be a system of special drawing rights—electronic funds transfer.

Monetary chaos is building across the world. I believe it will take a crisis of major proportion to get people around the globe to agree to give up their nationalistic, autonomous allegiances in the desperate hope that their comforts might be secured, preserved, or restored.

With the signals of the end of the age in every direction we look—including the addiction-prone characteristic of humanity we've just examined—we have good reason to wonder: Might the Rapture be about to serve as the instrument the Lord uses to bring about the crisis that will give Antichrist the excuse to produce his system of control foretold in Revelation 13:16–18?

May 31, 2010
U.S. Paving Way for Final Führer

Try as I might to get away from thinking on the stupefying swiftness with which the world's monetary crises are reshaping our existence, I can't. I consider only the so-called peace process being foisted upon Israel by the American administration and other members of the Quartet—the United Nations, the European Union, and Russia—to be of slightly more profound prophetic importance than the current economic chaos. So, please indulge me yet another swipe at the matters involved.

Most are aware that the Western world in particular is in unprecedented economic turmoil. While the Great Depression of the 1930s was terrible in its ramifications for the planet's inhabitants, the crisis was relatively simple in its cause-and-effect dynamics. Relatively simple, that is, compared to the complexities that the decades have wrought with the evolution of interlinkage between banking institutions and governments.

Computers, satellites, and myriad other technological wonders have intertwined the fiscal health of continents in a way that was impossible to imagine before the advent of such technology. Actions taken in London, Berlin, Paris, New York, or other such disparate financial centers can instantaneously cause global reverberations. This intimate linkage can and has included mechanisms to use in averting—perhaps better put, postponing—disastrous monetary crises. Manipulation by the wizards of finance has worked to this point. But now it seems their magic has fueled a gathering economic storm that is about to break upon a world ill-prepared to cope with what is coming.

Now for the conspiracy-theorist within your essayist. The question that leaps to the forefront is this: How much of the economic storm that is ready to break upon the world was fueled by the stumbling, bumbling machinations of those at the monetary controls, and how much was deliberately and masterfully contrived?

What follows provides a glimpse into the eye of that cyclonic economic turbulence:

> BRUSSELS—European Council President Herman Van Rompuy has said he is looking to establish a clearer "hierarchy" among the EU institutions and member states to make it easier to deal with any future crises in the eurozone....
>
> "We are working in order to have some crisis cabinet because we are a lot of players in the field—certainly

> when you are in crisis—and there is not much hierarchy or organic links between the main players and the main institutions.... Really, this is a problem," he told a gathering organised by European Movement International on Tuesday [May 25]....
>
> The tentative proposal comes after the EU's often torturous approach to the Greek debt crisis—a protracted response that widened the problem to the eurozone and almost made it a global crisis.
>
> As market-induced panic looked set to gain a foothold, and following the intervention of U.S. President Barack Obama, the sixteen-member eurozone agreed on a €750 million EU/IMF package earlier this month.
>
> But it is widely agreed that this is only a stop-gap measure and that the EU's budget discipline rules need to be tightened.[36]

Bible prophecy again asserts its truth into our daily headlines regarding breaking developments. Like the peace efforts that pressure Israel to give the international community and the Jewish state's enemies their way in dominating news headlines, powerful global economic rearrangements involving the reviving Roman Empire at the heart of the process now also command top headlines above the front-page folds of the world's newspapers.

Reuniting Europe and its first president demanding greatly increased powers to act in the present European and global financial meltdown hammer home the point. This generation almost certainly is witnessing the groundwork being laid that will assure Antichrist's eventual elevation to supreme authority prophesied in the thirteenth chapter of Revelation. The pace with which things are shaping up makes one wonder whether that man of sin might step onto the stage of history quite soon.

As has been said before, one of the most-often asked questions we get at prophecy conferences is: "Is America in Bible prophecy?" We most always answer in one form or another, "No, it is not mentioned by name." However, I must add that this, certainly the most materially blessed nation and one of the most spiritually blessed countries to exist on earth, is in Bible prophecy by implication. Our current president is at the very heart of influencing the two most critical headlines of these troubled days, both of which are at the top of the list as being Bible prophecy indicators for comprising world conditions at the very end of the age. The U.S. thus seems to be in the lead in helping pave the way for the world's final führer.

Terry James
JUNE 2010

Israel, Gog-Magog Nations at Stage-Setting Center

June 7, 2010

Phenomenal Prophetic Picture Emerging

One of the most consistent truths of our time is that no matter where the news cameras and microphones are pointed, they will always be turned again to the nation Israel and Jerusalem in short order.

Most recently, that truth has been proved before the eyes of the world. The financial upheavals in America and around the globe had the leaders of the nations and the journalists alike deeply engrossed in the threat to the world's economic stability. North Korea sank the South Korean naval vessel, killing a number of people, and Kim Jong-Il's "double dog dare" to do anything about it—after denying his regime's culpability—again had the diplomats and reporters fearing the possible outbreak of nuclear war. At the same time, the immigration law passed by the Arizona state legislature and signed by the governor made the mainstream news organizations and left-leaning politicians go ballistic. Then the oil rig exploded, killing eleven of the rig's crew in the Gulf of

Mexico and releasing into the waters a gusher that threatens the ecosystem of the Gulf Coast and beyond.

With consistency that is 100-percent faithful to some unseen force that suctions it toward the world's spotlight, Israel stands front and center once again, despite the momentous events in the headlines. The news cameras and microphones now are aimed at the sliver-sized nation that has raised the collective ire of the world with a single incident.

Israel, as most everyone knows by now, stopped and boarded a flotilla of ships loaded with, supposedly, activists and their cargoes of humanitarian aid items for the Palestinians of Gaza. The Jewish state, with the understanding of Egypt and other nations of the region, has placed a blockade on anything going to Gaza because of the terrorists who continue to inhabit that area. Israel has suffered continuing attacks by the forces supplied by Hamas and other terrorist organizations.

The Israeli naval personnel gave the six flotilla ships a warning that they were to go to a port as directed so that the cargo could be checked for weapons that might be intended for the terrorists of Gaza. The humanitarian aid, Israel promised, would then be shipped by land to the people of Gaza. The crews aboard the six ships refused, instead shouting curses and insults at the Israelis. After further warnings that they would be boarded if they didn't comply and receiving in return only more curses, the Israelis boarded the ships.

Israeli Defense Force (IDF) commandos were assaulted by the people who were on the boarded ships. The "activists" used iron bars, baseball bats, slingshots (firing steel balls), handguns, and rifles. Finally, for protection, deadly force was used by the

IDF, and reports have it that from nine to eleven of the so-called humanitarian activists, all speaking Arabic, were killed, and a number injured.

IDF spokesperson Avi Benayahu said this about the commandos boarding and the subsequent attacks by the people on the boarded ships:

> IDF forces met with pre-planned violence when attempting to board the flotilla. IDF naval personnel encountered severe violence, including use of weaponry prepared in advance in order to attack and harm them. The forces operated in adherence with operational commands and took all necessary actions in order to avoid violence, but to no avail.[37]

There is little doubt that it was a setup—a deliberate action to lure the Israelis on board, then make Israel appear as the bad players before the eyes of the entire world. The ploy cost the lives of a number of the ambushers, but what's a few dead fellow terrorists to those who have no compunction about strapping bombs onto their own children and women and sending them out to kill themselves and anyone around them?

The ambush was about as successful as the terrorists could have hoped. The Turkey-sponsored "activist humanitarian aid" flotilla instantly brought the diplomatic world to the boiling point of anger against the Jewish state.

Turkey froze military ties with Israel, promising "unprecedented and incalculable reprisals." The nation's leaders threatened to send yet another flotilla to run the blockade, this time using Turkey's navy as an escort. The Arab League called for a meeting to assess a response to the Israeli action, with the organization's leaders from Palestinian president Mahmoud Abbas to Arab League chief Amr Moussa calling Israel's action "a massacre" and a "crime." Egypt, heretofore quasi-supporting the blockade of Gaza, is leaning toward removing the blockade. Greece, a partner with Israel in military exercises, will likely withdraw from participating with the Jewish state.

Israel faces enormous outrage from around the world. UN chief Ban Ki-moon said he was "shocked" by the Israeli action against the peaceful flotilla and called for the Israeli government to "explain itself" for the move. Governments around the world summoned Israel's ambassadors. Britain, France, China, and Russia, all of which wield the veto power of the UN Security Council, called for the blockade against Gaza to be lifted and for an independent inquiry into the incident. The other veto-empowered member, the United States, hinted that the blockade should be lifted.

Ambassadors from the twenty-seven European Union countries strongly condemned Israel and called for a complete and independent inquiry.

It seems that about the only friends Israel has left at the moment are Christians who understand the real story about these astounding anti-Israel developments. Those developments are prophetic, make no mistake. The incident has put the end-times picture into clearer focus for all who study God's prophetic Word from a literal viewpoint.

Two main prophecies leap to mind when considering these developments. They are found in Zechariah 12:1–3 and Ezekiel 38 and 39.

Zechariah, the Old Testament prophet, foretold God's Word

on Israel versus all nations of the world at the very end of human history just before Christ's return. And Ezekiel made plain that the Middle East nations would specifically be formed against Israel at the time of the end.

The attempt to run the Gaza blockade and Israel's subsequent boarding of the flotilla ships bring both prophecies to the forefront of the hour. Turkey—comprising much of the area called Togarmah in the Ezekiel 38:6 passage—has gone from being a secular-based government to one that is heavily Islamic. Segments of Islam are trying to make it totally Islamic and one ruled by sharia law. That country has now turned totally against Israel, whereas only a couple of years earlier it was one of Israel's friends in the region.

All nations of the world—represented by the United Nations—have, in effect, condemned or come against the Jewish state. It is clear that Zechariah 12:1–3 is manifesting itself before the news cameras, thus before the eyes of all who have discernment to see and believe the veracity of God's Word.

June 14, 2010
EU as Reviving Rome in Question

Is the European Union on its way to dissolution? Do the developing economic cracks that seem all but impossible to repair mean that it's over for the EU?

More to the point of our concern here: If the EU were to fail, does it mean that we who believe we are seeing the Roman Empire reviving in the EU are wrong? Thus, will the area out of which Antichrist is foretold to emerge not be Western Europe, but rather somewhere else?

Are those correct who proclaim that the "prince that shall come" of Daniel 9:27 will emerge from the eastern leg rather than the western leg of Nebuchadnezzar's dream-vision (Daniel 2)?

These questions come across my e-mail quite frequently these days. Europe's economic problems are worse than those of the United States, it is generally agreed by monetary experts. Could it be that Humpty Dumpty, who fell apart with the decline and fall of the ancient Roman Empire, who was then patched together in the 1950s and has been coming back together in a major way since, is now on its way to taking another great fall?

I defer in matters of high finance to experts such as my friend Wilfred Hahn when it comes to precisely laying out the case for what is likely to happen in the precarious economic positions of Europe, America, and the world. But there are some important matters within what I believe we see happening from a biblically prophetic standpoint that should be interjected.

Hahn writes:

> The Bible tells us that a group of ten ally together out of common self-interest. They have one purpose and will give their power and authority to the beast (Revelation 17:13). The large multinational nation groups of today simply have too many conflicts of interest to be any effective consequence in today's geopolitical environment. Developments in Asia today also, we believe, play a decisive role in these last-day machinations of ten kings.[38]

It makes perfect sense that the many turf fiefdoms held by the powers large and small across the planet will never—under anything approaching normal circumstances—give in to a central authority. Such acquiescence will have to be wrested from their grip in a painful manner.

One thing is sure: The beast system of Antichrist (Revelation 13:16–18) will manage, ultimately, to get all governmental entities to give him their power and authority (Revelation 17:12–13). That power and authority will consist, at its base, of economic control. Hahn correctly surmises, because he relies upon Bible prophecy, that ten entities (called "kings") will ally out of common self-interest. Seven of the ten will willingly give up their power and authority, and three will have it ripped from their grip by the most powerful tyrant ever to draw breath (Daniel 7:24).

Whether the power is taken by willing acquiescence of the seven heads of the entities involved or by force, as seems to be the case of the three kings having their power and authority stripped from them by the beast in Daniel 7:24, the deed will be done.

It is no surprise. Recent crushing fiscal issues and events point to the inescapable reality that something is going to have to happen soon, or world economic implosion will result. Again, Hahn writes:

> Recent events are therefore of no surprise. What is always unpredictable in crisis situations is the specific catalyst that prompts a reappraisal of risk...the sudden awakening to reality.[39]

I believe that catalyst—the crisis that will cause all sovereign leaderships to realize they must come together to give up their desperately held-onto turf kingdoms—will be the Rapture. The ensuing chaos will cause most everyone left behind to rethink their worldviews. The prince that shall come will have the answers they seek—at least, they will believe him to have the answers.

As expressed before in this column, I'm convinced that a completely changed economic order based upon special drawing rights or a system of electronic funds transfer (computer units, not hard currency of any sort) will be acceptable to most leaderships around the world. The ten kings of Revelation 17:12–13 who correspond to the entities of Daniel 7:24 will perhaps be, in my scenario, ten pan-continental trading blocs modeled on the eurozone prototype. Thus, Daniel's prophecy of the ten-toed, final, humanistic system of government that Christ's return will smash to pieces will be fulfilled.

I agree with Wilfred Hahn that the current apparent crumbling of Europe in no way means the EU is finished as the prime candidate for the reviving Roman Empire. The crisis that will bring everything into perfect prophetic alignment, in regard to the 666 beast government, will, I'm more and more convinced, be the shout from heaven: "Come up here" (Revelation 4:1).

June 21, 2010
The Sea and the Waves Roaring in Gulf Gaffe

Let me begin by stating that I don't see Jesus' prophecy in His Olivet Discourse fulfilled in the Gulf oil fiasco. However, the process of fulfillment has begun, I believe. The prophecy to which I refer is the following:

> And there shall be signs in the sun, and in the moon, and in the stars; and upon the earth distress of nations, with perplexity; the sea and the waves roaring. (Luke 21:25)

It is obvious that the many people of the Gulf region are roaring in their distress—and rightfully so. The term "sea" is often used symbolically or figuratively rather than literally in biblical language. This is especially true in biblical prophecy. For example, in Revelation, John uses the term "sea" as follows:

> And I stood upon the sand of the sea, and saw a beast rise up out of the sea, having seven heads and ten horns, and upon his horns ten crowns, and upon his heads the name of blasphemy. (Revelation 13:1)

Later, John prophesies:

> And I beheld another beast coming up out of the earth; and he had two horns like a lamb, and he spoke like a dragon. (Revelation 13:11)

These references, of course, are to the political leader who will be Antichrist in the first instance, and to the False Prophet who will be his sidekick—his John the Baptist—in the second. Antichrist comes out of the sea; the False Prophet comes out of the earth, or land.

Antichrist "coming out of the sea" refers to the sea of peoples of the world—the Gentile world (non-Jewish world). The second beast, the False Prophet, comes out of the earth. This, most of the pretribulational view of Bible prophecy believe, means this character will come out of the land of promise—the land God gave to Abraham, Isaac, and Jacob. Many are convinced the False Prophet will be a Jew.

While the sea of humanity that this terrible accident so adversely affects is roaring in distress, the Gulf gusher is but a token of things to come. The Tribulation hour is looming just ahead in the murkiness of these strange times.

What leaps at the observer of the days in which we live—those who do so through the prism of God's prophetic Word—is the swiftness of the global, in-our-faces grab for power. And it is done overwhelmingly against the wishes of the American people. If I didn't absolutely know better from intensive study and prayer, I might join some of the wonderful, but not fully informed, folks whose e-mails I've received over the months since the last presidential inauguration.

These believe Barack Hussein Obama is the prime candidate for the first beast of Revelation 13. He isn't, of course, although I've been called at least twice by *The Daily Show* trying to get me to say he is, so Jon Stewart can have his version of fun with us Christian types. When I told the callers that I believe Mr. Obama is not the Antichrist, they asked me on each occasion to give them the name of someone—from among my colleagues, I presume—who does think he fits the bill.

The sea of humanity is indeed roaring, both here and around the globe. Not to the extent it will be in the coming Tribulation years, but it is roaring nonetheless, while governments seem to be striving to prevent people from working, in order to create a dependent class on a global scale. In this sense, the situation is in a very real way setting the stage for fulfillment of prophecy.

Economic desperation has the people and the world beginning to roar in distress. This is a major birth-pang convulsion, in my view.

June 2010

In these commentaries, we have detailed the many facets of America's multi-trillion-dollar indebtedness. We have chronicled Europe's even-deeper slide into the fiscal morass of these strange times. The Gulf oil spill and ensuing madness just exacerbate the conditions in which we find ourselves, and the sea thunders ever louder. Rioting over socialistic largesse being withdrawn illustrates the addiction to the proverbial free lunch among those on the government feeding spigot. Others in Europe and Asia roar with demands that their freebies be restored. There has been bloodshed in some cases, and the nations are in perplexity as to how to assuage the collective anger.

And now the president of the United States has made the brilliant decision to pile on the good people of the Gulf region who have been, perhaps catastrophically, damaged by the British Petroleum oil spill. His presidential edict seems to me not a bad decision by an incompetent, but a calculated geopolitical move to begin the process of instituting his agenda and that of the globalists-elite to bring the U.S. under a larger governance.

Remember the words of the president's chief of staff, who said that a crisis is something that must not be wasted. We saw and heard his boss put those words into action Tuesday evening, June 15, from the Oval Office. Obama went—not subtly—from talking about how the people of the Gulf were suffering and how BP would pay to talking about how it all means that America must convert to green energy. The agenda is still to deal dictatorially with global warming—or climate change, as the liberal ideologues now call it. Obama declared a moratorium on offshore drilling, thus making it certain that the Gulf population will suffer. In addition to the environmental and tourist impact, as well as the loss to the fishing industry, none of the oil production jobs of the region will exist any longer.

There is method to the madness, even if this president and the pundits who rant in every confused direction can't see it all in terms of the biblically prophetic picture. A supreme crisis is welling—not just in the Gulf of Mexico, but throughout the world. The sea is beginning to roar in increasing waves of volume and violence.

The crisis/storm will break in full fury, I'm convinced, when the Rapture takes the church to Heaven and the conscience of mankind is no longer restrained by the Holy Spirit. The apostle Paul foretold the following in that regard:

> For the mystery of iniquity doth already work; Only he who now letteth will let until he be taken out of the way. And then shall that wicked be revealed, whom the Lord shall consume with the spirit of his mouth, and shall destroy with the brightness of his coming,
>
> Even him, whose coming is after the working of Satan with all power and signs and lying wonders,
>
> And with all deceivableness of unrighteousness in them that perish; because they received not the love of the truth, that they might be saved.
>
> (2 Thessalonians 2:7–10)

When the Holy Spirit resident within the church—the body of believers—no longer restrains evil in mankind as before the Rapture, Antichrist will have the roaring-sea crisis that he will use to enslave most of the planet. The stage-setting process for that is well underway.

June 2010

June 28, 2010
Jesus' Critical Question for End-Times Believers

A recent news item about certain polling data grasped my attention. I'm sure many who peruse www.raptureready.com's news section had their curiosity piqued and read it as well.

After looking into matter, I found the poll wasn't as thorough as I would have liked—but it was fascinating nonetheless. Also, it was too one-sided in ethnic makeup. However, I give it enough credence to examine it here because I believe it revolves around a concern the Lord Jesus Christ expressed while teaching about conditions that will prevail at the end of the age.

A new survey finds that Americans are divided over whether they believe Jesus Christ will return by the year 2050.

Among respondents to the survey by the Pew Research Center for the People and the Press and *Smithsonian Magazine,* 41 percent said they expect Jesus' Second Coming in the next forty years, while 46 percent said it probably or definitely won't happen.

The poll suggests that 58 percent of white evangelicals believe Jesus will return by 2050, compared to only 32 percent of Catholics, and respondents with no college education were three times as likely as those with college degrees to expect Christ's Second Coming in the next forty years.[40]

To be honest, I was quite surprised that 58 percent of white evangelicals believe Christ will return by 2050. This disconnect in my mind comes from the fact that in looking for interest in Bible prophecy within the church today (by this I mean, of course, born-again believers—see John 3:3), my colleagues and I find no evidence to support that percentage.

Perhaps I should speak just for myself, but if my colleagues are honest, based upon conversations we've had among ourselves, they will confess that the interest just isn't there in those kinds of numbers.

So, a few cynical (I suppose) thoughts regarding the poll come to mind:

1) The poll is a complete "guesstimate"—even a prefabrication.
2) The poll is skewed because it was taken from among a limited group of believers thoroughly educated in Bible prophecy.
3) The poll reflects a flippancy that will agree that Christ could return within the next forty years because the possibility is far enough in the future that the respondents need not worry about changing their personal conduct.
4) My colleagues and I are wrong and the church—"white evangelicals," in this case—is expecting the Lord's return in majority numbers.

If the last point is true, then the fact that so many are looking for Christ is well hidden. I'm a blind guy, as many know, so I can't see things all that well. But interest in Christ's return—and in Bible prophecy in general, according to everything I hear—is confined to an extremely small number of folks in relationship to the tremendous number of people who claim the name of Christ.

Clicking through Christian TV networks (yes, we blind guys "watch" TV), I rarely come across a prophetic message. The majority of the viewing fare consists of the prosperity gospel or entertainment that is for the most part a rather poor knockoff of secular entertainment. The preachers who do present a sound gospel message and sound doctrine seldom, if ever, speak on Bible prophecy. And they certainly don't touch upon the pretribulational return of Christ in the Rapture.

When I've personally asked some of the preachers and teachers why they avoid presenting prophecy, they have said things like:

"The people just don't understand Revelation."

"The subject is just too scary to most people."

"We just concentrate on getting people the gospel so they will be saved."

Some honest preachers and teachers say: "I just don't know anything about prophecy. I've not studied it enough to preach on it."

What a tragedy, a travesty, this is! There is a singular hope (Titus 2:13) that God's people have in this swiftly degenerating age. Yet, their shepherds—the preachers and teachers, their suppliers of spiritual food—use every conceivable excuse for not telling Christians about their returning Lord.

Some accuse those of us whose mission we believe it is to concentrate on Bible prophecy of ignoring Christ's love and the Bible's life lessons for His people.

We in no way believe that prophecy should be taught exclusively. However, prophecy constitutes almost 30 percent of the whole Word of God, so the Heavenly Father obviously means for prophecy to be a generous part of the mix for His children's spiritual sustenance. This is especially true in these days when the signals of Christ's coming again are in every direction one looks.

Bible prophecy is being marginalized by many of those who

are supposed to shepherd their flocks, but who don't want to study it and/or don't want to risk scaring people out of the pews. This is because it is the feel-good and do-good, entertainment-oriented sermonettes that tickle itching ears and build many of the elaborate end-times edifices.

Understand that I recognize there are huge churches that hold to doctrinal truth and include God's prophetic Word as part of feeding their attending flocks. This is not to castigate these wonderful pastors, teachers, and staffs. God bless them! But these are in the minority. The dearth of interest in Christ's coming back in the Rapture, then in the Second Advent, demonstrates the lack of faith resident within Christ's body at this crucial hour.

Jesus asked the following profoundly troubling question in that prophetic context:

> Nevertheless when the Son of man cometh, shall he find faith on the earth? (Luke 18:8b)

The indifference so prevalent within the church is, itself, an end-times signal, it seems. The Lord obviously spoke to the fact that God's own children will in large part be indifferent to the prophetic signals. They will not be living as they should at the time of His coming for them, as He promised in John 14:1–3. As a matter of fact, He forewarned:

> And take heed to yourselves, lest at any time your hearts be overcharged with surfeiting, and drunkenness, and cares of this life, and so that day come upon you unawares.
>
> For like a snare shall it come on all them that dwell on the face of the whole earth.

June 2010

> Watch ye, therefore, and pray always, that ye may be accounted worthy to escape all these things that shall come to pass, and to stand before the Son of man. (Luke 21:34–36)

I pray more born-again pastors, Bible teachers, and God's children of this nation and the world will awaken en masse to the staggering implications of Christ's Second Coming.

Worldwide Worries in the News

July 5, 2010
Troubled Hearts in Troublous Times

Frightening news and expressions of worries stream minute by minute into my in-box, threatening to reach an unmanageable level. But the flow, unlike the oil gushing unstoppably into the Gulf of Mexico, is welcome. The messages are rich in information about the convulsions making up these troublous times, times that almost certainly presage the Second Advent of Christ.

For example, a dear friend of the Rapture Ready site is extremely concerned based upon a report she received from a ministry. The report reads, in part:

> A well-placed source in California told [a ministry I've omitted] that the California Emergency Management Agency (CEMA) has been briefed by its counterpart agencies in the Gulf coast states that there are plans to conduct a mass evacuation of millions of Gulf coast residents due to the catastrophic environmental and public health effects of the BP oil disaster....

> The Gulf states' emergency planners stressed to their California counterparts that they are dealing with a disaster of unprecedented proportions and that contingency plans are being constantly updated and revised on ways to deal with the transformation of the Gulf of Mexico into a deadly "toxic soup" of oil and Corexit 9500 oil dispersants and the atmosphere into a dangerous mixture of hydrocarbon gases.
>
> CEMA was briefed on the impending mass evacuation, since California would be expected to absorb a large number of evacuees from the Gulf states. CEMA officials did not say how the state of California, which is virtually bankrupt, would pay for the influx of hundreds of thousands, and perhaps greater, numbers of evacuees from the Gulf coastal region.[41]

The point is that it is but one of an incredible number of such reports appearing in my in-box from every direction. God's people are becoming increasingly troubled by the fearful things purported to be on the cusp of shattering their lives.

When one attempts to pin down the reporting entity as being from a source or sources with official credentials with which to present the supposed pending catastrophes, one finds little, if any, substantiation that the fountainhead of information has credibility.

One claim is that there is a gargantuan methane bubble building that will erupt and immediately cause all vessels in the Gulf near the site to instantly sink. The erupting gas will then send a tsunami of unfathomable height cascading as far inland as two hundred to three hundred miles.

This dire warning is made even more frightening by the reports of the evacuations and relocations the reporters of these matters say government will demand. At last, the crisis will have arrived that will give government the excuse to move people into the feared FEMA [Federal Emergency Management Agency] gulags warned about by the conspiracy theorists over recent years.

On another front in the e-mail deluge of fearful news, the methane-like economic bubble continues to grow. This is a 100-percent-verifiable catastrophe on the brink of exploding upon this nation and the world. Todd and I have discussed this growing monster many times and conclude that the only reason the U.S. and the world aren't in the darkest depression imaginable is due to the staying hand of God. By all accounting principles, the bubble should have exploded long ago.

The G-20 (Group of 20) nation leaders have just, in effect, told the president of the United States that they will not follow his lead in adding more stimulus funding to try to avert the inevitable economic implosion if spending isn't brought under control. Much of Europe has sown the seeds of socialistic insanity for decades, and now is reaping the destructive whirlwind.

Still, Mr. Obama insists we can spend our way out of the terrible situation. This he insists upon, despite the reality that every economic expert of late calls such profligate spending "unsustainable." People who send the e-mails are understandably in distress over what looks to be apocalyptic things to come.

Many messages I receive include articles on the Israeli-Iranian nuclear confrontation nightmare in the making. This, too, is a legitimate reason for worry, and from that worry comes the inflow of reports, many of which I sense, however, are based upon armchair surmising, rather than hands-on, on-the-scene reporting accuracy.

JULY 2010

One "news source" in particular has earned my skepticism over the years. Time after time this source—which I won't name here—has reported things that were made to sound like Armageddon-level events about to explode. Each time the mainstream media—for whom I have little regard, so far as unbiased news is concerned—proved to be accurate, and the source to which I refer, totally inaccurate. Thus, I very cautiously scrutinize whatever comes from that quarter.

Such is the case in the current reports from this questionable source—those reports of the third U.S. carrier group maneuvering in the waters near Iran.

The reports say that the USS Nassau (LHA-4) Amphibious Ready Group 24th Marine Expeditionary Unit, charged with supporting the Bahrain-based 5th Fleet area of operations, is cruising around the Bab el-Mandeb Strait where the Gulf of Aden flows into the Red Sea.

The USS Harry S. Truman Carrier Strike Group consisting of twelve warships is reported to be cruising in the Arabian Sea. The Dwight D. Eisenhower Strike Group is said to be cruising farther west in the Arabian Sea.

This source of some concern to me—so far as its credibility is in question—adds the strong intimation that these U.S. naval vessels are loaded to the brim with marines and other troops. They are, I sense we are expected to infer, just awaiting orders to take on the Iranian ground forces in a preemptive action.

The reports have it that Israel is in the mix with some naval vessels of its own, engendering fear of an imminent major crisis.

All of this is the grist of growing anxiety for those who write us at an ever-increasing rate. The notes are much appreciated, and

I encourage the senders to continue. These help us to stay on top of the rapidly changing conditions of these end times.

I'm not pooh-poohing any of these or any other areas of concern. Perhaps that oil disaster will explode into a greater catastrophe. Maybe the global economic implosion will take place soon. Possibly the current build-up in the waters around Iran will result in Middle East war.

What I wish for Christians to consider, however, is that Jesus made a very specific statement about just such a time as surrounds God's people today.

Fox News host Sean Hannity uses the Lord's exhortation in each of his nightly programs—although I don't know whether he has a clue about its powerful meaning. "Let not your heart be troubled," he says, I guess to assuage anxiety over the many snippets of bad news discussed on his show.

Jesus was most definitely telling His followers that we are to take heart, no matter how bad things look at the time of His return. His comforting words should embolden every believer:

> Let not your heart be troubled; ye believe in God, believe also in me.
>
> In my Father's house are many mansions; if it were not so, I would have told you. I go to prepare a place for you.
>
> And if I go and prepare a place for you, I will come again, and receive you unto myself, that where I am, there ye may be also. (John 14:1–3).

He said further; after giving an overview of the fearful signs that would come upon the world like birth pangs just before

He reaches down to snatch His people up into the clouds of glory:

> When these things begin to come to pass, then look up, and lift up your heads; for your redemption draweth near. (Luke 21:28)

We certainly are seeing these things begin to come to pass. Let not your heart be troubled.

July 12, 2010
Deadly Pressure for Peace

While much attention is concentrated upon the oil spill crisis in the Gulf of Mexico, an infinitely greater pressure than that feared to be beneath those waters threatens all of humanity. The threat is made more dangerous by its surreptitious nature. "Peace" is the word that veils the catastrophic eruption building just beneath the surface of the world's geopolitical stability.

Bible prophecy zeroes in on this end-times peace and the beast who will be history's most destructive tyrant. Daniel the prophet foretold the following about the one who will be Antichrist and the results of the diplomatic maneuverings he will employ when he comes to his ultimate power:

> And in the latter time of their kingdom, when the transgressors are come to the full, a king of fierce countenance, and understanding dark sentences, shall stand up.
>
> And his power shall be mighty, but not by his own

> power; and he shall destroy wonderfully, and shall prosper, and practise, and shall destroy the mighty and the holy people.
>
> And through his policy also he shall cause craft to prosper in his hand; and he shall magnify himself in his heart, and by peace shall destroy many. (Daniel 8:23–25a)

The embryo of the peace that "shall destroy many" is on the front pages of today's newspapers and at the top of the news in electronic media. The process that will produce that final humanistic effort at peace continues to bubble to the top of the end-times cauldron. Efforts to produce peace between Israel and those who would destroy that nation inevitably command the headlines over all other birth-pang signals of the end of days.

Israeli Prime Minister Benjamin Netanyahu returned to Washington D.C. on Tuesday, July 6, to meet—finally—with American President Barack Obama. The previous effort of the leaders to meet had been disrupted in June when Israeli Defense Force troops maintaining a blockade boarded a ship headed for Gaza and battled with Islamics who attacked them.

Unlike a meeting in Washington earlier this year when Mr. Netanyahu received a White House welcome about as warm as the iceberg that sank the Titanic, Tuesday's meeting was obviously staged to show Obama's supposed warm personal regard for the prime minister and for Israel as a valued ally. With the polls showing American sentiment to be positive and growing more so toward Israel, and with the president's favorability numbers falling, one has to look at the photo op smiles and backslapping with a cynical eye.

July 2010

Beneath the cordiality beats the satanic heart of the unending effort to force Israel into giving up its territory. This must be done—the international community of diplomats believes—so that peace can come to the Middle East. Make no mistake: The purpose of every meeting this president has with the Israeli prime minister is aimed at exerting pressure on the Jewish leadership to give in to his wishes regarding the Mideast "peace" process.

The major roadblock to the "Roadmap to Peace" at the moment is the Palestinians' refusal to see Israel stopping new construction in the West Bank as a gesture worthy of winning its agreement to come to the peace table.

Ghassan Khatib from the Palestinian Authority (PA) said that "settlement building is continuing everywhere," emphasizing that he considers the Israeli gestures hollow, with existing, even if not new, construction continuing.[42]

The PA is also angry over Israel's developments in East Jerusalem. The question to think upon is whether Obama considers Israeli efforts to placate the PA enough to bring about a meeting that might produce the peace agreement the international community demands. A larger question of likely prophetic significance is this: Will the president, if the Palestinians refuse to come to the table, put pressure of an intolerable magnitude on Israel to stop plans for demolition of unlawful Palestinian dwellings in East Jerusalem?

On the surface, the Tuesday meeting at the White House seems to have brought healing to the rift between Obama and Netanyahu, thus between the U.S. and Israel relations. Addressing reporters in the Oval Office, Obama said:

> The United States is committed to Israel's security. We are committed to that special bond. And we are going to do what's required to back that up, not just with words, but with actions.[43]

These are puzzling words from a president who has taken every opportunity, both personally and through his emissaries, to impart to Israel's avowed enemies that the U.S. is in a new era of dealing with Mideast problems. Since the Obama administration took office, the implication more often than not has been that the American government no longer looks on the Jewish state with favor.

A peace made with any humanist regime that demands Israel give up land it was granted by God Himself is a deadly agreement. It is deadly for Israel and for the purveyor of that luciferic peace. Such peace is not a blessing, but a curse, to all involved.

But look for the peace process to intensify, and for the president and his cronies within the Quartet of world power-broker nations to continue to pressure the Israeli government to give away what little of God's Promised Land they now possess.

The process will one day eventuate in the beast of Revelation 13 confirming the prophesied deadly peace agreement (Daniel 9:26–27). The foretold lethal peace agreement is called the "covenant with death, and with hell" (Isaiah 28:15; see also v. 18). That agreement will bring into effect the Tribulation, the last seven years of human history leading to Christ's Second Advent.

Today we are watching Israel being pressured by the most powerful leader of the world to submit to humanistic peace. It is a precursor of things to come.

July 2010

July 19, 2010
The Rapture Paradox

A woman from the Netherlands who is a frequent visitor to www.raptureready.com proposed we address a troubling thought she lives with as a Christian. It is a paradox I believe many Christians who look for Christ to come for believers in the Rapture have considered, at least to some extent.

The writer sent an article about the growing Islamic population in Europe and the threat Islam represents not only to Israel, but to the rest of the world that is not Islamic. She recognizes that Israel being at the center of world controversy indicates the lateness of the hour, prophetically speaking. She put it this way in her e-mail:

> Every time I see these articles, I am on one hand horrified at the treatment of the Jewish people but on the other hand full of anticipation as I know that with each event that pushes the Jewish people back to their homeland of Israel, the closer the Rapture is for Christians. I do feel badly that I am excited for the Rapture though.... I know what that means for those that will be left behind.... Should we be as excited as I am to know that we can (I believe "will") be raptured any second? I know this gives me an urgency to share the gospel with friends and neighbors, but I still always feel guilty for the anticipation and excitement I get when I see the current events played out daily.

The dichotomy within this believer's thinking is not unusual for those who truly look for Christ's any-moment call as prophesied by Paul the apostle:

> For the Lord himself shall descend from heaven with a shout, with the voice of the archangel, and with the trump of God: and the dead in Christ shall rise first;
>
> Then we who are alive and remain shall be caught up together with them in the clouds, to meet the Lord in the air; and so shall we ever be with the Lord.
>
> (1 Thessalonians 4:16–17)

Christians who believe the pretribulation Rapture is truth from God's Word yearn—without need to apologize—for the blessed hope that is found in Jesus Christ (Titus 2:13). At the same time, they know that when that call from their Lord comes, those left behind will soon endure a time of horror, about which the Lord Himself foretold:

> For then shall be great tribulation, such as was not since the beginning of the world to this time, no, nor ever shall be. (Matthew 24:21)

Those left behind will, the Christian knows, include perhaps close friends and beloved family members. So, the paradox of wanting the Rapture to take place, and at the same time dreading it for those who will stay on this planet that will endure God's judgment and wrath, is troubling to some.

The article this writer sent with her e-mail encapsulates just a small part of the building evil that the Lord of Heaven will judge with His righteous wrath. The matters point to the satanic rage represented within Islam, the number-one Israel-hating entity on the planet. Hatred for Israel and the desire of the international community to force the Jewish state to divide the tiny portion of its God-given land in order to come up with a formula for peace with its Islamic neighbors will lead to Armageddon:

> For, behold, in those days, and in that time, when I shall bring again the captivity of Judah and Jerusalem,
>
> I will also gather all nations, and will bring them down into the valley of Jehoshaphat, and will plead with them there for my people and for my heritage Israel, whom they have scattered among the nations, and parted my land. (Joel 3:1–2)

The article the e-mailer sent contains a speech by Geert Wilders, a Dutch member of Parliament for the Netherlands. He synopsized with stunning description how Israel's Islamic enemy is systematically infecting Europe, thus threatening world stability—or what little of it that remains.

Wilders, who is chairman of the Party for Freedom in the Netherlands, spoke at the Four Seasons in New York City, introducing an Alliance of Patriots and announcing the Facing Jihad conference in Jerusalem. He announced that Europe is in dire straits as it undergoes Islamization. America and the world, he warned, face the same fate as Europe if the threat isn't confronted and defeated everywhere it exists.

Wilders said that entire city sections throughout Europe are taken over by Islamics one street at a time. Local governments and police forces are often so intimidated that they dare not go into those areas to govern. Women, treated no better than slaves, according to the speaker, are covered from head to toe in tent-like attire, sharia law takes precedence, and women in sections of the cities that are not part of the Islamic communities more and more hear hate-filled shouts of "Whore!" from members of the Islamic population.

Wilders said in his speech:

> Jews are fleeing France in record numbers, on the run from the worst wave of anti-Semitism since World War II.... Many in Europe argue in favor of abandoning Israel in order to address the grievances of our Muslim minorities. But if Israel were, God forbid, to go down, it would not bring any solace to the West. It would not mean our Muslim minorities would all of a sudden change their behavior, and accept our values. On the contrary, the end of Israel would give enormous encouragement to the forces of Islam. They would, and rightly so, see the demise of Israel as proof that the West is weak, and doomed. The end of Israel would not mean the end of our problems with Islam, but only the beginning. It would mean the start of the final battle for world domination. If they can get Israel, they can get everything.[44]

Israel and its being targeted for extinction is the sure sign that the Tribulation is in view. The Rapture of the church is therefore an event that must be very near to occurring indeed. That being the obvious case, what should be the Christian's foremost priority? The answer is that it should not be considered a paradox for the believer, but an exhortation, a call to duty.

July 2010

There is nothing anyone can do to hurry or delay the coming of Christ for His saints in the Rapture. The timing of that great event is out of our hands. Therefore, longing for the blessed hope (Titus 2:13) to rescue us from the terrible time to come (Revelation 3:10) doesn't conflict with our concern and compassion for those who will be left behind if they don't come to Christ for salvation. It is time for those who name the name of Christ to recognize the lateness of the prophetic hour; witness to those around us of the truth that Jesus Christ is the one and only way to salvation; and live in such a way that we can earn our Lord's commendation, "Well done, good and faithful servant."

July 26, 2010
Harlot System in View

We can see on the prophetic horizon a monstrous beast lumbering in this direction with a woman astride it. Dave Hunt, you might recall, wrote the provocative—even controversial—book on the subject by the title *The Woman Rides a Beast.* The woman, most literalists (including Hunt) believe, represents the apostate religious system that will be Antichrist's mistress, as a counterfeit of the church, the bride of Jesus Christ.

The matters involved present a terrifying specter—a foreshadowing of bloody things to come, given John to record on the Isle of Patmos almost two thousand years ago.

> So he carried me away in the Spirit into the wilderness and I saw a woman sit upon a scarlet colored beast, full of names of blasphemy, having seven heads and ten horns.
>
> And the woman was arrayed in purple and scarlet

> color, and decked with gold and precious stones and pearls, having a golden cup in her hand, full of abominations and filthiness of her fornication;
>
> And upon her forehead was a name written, MYSTERY, BABYLON THE GREAT, THE MOTHER OF HARLOTS AND ABOMINATIONS OF THE EARTH.
>
> And I saw the woman drunken with the blood of the saints, and with the blood of the martyrs of Jesus; and when I saw her, I wondered with great admiration. (Revelation 17:3–6)

Historicists—those who believe that most prophecy, including this one, has been fulfilled historically—say this all took place during the Roman-based persecutions throughout early church history. The prophecy, they say, has nothing to do with things to come, except in the most general sense. Certainly, the prophecy has nothing specific to do with an end-times persecution leading to the most terrible time in human history. Such a view presents a torturous task for historicist adherents who try to explain the Revelation 17 prophecy of the wicked woman on the hideous beast.

> And the ten horns which thou sawest are ten kings, who have received no kingdom as yet; but receive power as kings one hour with the beast.
>
> These have one mind, and shall give their power and strength unto the beast.
>
> These shall make war with the Lamb, and the Lamb shall overcome them; for he is Lord of lords, and King of kings: and they that are with him are called, and chosen, and faithful. (Revelation 17:12–14)

This powerful, ten-nation entity and the beast have no historical basis as accomplished fact. Any dealing with this part of the prophecy from the perspective of any but the futurist view—that there is much Bible prophecy yet to be literally fulfilled—requires spiritualizing, allegorizing, or else applying pure sophistry to everything to do with these Scriptures.

Contemporary headlines, as they do for so many prophecies yet future, make the case for the Revelation 17 prophecy coming into view in our time. It is literally shaping up for fulfillment before the eyes of those with prophetic discernment. We have used these commentaries many times to dissect and examine news stories that show the governments of the world reconfiguring into what George H. W. Bush, Henry Kissinger, Zbigniew Brzezinski, Barack Obama, and many others have termed "New World Order." The dire global economic crises that have moved toward critical mass just within the past couple of years have shown the inextricable national fiscal interlinkages. It has become obvious that the world is being forced into a monetary mold that could easily morph into something like the ten-kingdom power bloc God's Word says will give its power and authority to the beast.

So, it is reasonable to expect the harlot who rides the beast—the agglomerate ten kings and kingdoms that comprise the beast of Revelation 17—to be somewhere in the prophetic picture, if indeed we are witnessing that ten-kingdom monster in the making.

> EUOBSERVER/BRUSSELS—Brussels is to hold an EU summit with atheists and freemasons in the autumn, inviting them to a political dialogue parallel to the annual summit the bloc holds with Europe's religious leaders. While the

> EU is a secular body, the three European presidents, of the commission, parliament and EU Council, alongside two commissioners, on Monday met with twenty-four bishops, chief rabbis, and muftis as well as leaders from the Hindu and Sikh communities. The annual dialogue, which has taken place since 2005, is for the first time this year made legally obligatory under Article 17 of the Lisbon Treaty.[45]

The report went on to inform that the atheist summit, a mirror of the annual EU religious summit, has within its ranks humanists who are "perplexed and annoyed" that the Freemasons were to be included as part of the strange eclectic mixture, due to pressure by Belgium. The Freemasons, a secretive fraternal organization, is given entrance under the rubric of being part of "non-religious groups." Humanists apparently find this a compromise of their non-religious summit, because Freemasonry holds to religious-like oaths and ceremonies that give allegiance to authority above that of man.

This brings home to my thinking how many of the mega churches within Christianity are, similarly to the EU "summits," contributing to setting up platforms that will produce the woman who will one day ride upon the back of the beast government of Revelation 17. Like in the EU get-together, there is compromise at the heart of these mega-efforts at man-made salvation.

The methodologies employed by such churches include the idea to bring together the saved and unsaved in a sort of "summit." The idea is one of thesis (Christian faith) and antithesis (the lost or unsaved), with the objective of producing synthesis. The "summits" in these cases aim to bring about dialogue between the two opposite worldviews to produce answers (synthesis) that both sides can live with.

The process is satanic at its core, denying that God's way to redemption and reconciliation is necessary. Apostasy is the result—the Laodicean model for the end of the age.

Be sure that you are not a part of helping that woman of wickedness climb upon the back of the beast that will one day be scarlet with the blood of the Tribulation saints.

Last-Days Diary

AUGUST 2010

Frightening Financial Crises

August 2, 2010
The Real Crisis

Politicians currently in majority power in the United States government have steered the American ship onto the deadly, rock-strewn shores of economic ruin. They have used the rudder of crises to do this dastardly deed.

They first created, whether unwittingly or deliberately, the so-called Fannie Mae and Freddie Mac housing disaster. They, in effect, made it mandatory for lenders to sell homes to buyers who had nowhere near the income or other means to secure the high-priced houses they purchased.

This led to the crisis of banks and other lending institutions facing defaults on payment, thus insolvency and/or bankruptcy in many cases. These banks and institutions were deemed too big to fail, in terms of importance to the national economy. Thus the politicians in charge, who also had the votes in Congress to do so, declared that national and worldwide economic catastrophe was inevitable if huge amounts of money weren't immediately voted to defuse the pending calamity.

Terry James

AUGUST 2010

The United States has come to the point of national shipwreck by years, even decades, of political chicanery. This scuttling has progressed more swiftly as of late through the federal government taking multi-trillions of dollars from nonexistent Treasury funds for bailouts and taking over some private companies, such as General Motors, Chrysler, and several large banks. Government has thereby indentured future generations of American citizens, saddling them with debt that can never be repaid.

Perhaps the following quote by presidential chief of staff Rahm Emanuel has been overused: "You never want a serious crisis to go to waste. And what I mean by that is an opportunity to do things you think you could not do before." But his declaration is quite telling in explaining the otherwise irrationality of this country's being steered through crises mismanagement toward an economic crash. In my view, the whole process is to bring America to European-style socialism, a course that has in effect wrecked—or is in the process of wrecking—all of Europe.

As disturbing as is the crisis America faces in so many areas of the nation's well being, there exists a crisis infinitely more intense. This one has profound, biblically prophetic import on an even greater scale.

The crisis is the almost-total blindness the church (born-again believers; see John 3:3) suffers from while America and the other nations reel and stagger toward the time of Tribulation. America's deliberately directed breakup and the nations of earth tearing apart in the aftermath of her carnage, as well as the church's deliberately directed, head-in-the-sand blindness, are major parts of the end-times picture. It's Bible prophecy in the final, stage-setting phase.

As stated previously, the blindness of the church constitutes the far more virulent of the crises. That is because the venom it injects is done so in a benign, peaceful, even soothing way by the crisis managers—the religionists who purvey feel-good sophistry. These, like their political counterparts in the case of directing America onto the shoals of destruction, steer the people in their pews toward the inward-turning course of destructive selfism. It is theological mumbo-jumbo that sequesters God's people within do-goodism and feel-goodism and immerses them in a Laodicean-like prosperity gospel.

The words of the resurrected Christ to John are chilling, considering the churches today who fall under the Lord's omniscient, condemning eyes:

> I know thy works, that thou art neither cold nor hot; I would thou wert cold or hot.
>
> So, then, because thou art lukewarm, and neither cold nor hot, I will spew thee out of my mouth.
>
> Because thou sayest, I am rich, and increased with goods, and have need of nothing; and knowest not that thou art wretched, and miserable, and poor, and blind, and naked. (Revelation 3:15–17)

This inward-turning, wealth-oriented, false theology is so egregious because it blinds its adherents to the real world around them—a world that needs Jesus Christ. He is the only remedy for the crises the people of earth face. Yet the people in churches whose leaderships seek to insulate Christians from the realities of the lost, perishing masses can think only of ways to make their own lives comfortable and entertaining.

Again, this is not to paint all large church bodies with the same broad brush. Many strive to teach and preach absolute truth from God's Holy Word. But the churches that fit the Laodicean mold create the crisis that is far greater than any spawned from political treacheries.

Such false teaching has dumbed down many of God's people to the point that there is little discernment of the prophetic times—the end times—in which this generation finds itself. Many of these congregants, for example, haven't any idea for the most part that Israel is the key signal of where we are on God's prophetic timeline. Or that the peace process Israel is being pressured to join, trying to force the nation to give up land God gave it to enemies who want to wipe the Jewish state from the earth, is the number-one signal that the Lord is very near the time when He will call the church to Himself in the Rapture.

These haven't a clue—except in the distant, disinterested sense—that Christianity has been invaded by those who make this the time of Jesus' words:

> Also as it was in the days of Lot; they did eat, they drank, they bought, they sold, they planted, they built;
>
> But the same day that Lot went out of Sodom, it rained fire and brimstone from heaven, and destroyed them all.
>
> Even thus shall it be in the day when the Son of man is revealed. (Luke 17:28–30)

A recent news item frames the crisis created by the church's inward-turning:

> SAN FRANCISCO—Seven pastors who work in the San Francisco Bay area and were barred from serving in the nation's largest Lutheran group because of a policy that

> required gay clergy to be celibate are being welcomed into the denomination.... "It's going to be an extremely glorious and festive ceremony because it's the culmination of decades of work to welcome LGBT [Lesbian, Gay, Bisexual, and Transgender] people into the ELCA [Evangelical Lutheran Church in America]," said Amalia Vagts, executive director of the Extraordinary Lutheran Ministries, a nonprofit that credentials openly gay, lesbian, bisexual, and transgender people for ministry.[46]

The crisis builds. There comes less and less outcry from the true church of Jesus Christ about the corruption within its ranks. It is a sure sign that the church is abdicating its assigned duty as being the salt and light in this dark, dying world. Jesus said of such a time as this:

> Watch, therefore; for ye know not what hour your Lord doth come.
>
> But know this, that if the goodman of the house had known in what watch the thief would come, he would have watched, and would not have suffered his house to be broken up.
>
> Therefore be ye also ready; for in such an hour as ye think not the Son of man cometh. (Matthew 24:42–44)

August 9, 2010
Handwriting on the Wall

Think with me for a moment—back to the time on September 11, 2001, when you first learned of the World Trade Center tower being hit by the commercial jet. All eyes quickly went to television screens everywhere in America. Then the second tower was hit, and we were awestruck at the ensuing carnage that took the lives of nearly three thousand people who couldn't escape the horror.

Remember when the huge monoliths collapsed to rubble with billowing clouds of smoke and dust—a holocaust of flaming fuel and the blood of crushed, burning humanity.

Those of us who look through the prism of God's prophetic Word couldn't at that stunning moment help but consider that we were witnessing an event that punctuated the fact that the very end of the age was upon us. The United States of America was somehow, in the collapsing of those giant towers, brought front and center into God's focus for judgment and wrath about to be unleashed upon a world that has rejected Him.

Fast forward to this week. Another God-rendered exclamation mark seems to have punctuated the handwriting on the wall that began the final sentence of human history. The message written across the New York City skyline this week is not just ironic or even eerie. It is, I think, staggering in its supernatural import.

The New York Landmarks Preservation Commission ruled by a vote of 9-0 that some buildings at 45 Park Place, a few blocks from where the World Trade Center towers stood before the attacks of the radical Islamists, will not receive historic status. This ruling opens the way for the construction of a huge mosque and Islamic complex on the site. The building that stands where the mosque will be built was struck by one of the commercial jet's landing gear after the plane crashed into one of the 110-story towers. But in my view, that is not the truly unfathomable thing regarding the matter of having a super-mosque erected right across from the place where thousands were murdered by those who claim Allah as their deity. The supernatural nature of all of this is wrapped up in the fact that the mosque builders are, as of this moment, claiming they will begin construction of the mosque itself on September 11, 2011. Imagine the audacity! And the mayor of New York City, an American—even more than that, a Jew—said the following in giving an approving nod to opening the way for the desecration of Ground Zero where so many died and where the Freedom Tower is scheduled to be constructed:

> [The World Trade Center site] will forever hold a special place in our city, in our hearts. But we would be untrue to the best part of ourselves—and who we are as New Yorkers and Americans—if we said "no" to a mosque in Lower Manhattan.[47]

One writer has encapsulated well the incredible foolhardiness of the action in allowing such a slap in the face to New Yorkers and to all Americans:

> Can you imagine back in 1950 if there had been an effort by Japanese-Americans to build a Shinto center honoring Emperor Hirohito just two blocks from Pearl Harbor? Furthermore, imagine that the building was planned to open on December 7, 1951, just in time to celebrate the tenth-year anniversary of this cataclysmic attack. Faster than you can say "Tora Tora Tora," one can hardly contemplate the absurdity of such a plan.

Fast forward to now and imagine the family of Timothy McVeigh. They have plans to build a thirteen-story addition to the Oklahoma City National Memorial and Museum, which opened in 2001, where the Murrah Federal Building once stood. The family would like to commemorate McVeigh's life and help foster understanding and tolerance to those who hate the federal government—in hopes that a future domestic terrorist would visit the McVeigh Wing and decide against blowing up a federal building killing 168 innocents like McVeigh did on April 19, 1995.

The perfect timing for the construction of this wing, the family says, would be April 19, 2015—the twentieth anniversary of the Oklahoma City bombing. I am sure the city council and the mayor of Oklahoma City would vote a resounding NO.

You know where I am going with this.

On September 12, 2001, do you think anyone in New York City could imagine that nine years later a mosque would be approved at 45 Park Place, to be completed in time for the tenth-year anniversary of 9/11? One would guess not.[48]

America and the world have long been holding a debauched banquet to which the God of Heaven was not invited. America disinvited Him in 1963 by the judicial act of doing away with prayer and Bible reading in public schools.

The True Deity and His prescription for living life, given through His love letter to humanity, the Bible, has been evicted from all public places, for the most part. Thus with this exclamation point of supernatural irony—Islam's achieving its mocking tribute to its symbolic conquest of America—the finger of God might be writing upon the wall America has erected to separate the nation from Him. The prophetic fate of this nation and the world might thereby be in the heavenly process of being sealed.

Tragically, the message might indeed be one like that Nebuchadnezzar's grandson, Belshazzar, saw being written across the wall of the Babylonian banquet hall that housed the party during his last day on earth:

> And this is the writing that was written, MENE, MENE, TEKEL, UPHARSIN.
>
> This is the interpretation of the thing: MENE; God hath numbered thy kingdom, and finished it.
>
> TEKEL; Thou art weighed in the balances, and art found wanting.
>
> PERES; Thy kingdom is divided, and given to the Medes and Persians. (Daniel 5:25–28)

It's time to do what we can, for the cause of Christ might be very short. The time to do the Lord's business is fleeting swiftly. Whatever contributions we have to put into heavenly bank accounts must be done now:

> I must work the works of him that sent me, while it is day; the night cometh, when no man can work. (John 9:4)

Terry James

AUGUST 2010

August 16, 2010
Prophecy with Purpose

One of the most false and cutting accusations launched at the belief that the Bible teaches that a person cannot lose his or her salvation when truly born again (John 3:3) is: "If you believe once saved, always saved, you are saying that people can live any way they want without fear of punishment." Or so the line of condemning criticism goes.

The absolute assurance of eternal security, of course, engenders no such thought within the mind truly regenerated by the saving power of Jesus Christ. The Bible teaches that the Lord convicts His children in their spirits, and that habitual, unrepented-of sin will result in severe penalties—even physical death, in some cases. The Heavenly Father's patience is longsuffering, but not infinite.

A person who is a child of God cannot sin without severe repercussions if repentance isn't forthcoming. But, that person will never be kicked out of God's family. Never.

A kindred sort of accusation is thrown at those who believe in the pretribulational view of Bible prophecy. This view, of course, is the one we at Rapture Ready believe God's Word teaches. It is the view that Jesus Christ will call all who are born again to Himself before the Tribulation, which is the last seven years of history leading to the Second Advent (Revelation 19:11).

The angry diatribe against this view—by even genuine Christians, in many cases—usually goes something like this: "People like you, who believe that the Lord is going to rapture them before the Tribulation, think you can live however you want, because you think and teach falsely that you are going to be rescued before God's judgment and wrath fall, no matter what."

The non-Christian accusers who castigate those of us who hold the pretribulational Rapture view have their own version. It goes something like: "Christians who believe like that don't care anything about making the world better. You even hope for things to get worse and worse. You wish for earthquakes, famines, pestilence, war in the Middle East, and for Armageddon to hurry up and get here so you will go to your pie in the sky, and watch the rest of us get ours."

Although the first criticism is absolutely not true, I have to admit that, regarding the second, too often I've sensed—even heard—such sentiments from some of those who believe in the pretribulational Rapture. And, it is entirely the wrong attitude for the Christian to hold. There are no excuses for wanting the Christ-rejecting world of non-believers to be the recipients of God's judgment and wrath. It is only by God's unfathomable grace that every one of us isn't headed into that time of unprecedented horror.

No matter how—to use Lot's King James Version word—"vexed" we become by the debauched, debased actions of the lost world around us, our job as Christ's children—His representatives here on earth—is of a completely different nature than wanting to see them "get what's coming" to them. The changed nature produced by being born again into God's eternal family should make us do just the opposite of wanting them, in our vexation, to get what we see as "coming to them."

The Christian whose spirit is attuned to the Holy Spirit's desire for the lost doesn't want to see them "get what's coming to them" either during the Tribulation or upon death. Rather, we want to do all within our power to keep them from having to go through the coming time of God's judgment and wrath. That's what Christ's Great Commission to His disciples before He ascended to sit at the Father's right hand is all about, you see. That is what God's love—love that those who have Christ indwelling them possess—is all about. (Read Matthew 28:18–20.)

In the same vein, that's what Bible prophecy is all about. Prophecy given in God's Word has purpose—profound purpose. Bible prophecy has at its center the commission from the Lord to forewarn of God's judgment and wrath to come upon all who oppose Him—the Lord of Heaven and Creator of all things. It is not the hatred of God for the lost people of this fallen planet that drives prophecy. It is the love of God that powers His prophetic Word. It must be the Christian's desire, therefore, to study Bible prophecy and put forth those forewarnings out of a spirit of God's love, not through an anger-filled abhorrence of those who are lost.

Christians who do study prophecy—and they seem to be few these days, I'm sad to have to say—are often heard wondering about when Christ will call the church in the Rapture. Everything seems so ripe for His plucking His people from this sin-darkened sphere.

Nothing and no one can change God's timing for His next catastrophic intervention into earth's history. It will happen exactly on time, as He has determined since before the foundation of this world. However, we might as believers look to ourselves for the Lord's—often in our view—delay in calling us as outlined in 1 Corinthians 15:51–55 and 1 Thessalonians 4:13–18.

The apostle Peter gave the heart of the reason Christ hasn't raptured His church:

> The Lord is not slack concerning His promise, as some men count slackness; but is longsuffering toward us, not willing that any should perish, but that all should come to repentance. (2 Peter 3:9)

The purpose of Bible prophecy is to show the love of God to a lost and otherwise doomed world. God is not willing that anyone should die in his or her sins, but that all should accept Jesus Christ as the one and only sacrifice for sin that God will accept.

The Lord is "longsuffering." The reason that the Lord seems so "slack" to many in His coming is because those same people have neglected their duty to share the love of God with the lost—the lost whom God loves so very much that He sent His only begotten Son in order that they not perish.

It is well past the time for God's people to begin investing in getting the message of the love of God to those who will otherwise not hear the warning of deadly things soon to befall this Christ-rejecting planet. Considering these times that so dramatically are signaling the coming Tribulation, Bible prophecy can and must be used as a productive tool for evangelism.

August 23, 2010
Israel Here to Stay?

My in-box and the news from Bible prophecy circles bulge with talk of Israel's almost-certain attack on Iran's nuclear facilities.

Terry James

AUGUST 2010

The scuttlebutt has been coming hard and fast since 2007 or even earlier. Each summer was going to bring an assault by Israel, and all-out Mideast war was sure to ensue.

As I write this, the predictions are at fever pitch. John Bolton, former American UN ambassador, declared that Israel had until Saturday, August 21, to take out Iran's nuclear plants, or risk—by their bombing—the spreading of radiation contamination across the area and into the Persian Gulf.

The flood of e-mails proclaims that this is it. The region is going to go up in flames, with Russia coming to the aid of Iran, because the Russians are so heavily invested in the Iranian nuclear program. There will be Russian nuclear technicians installing the radioactive rods necessary to fuel and power up the facility. They will be in harm's way, and Moscow—from which Gog of Magog prophetic infamy will come—will not abide such an insult. The thought frequently conjectured: Could this be the beginning of Ezekiel 38–39…the Gog-Magog attack?

Israel cannot afford, the argument goes, to allow the facility to come online. This, because the spent fuel rods will provide plutonium and other byproducts to give Iran the materials from which they can produce nuclear weapons. That's a simplification of the matters involved, but should suffice, I hope, in making the point of this commentary.

This attack by Israel will be, the e-mailers apparently believe, prophecy being fulfilled. This preemptive attack by the Jewish state upon the land of ancient Persia surely will, the messages exclaim, instigate a chain reaction of events. These events will bring the Gog-Magog attack, and perhaps Isaiah 17:1 will also be fulfilled. Some even believe it will provoke the long-pondered-over Psalms 83 war supposed by many to be in the offing.

Last-Days Diary
AUGUST 2010

I could have waited until Saturday, August 21, had passed to write this piece, but chose not to do so. My reason for not waiting until after that time is primarily that I don't believe this is the time for the Gog-Magog War, or for the proposed Psalms 83 conflict, should it be an actual prophecy. Exigencies just aren't ripe for producing the horrific results such conflicts as the Gog-Magog or the supposed Psalms 83 conflagrations would inflict. At least, that's my view from my present perspective.

More than that, I believe that's the way it is presented from the perspective of Bible prophecy. One thing I do think is an almost 100-percent certainty is that Israel isn't going anywhere. Iranian tyrant Mahmoud Ahmadinejad's promises to erase Israel from the face of the Middle East and the world map are empty threats. It will never happen—not even with the help of the Gog nation, Russia.

Why do I say "an almost 100-percent certainty"?

This goes to the argument of those who say that it is possible that Israel could be removed from its land yet again. Then all would have to again rearrange in order to get the prophetic indicators into place like they are now. God might allow Israel's enemies to again take the Jews from the Promised Land because of their unbelief.

Zola Levitt and I were once discussing the hatred of the Arab nations for Israel. I mentioned that the late Dr. J. Vernon McGee didn't think that the Jews being back in the land was necessarily a major signal of the nearness to Christ's return. My friend Zola, a very passionate man when it came to Israel, got pretty exercised, as I recall. He said that he and Dr. McGee "got into it"—as the southernism goes—over this subject.

Zola said Dr. McGee said it could be that Israel might yet be removed from the land of promise. Zola didn't like that at all, so they had a rather lively discussion on the matter, on camera. I said, "Well, Dr. McGee [who went to be with the Lord in 1988 at age eighty-four] knows now, that's for sure." That seemed to calm Zola a bit.

Dr. McGee would no doubt agree that Israel is back in the land to stay, if he could have watched developments of the years since his leaving the planet. Israel is the center of most all controversy so far as issues of war and peace are concerned; it is pressured by the international community to give up God's land; and it is at the center of a forced, phony peace process, with Iran (ancient Persia) threatening from the north. How could he or anyone being privy to such facts say otherwise?

Whatever happened last Saturday—as you read this on August 23 or later—Israel isn't going anywhere. So, I'll change my "almost" to an absolute 100-percent certainty.

Although Israel—and the world—are in for some terrible times ahead, I firmly believe that we have the very Word of God about the current and future disposition of His chosen nation. Israel is here to stay.

> And I will bring again the captivity of my people of Israel, and they shall build the waste cities, and inhabit them; and they shall plant vineyards, and drink the wine thereof; they shall also make gardens, and eat the fruit of them. And I will plant them upon their land, and they shall no more be pulled up out of their land which I have given them, saith the LORD thy God. (Amos 9:14–15)

Last-Days Diary

AUGUST 2010

August 30, 2010

Economy Nucleus of Tribulation

One prophetic element stands out in considering the seven-year Tribulation era with regard to the Antichrist regime. That is the economic platform prophesied to be at the heart of the beast system.

With so many signals in view that point to the brewing Tribulation tempest, we should expect—if we are reading the end-times signals correctly—that this heart of the beast should be well along in its construction. We have covered all of the indicators found within current issues and events that we believe are signals like those given by Jesus and the prophets. National and world economies have been dealt with in our efforts to make prophetic sense of the dynamic rearrangements taking place in recent years, months, weeks, and days.

America's staggering weight of debt and swift economic decline are front and center in pointing to the fact that this generation stands at the end of one dispensation—the Church Age—and upon the precipice of the next–the Tribulation. Each hour seems to bring additional confirmation that the Tribulation storm is about to break upon an uncomprehending world. Such confirmation is present in abundance in the realm of geopolitics and global economics.

Since Bible prophecy clearly foretells that the Antichrist government, thus the economic engine that will power that absolute dictatorship, will emerge from Europe, we need keep our prophetic antennae pointed in that direction—i.e., we must be especially alert to news involving movement within Europe to cause significant changes to the global economic structure.

August 2010

The following excerpt from the *Wall Street Journal* registers an interesting blip on my own end-times radar screen.

> Paris—French President Nicolas Sarkozy called on the world's twenty largest economies to work together to reform global monetary order.
>
> "We must define a new framework for discussing currency movements," Mr. Sarkozy said, adding that it is "nonsense" to talk about exchange rates without including China, which has accumulated huge foreign exchange reserves.
>
> He said stabilizing erratic foreign exchange and commodities markets will feature high on France's agenda when it heads the Group of 20 [in] November. He added there is a need to reduce the U.S. dollar's dominance as the reserve currency of choice.[49]

Prophecy scholars and others have long pondered why the U.S., the most powerful nation in history, isn't mentioned by name—or even by significant reference—in God's Word. We continue to flounder in attempts at finding an exact answer for that question. However, with the recent astonishing changes nationally and abroad, the answer seems to be in the process of forming.

Monetary manipulation is at the root of the change taking place. The American dollar must be removed as the currency standard so that a global currency not underwritten by any national monetary unit can be established. This is precisely the beast economic order I'm convinced Bible prophecy describes as outlined in the following:

> And he causeth all, both small and great, rich and poor, free and bond, to receive a mark in their right hand, or in their foreheads,
>
> And that no man might buy or sell, save he that had the mark, or the name of the beast, or the number of his name.
>
> Here is wisdom. Let him that hath understanding count the number of the beast; for it is the number of a man; and his number is Six hundred threescore and six. (Revelation 13:16–18)

This speaks to me of a computer system—a hybrid Internet whereby all citizens of the global economic order will be absolutely controlled at every level of life. Probably, it will consist at its heart of electronic funds transfer—a system of special drawing rights. Anyone refusing to toe the mark of the Antichrist's regime will face having his or her account blocked or removed completely from the system. Fear of starvation is a mighty motivator to comply.

Pressures are mounting for a completely changed global economic order. Even the king of the kings of the East, China, is at the center of the dynamics driving the changes.

Most economists who are honest will admit that the current building economic heap of debt cannot continue to accumulate. They are amazed, in fact, that everything hasn't already collapsed into total, worldwide depression. I again offer my belief that it will be the Rapture that causes the ultimate implosion and collapse.

The great world leader called in Revelation "the beast" will be there to implement a satanically inspired economic scheme that will at first offer hope—that will for a time "cause craft to prosper" (Daniel 8:25). But Antichrist's plan will achieve what it will be designed to do: enslave most of the world in electronic bondage.

Jesus offers the opposite of what the counterfeit, Antichrist, will produce. Jesus promises: "If the Son, therefore, shall make you free, ye shall be free indeed" (John 8:36). We must at every opportunity lift up the Holy name of Jesus before the eyes of a world headed into the terrors of the Tribulation.

Last-Days Diary

SEPTEMBER 2010

Tribulation Tremors in Evidence

September 6, 2010
End-Times Kaleidoscope

We have all done it one time or the other as children—and maybe even as adults. We have looked into a long tube and watched a constantly changing picture of colorful shapes and patterns. Kaleidoscopes with colored glass prisms rearranging while we turned the cylinder and watched through the little hole were a source of entertainment—well, before technology made such entertainment *quaint*, for lack of a better word.

I would like to revive the use of the kaleidoscope—at least the concept of the kaleidoscope—to briefly view the shapes and patterns of these prophetic times. The twists and turns of hourly news indeed bring into view biblically prophetic reminders—shapes and patterns of what God's Word says about things to come.

And remember, God's Word is all-important in our viewing tube. We must have a bright light at the end of the kaleidoscope to fully illuminate the details of the display.

Looking into our kaleidoscope just within the past week, the specter of Tribulation-like developments begins to take on form and substance. Let's twist the instrument just slightly to bring into some degree of focus the distinctive points within each news item.

The Middle East peace process continues to be the centerpiece of the watchman's attention. It takes no more than a nuance of eye movement across the headline to bring this most important end-times matter into a definitive prophetic image.

> Ahead of [the] start of direct peace talks in Washington, Defense Minister Ehud Barak says Jerusalem's Arab neighborhoods will be part of a Palestinian state; a "special regime" to govern holy sites.... The defense minister believes in the 2010 peace summit even more than the principals taking part in it.... From his office at the Defense Ministry headquarters in Tel Aviv, his sense was that there is a good chance that Netanyahu will surprise us....
>
> "In the current reality that is encircling us, there are remarkable changes underway. Thirty years ago, the Arabs competed amongst themselves in spouting rejectionist slogans.... Today the Arab states are competing amongst themselves in arguing over which peace initiative will be adopted by the international community. The same situation is taking place with us....
>
> "Netanyahu leads a process, a significant number of rightist ministers will stand with him. So what is needed is courage to make historic, painful decisions. I'm not saying that there is a certainty for success, but there is a chance. This chance must be exploited to the fullest...we cannot be deterred from working toward the success of the peace negotiations."[50]

The light behind this kaleidoscopic picture of the peace process, in which the Obama administration and the international community are pressuring Israel to cede God's land to the enemies of the Jewish state, is effulgent with forewarning.

> Wherefore, hear the word of the LORD, ye scornful men, that rule this people who are in Jerusalem.
>
> Because ye have said, We have made a covenant with death, and with hell are we at agreement, when the overflowing scourge shall pass through, it shall not come unto us; for we have made lies our refuge, and under falsehood have we hid ourselves....
>
> And your covenant with death shall be disannulled, and your agreement with hell shall not stand; when the overflowing scourge shall pass through, then ye shall be trodden down by it. (Isaiah 28:14–15, 18)

Whatever peace agreement the current process brings about might presage the covenant that will initiate Daniel's seventieth week.

We slightly twist the instrument again, and yet another ominous shape moves into view.

> BRUSSELS—European Union foreign policy chief Catherine Ashton said Saturday she could not attend next month's Middle East peace talks because of a China trip, and she had no place there anyway.
>
> French Foreign Minister Bernard Kouchner said Friday the EU should be at the table when the Israeli and

> Palestinian leaders resume direct peace talks in Washington on Thursday.
>
> "It would be a shame if there was no European representation," Kouchner said, suggesting it should be Ashton.
>
> He referred to the fact that EU countries are the major contributors of Palestinian aid, but the EU plays second fiddle diplomatically behind the United States.[51]

A fire is burning within the heart of Europe, the nucleus out of which the beast system of Revelation 13 will emerge. That burning desire is to become a power along the lines of ancient Rome. This will eventuate, many of us believe Bible prophecy foretells.

God's prophetic light reveals the reshaping European behemoth with regard to the ongoing pressures for Israel to acquiesce in dividing the land to achieve Middle East peace. The "prince that shall come" (Daniel 9:26) will come out of this reviving Rome–Europe: "And he shall confirm the covenant with many for one week" (Daniel 9:27a).

A half-turn or so of our end-times kaleidoscope gives the next visual of prophetically shaping events.

> The Israeli Prime Minister, in his opening statement ahead of the talks, said real peace could only be achieved by "painful concessions from both sides," stressing that security for the Israelis was paramount to reaching an agreement.
>
> "Achieving security is a must. Security is the foundation of peace. Without it peace will unravel," [Benjamin] Netanyahu said.[52]

This Israeli prime minister, in my estimation, is the strongest in quite some time, in terms of resisting the incessant call for his nation to give in to the insane notion of giving up more territory for a peace process that seems to have no end. Yet, it is as if Mr. Netanyahu—if he is genuine with his words—can't resist the same trap other Israeli leaders have fallen into.

Biblically prophetic illumination tells us that at the end of this age and the beginning of the next—the Tribulation (Daniel's seventieth week)—Israel's leadership will give in to the covenant of the false, deadly peace that the "prince that shall come" will confirm. The concession those leaders make will come as a result of a cry for peace and safety by Israel and the other nations of the world. We are hearing that cry frequently and loudly today:

> For when they shall say, Peace and safety, then sudden destruction cometh upon them, as travail upon a woman with child; and they shall not escape. (1 Thessalonians 5:3)

At any moment, the resplendent image we see when looking into our end-times kaleidoscope might be the face of Jesus Christ as He shouts, "Come up here!" (Revelation 4:1).

September 13, 2010
End-Times Odds and Ends

Major prophetic ponderings deserve and get primary attention in the "Nearing Midnight" forum. That's as it should be. Profound issues like Israel's being pressured toward giving up land for peace and Russia, Iran, and now Turkey coming into alignment that looks to be the forerunner of the Ezekiel 38–39 Gog-Magog coalition that will storm southward toward the mountains of Israel are often front and center on the Rapture Ready radar.

Odds-and-ends issues and events, however, can—analyzed collectively—present an end-times reality nearly as revealing of the denouement of the age during which we live as those more dramatic geopolitical dynamics. One particular area of such issues and events in development deserves a closer examination.

Three matters of concern in this regard, taken collectively, are: 1) France's president making increasingly strident attempts to effect monetary rearrangements globally; 2) Science and industry conjoining with government to produce instrumentality that can bring about electronic bondage; and 3) Orwellian surveillance moving from fiction to fact.

Sarkozy's Monetary Meddling

President Nicolas Sarkozy of France has set a political course he apparently hopes will bolster his flagging popularity.

> President Nicolas Sarkozy has set an ambitious agenda of creating a new international monetary system and taming commodity speculation for France's presidency of the G-20 global economic leadership forum from November....
>
> It also has a domestic payoff for a president hoping to leverage his international statesmanship to revive his battered popularity, and neutralize a highly popular potential rival, ahead of a tough 2012 re-election campaign.[53]

Perhaps the most intriguing element of Sarkozy's monetary meddling, from the standpoint of prophetic implication, is that this leader is a mover and shaker within the European sphere of influence. He observably intends to lead the way in wresting a large degree of influence from the seven industrialized economies—the U.S., Japan, Britain, France, Germany, Italy, and Canada. By, in effect, diverting the fiscal hegemony wielded by those seven power brokers, he raises his stature among the wider agglomeration of twenty nation economies. It is more than interesting to consider that at the heart of his ideas for moving away from the dollar as the world's reserve currency to a neutral economic unit is proposed computer currency–an International Monetary Fund special drawing rights system.

This doesn't mean I believe Sarkozy will be Antichrist—please understand. But his wheeling and dealing gives an inkling of the kind of monetary/economic rearrangements developing now that will likely increase many times over. Such maneuverings will ultimately bring to power the beast regime outlined in Revelation 17:12–13.

France Strikes Again

Following on the heels of Mr. Sarkozy's attempts to manipulate all things monetary, technology founded in France seems to be at the leading edge of changes in the offing:

> A French firm has designed a new interface which could increase the processing speed of contactless smart card technology.... However, faster transfer rates are needed to support more complex technologies such as contactless biometric data transfer and multimedia file downloads.

> CEA-Leti has been researching the new interface with sixteen European companies and research organisations since 2003. The firms also aimed to develop a universal standard for all electronic identity and mobile transactions.[54]

Again, it is fascinating to note that the political will and the technological acumen to control buying and selling on a global scale beat within the heart of Europe—out of which, we believe, will come the "prince" of Daniel 26–27.

Big Brother Watches

My next book, *The Departure,* to be released this month, is a book of compilation. That is, a number of authors and I have written chapters on crucial prophetic topics. One such chapter by my friend Alan Franklin is about the almost inconceivable number of surveillance cameras in his country.

It is eerie to me that George Orwell, author of the famous novel, 1984, used London as the center of his fictional Big Brother surveillance society. Alan Franklin writes the following about the England of his own time:

> If you want to be a film star, come to Britain. We're all on camera. All you have to do is walk through any town or drive down any road and you are watched, filmed, and monitored. When my wife, Pat, and I tour America, we feel neglected because the roadside cameras are no longer ever-present—not yet.
>
> As the world moves towards a "Big Brother" society beyond the nightmares of author George Orwell, who

> predicted a world in which the state watched everyone in his 1948 classic novel, 1984, it is like we are inmates of a high-tech prison. Big Brother really is watching us in Europe. The rest of the world is not far behind.[55]

Indeed, cameras are literally everywhere. Practically every cell phone has one. They are getting more and more sophisticated. Governments are on the cutting edge of video and other surveillance/tracking technologies. Computers are taking over.

It doesn't take much stretching of the imagination to understand that the real Big Brother will be able to control all buying and selling—and everything else—as prophesied in Revelation 13:16–18.

September 20, 2010
Promise of His Coming

A biblically prophetic reality that perfectly fits our present day and that has been looked at a number of times is the forewarning given by the apostle Peter especially to the generation alive at the end of the Church Age:

> Knowing this first, that there shall come in the last days scoffers, walking after their own lusts,
>
> And saying, Where is the promise of his coming? For since the fathers fell asleep, all things continue as they were from the beginning of the creation. (2 Peter 3:3–4)

In almost every case of looking at this prophecy, the point has been exclusively dwelt upon that both the religious and non-religious of the world mockingly chide those of us who believe Jesus

Christ will return to planet earth. This prophecy has observably come to pass in our time.

However, it is the phrase "promise of his coming" that I would like to consider here, rather than the chiding sarcasm of the mockers.

Like the 2 Peter 3:3–4 prophecy, so many other things we can see developing in these troubling though exciting times testify mightily to the evidence that God absolutely keeps His Word. Scripture promises, for example, that ultimately, no matter how scattered and oppressed the Jewish people have been throughout history, Israel will be a nation forever:

> And yet for all that, when they are in the land of their enemies, I will not cast them away, neither will I abhor them, to destroy them utterly, and to break my covenant with them; for I am the LORD their God.
>
> But I will for their sakes remember the covenant of their ancestors, whom I brought forth out of the land of Egypt in the sight of the nations, that I might be their God: I am the LORD. (Leviticus 26:44–45)

Israel was restored to the land after centuries of the people being removed from their own land and being persecuted unmercifully in the nations to which they were scattered. They were regathered and established again as a nation in a single day, just as foretold.

> Who hath heard such a thing? Who hath seen such things? Shall the earth be made to bring forth in one day? Or shall a nation be born at once? For as soon as Zion travailed, she brought forth her children.

> Shall I bring to the birth, and not cause to bring forth? saith the LORD. Shall I cause to bring forth, and shut the womb? saith thy God.
>
> Rejoice with Jerusalem, and be glad with her, all ye that love her; rejoice for joy with her, all ye that mourn for her. (Isaiah 66:8–10)

That miracle rebirth took place May 14, 1948, following perhaps Israel's most horrendous persecution—that suffered under the Nazis. No other nation has been so torn apart and scattered to the winds of history, then regathered, having its original language restored. The Lord proved He alone is God. His promise to Israel goes into the future for His chosen people:

> And I will bring again the captivity of my people of Israel, and they shall build the waste cities, and inhabit them; and they shall plant vineyards, and drink their wine; they shall also make gardens, and eat the fruit of them.
>
> And I will plant them upon their land, and they shall no more be pulled up out of their land which I have given them, saith the LORD, thy God. (Amos 9:14–15)

Israel's God is God! There is no other God. He continues to prove who He is through Israel. This, doubtless, is one extremely important reason He chose that people: to demonstrate the absolute veracity of His Holy Word. That same Word—who is the very person of the Lord Jesus Christ (John 1:1)—has made a promise of staggering importance to His other chosen people:

SEPTEMBER 2010

> Let not your heart be troubled; ye believe in God, believe also in me.
>
> In my Father's house are many mansions; if it were not so, I would have told you. I go to prepare a place for you.
>
> And if I go and prepare a place for you, I will come again, and receive you unto myself; that where I am, there ye may be also. (John 14:1–3)

His coming again for God's other chosen people—the church (every born-again member of Christ's body during this Age of Grace)—is assured. It is a 100-percent certainty, because He continues to prove His faithfulness through the nation Israel, and through keeping every prophetic promise He has made.

Jesus tells us who constitute His chosen bride:

> Because thou hast kept the word of my patience, I also will keep thee from the hour of temptation, which shall come upon all the world, to try them that dwell upon the earth. (Revelation 3:10)

And He promises:

> And when these things begin to come to pass, then look up, and lift up your heads; for your redemption draweth nigh. (Luke 21:28)

Jesus is coming. It could be the very next moment!

September 27, 2010
Who Goes in the Rapture?

Our new book, *The Departure: God's Next Catastrophic Intervention into Earth's History,* will be officially released October 2, God willing.[56] I say "our" book" because a number of the most knowledgeable authorities in Bible prophecy have written chapters on the most relevant topics of our day. All issues and events involving what we consider to have prophetic import are, of course, looked at through the supernatural prism of God's Word. I consider it "our" book, not just mine.

More than that, I believe each of us who wrote for it considers it to be a volume devoted to the Lord Jesus Christ for these troubling although exciting times. We trust it will be a tool to help edify those who are in God's family by pointing to the very real evidence that proves the coming of "the blessed hope" of Titus 2:13 is likely very near. To that extent, that's another reason I call it "our" book. It's written for all believers alive today, with the prayerful hope God's family will awaken to Christ's imminent coming.

With the book on the cusp of its release, I thought it good to use the this week's column to look at exactly who I believe will go in the Departure—the Rapture, when Christ gives the command to "Come up here" (Revelation 4:1).

There might be some among the authors who would disagree on a couple of my views about specifically who will go to be with Jesus at the time of the Rapture. However, I will let them answer for themselves in their own forums and in their own ways. My own feeling on the differences we might have is like that of the late Dr. J. Vernon McGee, who more than once said that you can believe the way you want to believe. But, if you want to be right, you'll want to come along with me on this…

Dr. McGee said that with a chuckle, and I hope you can hear the chuckle in my written expression, regarding my borrowing from that grand old Christian man's humor.

First, I will state that God's Word says without equivocation just who will go in the Rapture—the Departure:

> Behold, I show you a mystery: We shall not all sleep, but we shall all be changed,
>
> In a moment, in the twinkling of an eye, at the last trump; for the trumpet shall sound, and the dead shall be raised incorruptible, and we shall be changed. (1 Corinthians 15:51–52)

So, it is plain that Paul the apostle was saying two major things about one classification of people. He was writing to the believers at Corinth. But, he was also writing to every believer who would come along during the Church Age. Every believer at Corinth during Paul's day is long since dead. So he had to be addressing those who would be living at the time when Christ would call for them, as well as those alive at the time this letter was written.

The context of the letter is that of informing those Christians about a mystery regarding a stunning event in their future. His words were to put to rest some of their worries about what would happen to those Christians among them who had died. What would happen to them in terms of their going to Heaven?

Paul was saying that: 1) Not all believers would die; some would not have to die, but would be alive at the time of a stupendous event; and 2) All believers, however, would be changed.

They would be changed in one single moment of time. The dead would be made alive and put into supernatural bodies. Those alive at the time of the event would be changed into supernatural bodies while living.

The "mystery" Paul was revealing was the one wrapped up in Jesus' words as recorded by John the apostle:

> Let not your heart be troubled; ye believe in God, believe also in me.
>
> In my Father's house are many mansions: if it were not so, I would have told you. I go to prepare a place for you.
>
> And if I go and prepare a place for you, I will come again, and receive you unto myself; that where I am, there ye may be also. (John 14:1–3)

Paul further expanded on this "mystery" in his letter to the Thessalonians:

> For the Lord himself shall descend from heaven with a shout, with the voice of the archangel, and with the trump of God; and the dead in Christ shall rise first;
>
> Then we who are alive and remain shall be caught up together with them in the clouds, to meet the Lord in the air; and so shall we ever be with the Lord.
>
> (1 Thessalonians 4:16–17)

So, the thing to consider is that believers of the Church Age (Age of Grace)—and Paul was talking to believers of this dispensation—will ALL go to be with Jesus when He calls them in that "twinkling-of-an-eye" (*atomos* of time) moment—the Rapture. ALL believers of this dispensation will go to be with the Lord! Not a single individual who has accepted Christ for salvation will be left behind.

This truth includes every individual who never reached the intellectual ability—through brain incapacity or because of being too young—to understand that he or she must accept Christ for salvation. These are all under the blood of Christ for redemption and reconciliation to God, the Father. All will go to be with Jesus at the Rapture.

Some believe and teach that only those believers who are living in the will of God will go to be with Christ at the Rapture. Those living "carnal" lives, they believe, will be left behind to go through a time of God's judgment and wrath, along with the unbelieving earth dwellers. But God's Word doesn't teach that some will go and some will stay. ALL believers, Paul plainly writes, will go to be with the Lord at the Departure. Paul writes further to the Thessalonians:

> For God hath not appointed us to wrath but to obtain salvation by our Lord Jesus Christ,
>
> Who died for us, that, whether we wake or sleep, we should live together with him. (1 Thessalonians 5:9–10)

It is true that we are told by the Lord as recorded in Luke 21:36 that we are to watch and pray always that we may be accounted worthy to escape all of the things of the Tribulation. But "worthy" in this sense means that we should be living in such a way that we will not be ashamed when we stand before Him at the judgment seat—the bema. We should desire to hear our Lord say, "Well done, good and faithful servant."

This might not seem fair to those who disagree with me on this—those who believe they are living their own lives within God's prescription for Christian deportment. But, it's not what we think is fair that matters. It's what the Word of God says that matters in any question of spiritual truth. God's truth—His Holy Word—says plainly that ALL believers who have died or are living during this present dispensation will go to be with the Bridegroom, the Lord Jesus Christ, when He makes that shout heard around the world to His bride: "Come up here!"

"Roadmap to Peace" Puzzles Politicians

October 4, 2010

Israeli Leaders' Lethal Liability

Bible prophecy's most profound current issue simmers on the Jerusalem horizon, but there seems little notice even by the usually observant prophecy ministries. It is the peace process to which I refer.

Israeli leadership at the very top is in conflict internally, as it is with the Palestinian leadership. Controversy rages over exactly how to formulate a process that might have a chance at securing peace between Israel and its enemy-laden neighbors.

The following frames the internal Israeli struggle:

> Foreign Minister Avigdor Lieberman on Tuesday presented the United Nations with his draft for a population and territory swap, as part of an eventual peace deal between Israel and the Palestinians. Under Lieberman's controversial scheme, part of Israel's Arab population would be moved to a newly created Palestinians state, in return for evacuation of Israeli settlements in the West Bank.... But

his decision to place them before the General Assembly in his role as foreign minister will raise speculation over whether they are his private plan, or the official policy of the Israeli government, and Netanyahu is likely to face international calls for clarification.[57]

Prime Minister Benjamin Netanyahu countered Lieberman's stated preference for the way peace should be pursued. The prime minister rejected the foreign minister's idea of a land swap and asserted that he felt peace might be achieved between Israel and the Palestinians within one year through talks with Palestinian Authority President Mahmoud Abbas.

Netanyahu reportedly said, "It is vital, and I wholeheartedly believe that it is within our power to reach a framework agreement within a year and change Middle East history."[58]

I have noted with great interest that the current Israeli prime minister seems to be an adherent of the saying, "Fool me once, shame on you. Fool me twice, shame on me." This, based on the way he conducted his first stint as the Jewish state's top post, versus his present *modus operandi.*

Netanyahu, in the first go-around as prime minister, held firm at most every juncture in dealing with Israel's enemies. At the same time, I believe he observed and took to heart a number of critically valuable lessons: 1) He saw that the international community as a whole turned ever more anti-Israel with each of his own hard-line stands; 2) He came to understand how the Arab-Islamist mind works; and 3) He formulated from his first run-in with his enemies' intransigence how to deal with them when his next opportunities presented themselves. He had opportunity to analyze his predecessor prime ministers during his second ascension to that post. He is a quick learner, I've come to observe. This is what I mean.

The Palestinian thugs, from Yasser Arafat to present—as well as every Arab leader who has dealt with Israeli leaders—will agree to any number of proposals, so far as the process of agreement is concerned. That is, once they enter a negotiations process, they always present a surface reasonableness—a willingness to be part of the process, as long as they don't have to make the iron-clad agreement that can be confirmed or ratified by the international powers that be. When this point is reached, they will find reasons to break off the negotiations. One glaring instance of this was when Arafat broke off negotiations after achieving 98 percent or so of what the Palestinians wanted during the Oslo talks.

When Israel wouldn't turn all control of the Temple Mount in Jerusalem over to Arafat, he got up and stormed out of the talks in a rage, despite the fact that he had been given everything else he had demanded—i.e., he didn't want peace. He wanted the complete eradication of the Jewish nation, as does the leadership of Israel's Islamist enemies today.

The process of feigned peacemaking is the weapon of choice of Israel's Arab enemies when military action isn't an option. They are masters at stringing out that process interminably.

Again, Benjamin Netanyahu is, if anything, a fast-track learner. I sense that he is playing the process of peace-making the same way the surreptitious Arabs have always played and now the Palestinian leaders play the process. While his own foreign minister is willing to give territory for the hope of peace, the prime minister just promises that he wants to negotiate peace. He is simply dragging out the process, thereby giving the international community Israel-haters nothing in the way of negative diplomatic ammunition to hurl at him. He is holding out on any land swap for a peace he knows is not likely ever to be established with those blood-vowed to murder every Jew on the planet.

Tragically, however, Bible prophecy indicates that it is methodology akin to that of Foreign Minister Lieberman, not of Mr. Netanyahu, that will be utilized by the Israeli leadership at the beginning of the Tribulation era (Daniel's seventieth week).

God's Word says that an end-times Israeli leadership will make a covenant with "the prince that shall come" (Daniel 9:26–27).

That covenant will almost certainly involve Israel's leadership giving up land, based upon Joel 3:2:

> I will also gather all nations, and will bring them down into the valley of Jehoshaphat, and will plead with them there for my people and for my heritage, Israel, whom they have scattered among the nations, and parted my land.

God will Himself bring all nations to Armageddon, in part because they have divided the land He promised His chosen people. The land-for-peace deal that end-times Israeli leadership consummates with Antichrist and the nations of the world will make them liable for judgment. The peace will be a lethal transaction to be sure.

> Wherefore, hear the word of the LORD, ye scornful men, that rule this people who are in Jerusalem.
>
> Because ye have said, We have made a covenant with death, and with hell are we at agreement, when the overflowing scourge shall pass through, it shall not come

> unto us; for we have made lies our refuge, and under falsehood have we hid ourselves.... And your covenant with death shall be disannulled, and your agreement with hell shall not stand; when the overflowing scourge shall pass through, then ye shall be trodden down by it. (Isaiah 28:14–15, 18)

I'm convinced we are witnessing the prophesied lethal peace process in the making.

October 11, 2010
Stuxnet—Foe or Friend?

The warnings have come for months—for several years, actually. Each time the e-mail articles have contained the almost-guaranteed certainty that the summer months would bring a preemptive attack on Iran's gestating nuclear facilities by Israel or the U.S. Mideast war would ensue, perhaps even lighting off the Ezekiel 38–39 Gog-Magog attack.

The number of articles I've received on this fearful matter have eclipsed the number received on any other.

Then, you might recall, the deadline was reached. If Israel didn't take out the Iranian nuclear sites by a certain day, the facilities would go online, making any strike against them too dangerous. Radiation would devastate populations surrounding the areas hit. Destruction of Iran's feared nuclear weapons effort could not be carried out. Iran would thus achieve the means by which to produce plutonium and other byproducts necessary to bring atomic weaponry into its military repertoire. The strike was imminent, the articles I continued to receive warned. The attack had to be accomplished before the nuclear facilities came online. This was it! All-out war in the Middle East!

But the deadline came and went. Neither Israel nor the U.S. struck Iran's atomic weapons development facilities. The inevitable was thus merely delayed. The war was averted, but the refusal of Israel or the United States to risk setting off conflict only assured that when the war did finally erupt, the world would then face a more deadly foe. The Iranians would now be a nuclear power—or so the fearful rhetoric goes.

How could Israel let such a thing eventuate? How could a madman like Iran's Mahmoud Ahmadinejad be allowed to have the power that now will guarantee the destruction of Israel at a point, perhaps in the not-too-distant future?

Enter the hand of God. The intervention was unwittingly carried out by the human sort, no doubt, but the handiwork of the God of Israel is all over the matters involved. An unseen entity suddenly has manifested itself in a way that has all but shut down Iran's nuclear energy/possible atomic weapons production capability. While it is a mysterious cyber bug that could devastate, particularly, the most highly technical and sophisticated of industrial infrastructures, such as those of America and Israel, it is a number of other nations that are experiencing the illness.

Stuxnet is called a malicious cyber weapon—a software or malware program that was apparently first discovered in June of 2010. It has appeared in China, Indonesia, Pakistan, and India, but Iran seems to have been affected most. The cyber bug has particularly devastated Iran's industrial complexes, including its nuclear installations.

Stuxnet, which acts as a computer worm, is inserted into a computer system through a USB port. Since it is introduced this way, rather than through the Internet, the worm is capable of infiltrating networks not connected to the Internet.

This worm is a quantum leap in cyber-bug terrorism, having the ability to determine what, where, and when it wants to attack upon entering a system. It invades, then assaults, industrial computer systems that control infrastructures such as those of power plants and refineries.

According to experts, Stuxnet, after recognizing its target, does what no other malware program has been able to do. It takes over the industrial target's supervisory control and data acquisition system (SCADA), and, working within this system, manipulates controls and even destroys the facility.

This is what has happened to Iran's computer, thus the nuclear program, at Bushehr. Iran was poised to start up the plant next month, but has announced the launch has been set back at least several months.

Deputy head of Iran's Information Technology Company, Hamid Alipour, told reporters that the malware operated undetected in the country's computer systems for about one year. He said later that efforts to mitigate its destructive effects have been unsuccessful.

"We had anticipated that we could root out the virus within one to two months," Alipour said. "But the virus is not stable and since we started the cleanup process, three new versions of it have been spreading."[59]

Speculation is rampant that Israel introduced Stuxnet to Iran's computers to cause this malfunction. I would really like to think so. Ah…it would indeed be poetic justice. Regardless, it is a welcome relief. Rumors of Mideast war because of Iran's atomic threat can be pushed down the road for the moment.

Perhaps it will be pushed down the road until the Iranian hordes are destroyed by God when they come with Gog to try to make good on Ahmadinejad's threat to wipe the chosen people off the earth. Certainly, there is no mention of the Persian forces (Iran) or any other of the Gog-Magog coalition nations using atomic weaponry on Israel.

Quite the opposite will be the case, according to Bible prophecy. It is those attacking satanic forces that will lose five-sixths of their troops—and by weapon power that will far exceed anything human scientists have been able to devise. Maybe Stuxnet is the first small volley in Jehovah's battle plan for that coming event. Stay tuned...

October 18, 2010
Strange Prophetic Silence: Part 1

Todd Strandberg often observes these days a strange lack of prophetic activity; nothing in the news rivets the observer in the dramatic way, say, that an attack on Iran's nuclear facilities might grab one's attention.

This perception of a "lull in prophetic progression," as he calls it, might seem at first nonsensical, considering the tremendous procession of probable end-times issues and events that we address each week. Geopolitically, there are many signals of biblically prophetic significance. The European Union continues to consolidate power while remaining at the same time loosely confederated. Certainly, we legitimately can and do make the case for this strange entity being the likely candidate for producing revived Rome—the ten toes of iron and miry clay given in Nebuchadnezzar's dream-vision of the final world empire (Daniel 2).

October 2010

Russia is a brooding giant to Israel's north, and at every opportunity, Iran threatens the Jewish state with oblivion. These nations combine with Turkey and others to constitute a coalescing agglomerate that has the characteristics of the Gog-Magog military machine described in Ezekiel 38 and 39.

Russia's Vladimir Putin openly displays ambition that easily qualifies him as one who might aspire to be the Gog of the Ezekiel prophecies. Iran's Mahmoud Ahmadinejad spouts the kind of hatred for God's chosen people that the prince of Persia no doubt will use to inspire Iran's (Persia's) leader to join with Gog in raging against Israel in that satanic attack (Daniel 10:20).

Recently, Turkey's prime minister, Recep Tayyip Erdogan, has brought his nation into the Iranian and Arab world's mantra for Israel to, in effect, be neutralized—eradicated as an entity in the Middle East. Thus, Ezekiel's prophecy about the Gog-Magog forces continues to congeal, with the ancient area of Togarmah now firmly within the foretold mix of peoples that will storm over the mountains of Israel to meet their God-ordained doom.

So, again, it seems nonsensical to say that there is a lack of prophetic progression, based upon such spectacular developments. Yet, Todd and I have agreed with his assessment during our conversations. Even so, the signals of this being the very end of the age continue to accrue.

Socioeconomically, the end-times signals are prolific, with the whole world in economic distress. The 2008–2009 U.S. and international monetary crises were nothing short of earth-shaking. With the global financial structure intricately linked to the U.S. dollar and its economy, America's banking meltdown and all attendant to it suddenly had the Western nations in panic. The panic is unabated, despite America throwing trillions of dollars that don't really exist into the fiscal fiasco.

Rioting in Greece, Spain, Italy, and other so-called "civilized" countries displayed in blatant fashion the economic turmoil. Rage over government-provided social services being withdrawn and jobs cut from government, along with unions losing their funding, caused—and continue to cause—withdrawal spasms like those suffered by addicts needing their heroin fixes.

The nations are in distress with perplexity, just as Jesus prophesied (Luke 21:25). There is a call for a rearrangement of the economic order. It is just such an order that will serve Antichrist's dastardly regime as he sets about to enslave the world. His 666 numbers-and-mark system as found in Revelation 13:16–18 can be seen in the making in these very days in which we live.

The electronic means to produce such a system exists, too. The computer-satellite capabilities and linkages—with Internet connecting practically every place on earth—doubtless will be all brought together in some spectacular way to produce the beast system of economic gulag.

Ironically, about the only area of the world that seems to be progressing economically is part of Asia—particularly one specific nation that almost certainly has a prophetic destiny. While the economic and technological apex nation of the world—the United States of America—is suffering, causing the other industrial nations and socialist countries to suffer, that great prophetic Oriental region of the world benefits mightily from the distress and perplexity. China holds much of the debt owed by the most economically powerful nation ever to exist!

China will almost certainly be the "king" of the "kings of the

East" mentioned in Revelation chapters 9 and 16. It is even now apparently acquiring the level of wealth that will assure the accumulation of military strength with which to (along with demonic assistance of major magnitude) kill one-third of the world's population (Revelation 9:15–16, 16:12).

It seems beyond irony that it is the U.S. that is funding most of the Sino monster. It is the American technological/wealth base that has been primarily instrumental also in providing the financial wherewithal for paving Antichrist's future kingdom. It is perhaps within these fiscal facts that can be found America's own ultimate judgment for straying so far from the godly founding principles upon which it was based. Yet there is this strange silence of prophetic progression that bugs Todd and me. We will further examine the matter in upcoming columns.

October 25, 2010
Strange Prophetic Silence: Part 2

So, again, we come to the seeming disconnect—the tremendous number of biblically prophetic indicators from a strange prophetic silence that surrounds these signals.

Todd and I analyze these matters without ceasing. The signs are everywhere that we are at the end times as given by Jesus when He foretold, for example, that it will be like the days of Noah's pre-Flood time and Lot's days in Sodom at the moment He will break in like a thief in the night on an unsuspecting world. And, yet, we are both amazed that the "prophetic progression" seems strangely slow—even to the point of causing us to constantly ask why things seem at a standstill.

How can we ask that question when every one of the apostle Paul's 2 Timothy 3, perilous-times characteristics of end-times man is observably on the front burner of society today? People are lovers of themselves, boasters, and proud. Children are disobedient to parents, with the assisted rebellion built in to the public school systems of America. We are a people—worldwide—who are unthankful and, certainly, unholy. The government-backed—even church-organization-backed—homosexual agenda, with hate crimes being legislated and implemented to punish those who dare to say God's Word teaches homosexuality is a sin, shows the perilous-times characteristic "without natural affection" is in our faces today.

Abortion takes the lives of more than four thousand babies per day in America. This, too, speaks to the "without natural affection" characteristic Paul prophesied would mark the end-times generation. We only have to look at the divorce rate today to see that the characteristics Paul gave in prophecy are exhibited within marriage. Infidelity is rampant. People are traitorous to their marriage partners; they are false accusers and truce-breakers. We are a generation prone to incontinence, or addictions, whether thinking on illicit or prescription drugs or on pornography that sears the minds of those who spend hours before computer screens. Also, we are addicted to spending money to satisfy ever-increasing and insatiable material desires.

People love pleasures more than they love God. Mankind is fierce, while at the same time many have a form of godliness, but deny Jesus Christ—the power of godliness. The holy name of Jesus is used far more as an invective than as a term of reverence and praise in this end-of-the-age hour. The name that God says is above every other isn't even allowed in many of America's workplaces, public schools, or government facilities—another panoply of reasons the nation's judgment is certain.

Why do Todd and I see this as a time of slow prophetic progression, considering this avalanche of prophetic markers? How can we say this when Israel is in position precisely as biblical prophets foretold it would be as history draws to a close and Armageddon nears?

Isaiah and Daniel said that Israel would be involved in a peace process at the very end of things to come. Zechariah, many other prophets, and the Lord Jesus Himself prophesied that Israel would be surrounded by and hated by all nations of earth at the time of the end. All of those developing prophecies regarding God's chosen people are front and center right now!

There is a prophetic silence at present. But it is a perceived rather than an actual silence, I think. It is part of the strange cognitive malady with which we all suffer, perhaps.

Overload of day-to-day human activity causes desensitization to even the most traumatic of injuries. "Time heals all wounds" is one common explanation of this cognitive condition. We lose a loved one, and while we will often recall memories of him or her and suffer anew, the overloads of life continue to cause the scar tissue to thicken. The pain fades, to some extent.

So it is in the matter of being watchful in the sense of Mark 13:37. We are so saturated with issues and events of our time that look like prophecy in stage-setting for fulfillment that we develop a malaise. We become desensitized to the phenomenal crush of end-times exigencies.

This is so disconcerting to those who work within prophecy ministries such as Rapture Ready, I think, because it is a solitary feeling at times that comes from such lack of interest among true believers. We find ourselves almost hoping something dramatic will happen to shake believers into understanding exactly how late the prophetic hour is.

Come to think of it...Jesus foretold a strange prophetic silence. He said it would be at just such an hour that He would break in upon a world in darkness. Because our time is so saturated with indicators of Christ's Second Coming, the apathy-ending event isn't in the offing. Or maybe it will be the most lethargy-ending event possible that will do the shaking up. Maybe the next prophetic indicator that will end this strange prophetic silence will be the Rapture itself:

> Watch therefore; for ye know not what hour your Lord doth come.
>
> But know this, that if the goodman of the house had known in what watch the thief would come, he would have watched, and would not have suffered his house to be broken up.
>
> Therefore be ye also ready; for in such an hour as ye think not the Son of man cometh. (Matthew 24:42–44)

NOVEMBER 2010

Antichrist's Warm-Up Acts on the World Stage

November 1, 2010
Antichrist's Warm-Up Act

Top entertainers, no matter how personally charismatic and mesmerizing, often prepare their audiences with warm-up acts in order to work their magic more effectively when they finally burst into the spotlight. Many of these started out as warm-up acts themselves before they made the top billing.

Bible prophecy foretells this most charismatic personality of human history basking in the end-times spotlight:

> Let no man deceive you by any means: for that day shall not come, except there come a falling away first, and that man of sin be revealed, the son of perdition;
>
> Who opposeth and exalteth himself above all that is called God, or that is worshipped; so that he, as God, sitteth in the temple of God, showing himself that he is God. (2 Thessalonians 2:3–4)

This supremely arrogant "beast," as he is called by God's Word in Revelation 13, will serve as his own sort of warm-up act immediately following the Rapture of the church. The "prince that shall come," as Daniel terms him, steps onto the stage of geopolitical diplomacy as a purveyor of peace.

> And he shall confirm the covenant with many for one week; and in the midst of the week he shall cause the sacrifice and the oblation to cease, and for the overspreading of abominations he shall make it desolate, even until the consummation, and that determined shall be poured upon the desolate. (Daniel 9:27)

Antichrist, empowered by Satan, will pave his own road for reaching his destiny as the object of forced worship by earth's inhabitants. This warm-up act—a roadmap for peace, of sort, that he will perform himself, with the assistance of another "beast" (the False Prophet)—will consist of impressive, if nefarious, accomplishments:

> And his power shall be mighty, but not by his own power; and he shall destroy wonderfully, and shall prosper, and practise, and shall destroy the mighty and the holy people.
>
> And through his policy also he shall cause craft to prosper in his hand; and he shall magnify himself in his heart, and by peace shall destroy many. (Daniel 8:24–25a)

Actually, the Man of Sin, as Antichrist is also called, has already had a number of warm-up acts. These have been put upon the world humanistic stage by Lucifer, the master orchestrator of evil. Theologians and even philosophers and soothsayers through the ages have thought some of these warm-up acts to be Antichrist fulfilling his prophesied role.

Perhaps even Satan himself has believed some of these evil characters that seemed like the predicted first beast of Revelation to be the foretold man whose number equals 666. Such lesser beasts as Nero, Hitler, Stalin, and others come to mind. Even U.S. presidents like John F. Kennedy, Ronald Reagan, and Franklin D. Roosevelt have been thought possible candidates for earth's final and most terrible tyrant.

Concerning Antichrist's eventual emergence, most all of today's end-times stage props form the setting for the final act of human history: The Gog-Magog forces are coming together in a swiftly coalescing cabal determined to move against Israel when the time is right. The kings of the East, which will trouble the beast as they will be a threat to his plans from the North and East, already can produce a two-hundred-million-troop military force. The European Union is almost certainly the reviving Roman Empire, out of which the dark prince will come.

Antichrist's geopolitical warm-up act has been preparing the way for his prime-time prophetic performance for decades. The past several years have brought dynamic rearrangements in preparation for his appearance. One thing within the eschatological mix is often overlooked when thinking about how near Antichrist's appearance might be. Again, this ingredient is found in the apostle Paul's second letter to the Thessalonians. The ingredient itself is difficult to identify because it involves deception from the father of all lies, which Satan will perpetrate upon those who reject God's righteousness.

And with all deceivableness of unrighteousness in them that perish; because they received not the love of the truth, that they might be saved. And for this cause God shall send them strong delusion, that they should believe a lie: That they all might be damned who believed not the truth, but had pleasure in unrighteousness. (2 Thessalonians 2:10–12)

Satan's present-day warm-up act, designed to mesmerize people of planet earth, has at its heart great deception that will delude most who are left behind following the Rapture. The Holy Spirit resident within the church will remove from acting on the consciences of mankind as He has been doing during this present Age of Grace.

Following the removal of the church, it will apparently be impossible for those who deliberately rejected the Holy Spirit's call to salvation before the Rapture to have any chance for redemption. The Lord will not let those people escape the delusion Satan's man, Antichrist, will produce. They will be doomed to believe a specific lie, Paul's prophecy indicates.

Some prophecy watchers observe Satan's preparations for bringing to the world's attention the man who will be his most infamous protégé. These—and I include myself—consider decades of fascination with extraterrestrial sightings to possibly be key to the old serpent concocting the "lie" of 2 Thessalonians 2:11.

Documentaries continue to fill cable TV networks, raising questions about whether we are alone in the cosmos. Reports of UFO sightings titillate the imaginations of brains already prepped by fictional accounts of invaders from far-flung places in space, such as in the current TV show titled *V*.

NOVEMBER 2010

The latest such silver-screen fiction about intruders from space is the film *Skyline.* Its story line is most fascinating, as the Star Trek Enterprise's first officer, Mr. Spock, might say.

One official synopsis of this movie about visitors from space states the following:

> After a late-night party, a group of friends are awoken in the dead of the night by an eerie light beaming through the window. Like moths to a flame, the light source is drawing people outside before they suddenly vanish into the air. They soon discover an otherworldly force is swallowing the entire human population off the face of the earth. Now our band of survivors must fight for their lives as the world unravels around them.[60]

Sounds eerily familiar to something from the Bible we address frequently on Rapture Ready, doesn't it? But God's Word is non-fiction–absolute truth. Such a scenario is prophetically scheduled to happen. Revelation 12 foretells that Satan and his fallen angelic horde will be cast to earth for the final time. John was told to write "Woe to the inhabiters of the earth" when that happens (see Revelation 12:12).

The second beast—the False Prophet—will call fire down from Heaven (Revelation 13:13) in the sight of men. Many students of Bible prophecy who observe these strange times in which we live think these things will likely be part of the lie of 2 Thessalonians 2:11, which earth dwellers will believe—i.e., the major part of the lie will be that those who have disappeared from earth have been taken for reasons held by the "extraterrestrial" entities.

Today, we are being "entertained" by Antichrist's warm-up act. But, it will be the Lord of Heaven—Jesus Christ—who will bring down the final curtain on Satan's great imposter.

> And then shall that wicked be revealed, whom the Lord shall consume with the spirit of his mouth, and shall destroy with the brightness of his coming. (2 Thessalonians 2:8)

November 8, 2010
Foreshadows of Ferocity

The San Francisco Giants won the 2010 World Series Monday, November 1. It was the first time the team has won the Series since 1954, when the franchise was playing as the New York Giants in the Polo Grounds. It should have been a reason for happiness, right? At least, if you were a Giants fan, and weren't a Texas Rangers fan. Certainly, it should have been a time of jubilation on the streets of San Francisco, one would think.

The victory was acknowledged by many, with congratulations all around. However, the dark side of humanity showed up—as it always seems to do—in demonstration of the malevolent side of humankind.

> As fans packed the streets, some violent incidents were reported such as fires, several fistfights, and a mob attack on a vehicle that was driven into a crowd. [The website] www.KTVU.com posted stunning helicopter footage of a large fire that was started at an intersection, followed by a driver's attempt to steer into the crowd. The car was

> stopped, its windshields were smashed, and passengers were attacked. Riot police arrived soon after the melee and the crowd began to thin out.[61]

The rioting is, of course, not without precedent. We have witnessed it time after time in large cities whose sports teams have won world championships. We have only to recall Chicago during the time when Michael Jordan ruled the NBA courts with the Chicago Bulls, and the victories of the Los Angeles Lakers and the rioting aftermath in some areas of that city. One can but look in open-mouthed wonder upon such obstreperous behavior—all in the name of celebrating something that's supposed to be fun and good.

The Founding Fathers of this nation wrote the Declaration of Independence and the Constitution with almost consensus acknowledgement that man's nature is depraved—fallen from the time of Eden. Peoples around the world have consistently validated that view of the human condition by exhibiting unseemly comportment. Except in the most tyrannical and oppressive of regimes, people often become unruly if things push them to the limits. Even such fear as those governments can present sometimes can't assuage the masses.

People will face down tanks and machine guns in some extreme cases, as in the Tiananmen Square uprising during the Olympic Games held in China some decades ago. Those Chinese faced down the murderous red military in a righteous cause of seeking liberty by demonstrating through the cameras of the world how brutal their masters were.

So, it is not against these courageous sorts that I write for our purposes here. There is a time for protests—for righteous uprisings. I put much of the civil rights protests of Martin Luther King Jr.'s day in that category to some extent. Although some of it was for the sake of crass political power grabs among certain left-wing politicians and community organizers, much of the demonstrations and actions were necessary to break the oppressive grip of racial bigotry.

Those who riot simply because they are riotous—unbridled in their "if it feels good, do it" hedonism—fit, in my view, into the category that is the subject of this commentary. They are of the classification I believe the apostle Paul was writing about in his second letter to Timothy, in which he said that "in the last days perilous times shall come," and described people alive during those times as "incontinent" and "fierce" (2 Timothy 3:1–3).

Out of sheer, uncontrolled determination to smash their way through life no matter what they break or who they hurt, those who live riotously prove the Founding Fathers right. The depravity of man is front and center for all to witness. It is an end-times signal manifest time after time in this generation.

That brings us to the purpose of our Constitution, our laws. No individual or class of individuals has the right to trample on the property or person of others. It is codified; it was put there by George Washington, Thomas Jefferson, John Adams, Benjamin Franklin, and all the rest. They got these precepts from the Word of God.

We have recently watched the riots in Greece, Spain, and other places where populaces, being weaned off the spigots of socialistic largesse, have acted as riotously as the mobs that burn down parts of their cities because their teams won. Governments are no longer capable of taxing the income-producing, working people of those nations enough to pay for the welfare and various other social programs politicians vote in time after time in order to gather support for themselves.

Governments, hopefully, have enough funds to defend against violence in the streets. One American city is so doing, it seems.

> INDIANAPOLIS—Armed security guards will be on hand at thirty-six unemployment offices around Indiana in what state officials said is a step to improve safety and make branch security more consistent…[Marc Lotter, Department of Workforce Development spokesman] said the agency is merely being cautious with the approach of an early-December deadline when thousands of Indiana residents could see their unemployment benefits end after exhausting the maximum ninety-nine weeks provided through multiple federal extension periods.
>
> "Given the upcoming expiration of the federal extensions and the increased stress on some of the unemployed, we thought added security would provide an extra level of protection for our employees and clients," he said.[62]

Let's pray that economic conditions in America don't become so desperate that they eventuate in violence like that seen in other countries. However, the fierce nature of fallen man hasn't stopped raising its hideous head since the first man rebelled and determined to do what was right in his own eyes, rather than what God chose for him. The ferocity is prophetically scheduled to get infinitely worse, when the Holy Spirit withdraws from governing the consciences of mankind in the way He does at present:

For the mystery of iniquity doth already work; only he who now letteth will let until he be taken out of the way. (2 Thessalonians 2:7)

The Restrainer—the Holy Spirit—will remove as governor of the unbridled evil of mankind when the Rapture takes place. God will allow the "mystery of iniquity" to strongly influence all who will not come to Christ for salvation during the last seven years of human history leading up to Christ's Second Advent (Revelation 19:11). The foreshadows of that luciferian evil are darkening our daily lives as never before. Each person who follows Christ must shine truth from His Word in order to illuminate the pathway to Jesus in these closing days of the age.

November 15, 2010
Israel's North American Friend

While preparing to speak at a Bible prophecy conference in Canada last month, I discovered some interesting facts and figures about those fellow North Americans. I also learned of stark contrasts between the leadership of Israel's North American key present-day "proponents."

I put the word "proponents" in quotation marks because support for the Jewish state is subject to slippage these days as never before. It is becoming increasingly difficult to find a true proponent of that prophetic nation. The North American continent encompasses the two national entities that have most been supportive of Israel's right to exist—the United States of America and Canada. This support is in contravention to attitudes and policies of most other nations of the world. The United Nations pulses with collective hatred for the Jewish state. Pressures are on the rise to change the North American support for Israel from one that is more and more tenuous to that of support for enemies blood-vowed to wipe the Jews from the earth.

It shouldn't surprise students of Bible prophecy who study eschatological matters from a literalist perspective that the European Union is among those who want Israel marginalized. The EU is believed by many to be the nucleus of the reviving Roman Empire—the region of Europe out of which Antichrist will one day step onto the stage of false peacemaking (Daniel 9:26–27).

The geopolitical reason for the Europeans taking the side of the Arab countries is most often given as the desire to keep oil flowing to the EU energy-thirsty member states. But the real reason behind the support for the Islamist regimes is satanic rage that is destined to bring all nations of the world against God's chosen people (Zechariah 12:1–3).

We can see in today's headlines the political ringmasters of that very region of the world beginning to bring to bear increasing pressure on America to come down on the side of Israel's enemies.

> WASHINGTON—U.S. policy toward Israel has been increasingly influenced by the hostility of the European Union, a report said. A report by a leading analyst said the EU has become the most influential lobby in the United States regarding Israel. Steven Rosen, a director at the Middle East Forum, said EU leaders were pushing Washington away from Israel and toward the Arab world.

"European leaders are the most effective external force urging the U.S. government to move away from Israel and closer to the Arabs," the report, titled "The Arab Lobby: The European Component," said.

"The strongest external force pressuring the U.S. government to distance itself from Israel is not the Arab-American organizations, the Arab embassies, the oil companies, or the petrodollar lobby," the report said. "Rather, it is the Europeans, especially the British, French, and Germans, that are the most influential Arab lobby to the U.S. government. The Arabs consider Europe to be the soft underbelly of the U.S. alliance with Israel and the best way to drive a wedge between the two historic allies."[63]

The current U.S. presidential administration seems to have little problem with falling in line with the pressures being applied. President Barack Obama, while on a ten-day trip to India and Indonesia, where he reached out yet again to try to show his country's desire to embrace the Muslim world in friendship, expressed his displeasure with Israel for continuing with construction of homes within its sovereign territory. He complained that he had not been given a heads-up about the building of the thirteen hundred new homes in East Jerusalem. The announcement was made while Israeli Prime Minister Benjamin Netanyahu was in New Orleans on an official visit.

"This kind of activity is never helpful when it comes to peace negotiations," Obama said.[64]

The Europeans were unhappy, too.

EU foreign policy commissioner Catherine Ashton said, in

commenting on Netanyahu's announcement, that the plan "contradicts the efforts by the international community to resume direct negotiations." She called for the decision to be reversed, adding that "settlements are illegal under international law, constitute an obstacle to peace, and threaten to make a two-state solution impossible."[65]

The U.S. State Department fell in line with European diplomatic expression of anger. Philip J. Crowley, spokesman for the State Department, expressed his deep disappointment because of the announcement and called the plan "counter-productive to our efforts to resume direct negotiations between the parties."[66]

The stark contrast I mentioned to begin this commentary—that I saw while preparing for my Canada speaking trip—was that between the American administration and Canada's top leader. While President Obama has consistently shown what I feel to be diplomatic disrespect to Israel and Netanyahu, Canadian Prime Minister Steven Harper has unwaveringly stood by the nation that should be North America's closest ally.

On Monday, Harper gave a speech dealing with ways to fight anti-Semitism. A report on that stated:

> Harper implied that his country did not secure a seat at the United Nations Security Council due to its failure to cooperate with an anti-Israel policy.
>
> "And like any free country Israel subjects itself to such criticism, healthy, necessary, democratic debate," he said. "But when Israel, the only country in the world whose very existence is under attack, is consistently and conspicuously singled out for condemnation, I believe we are morally obligated to take a stand. Not just because it is

the right thing to do, but because history shows us, and the ideology of the anti-Israel mob tell us all too well, that those who threaten the existence of the Jewish people are in the longer term a threat to all of us," he said.

"Whether it is at the United Nations or any other international forum, the easiest thing to do is simply to just get along and go along with this anti-Israel rhetoric, to pretend it is just about being even-handed, and to excuse oneself with the label of honest broker," he added.

Harper stated in his speech that "as long as I am prime minister...Canada will take that stand, whatever the cost."[67]

The nations of the world will be judged by Israel's God—the only God who exists. How world leaders deal with the Jewish state determines the fate of their own nations, in the ultimate sense. That time of reckoning, according to the deluge of end-times signals to which this generation is witness, can't be far off.

November 22, 2010
Scanning a Fearful Future: Part 1

Commentators, secular and religious, weigh in incessantly on all aspects of the issues of greatest concern for these angst-ridden times. Those issues of most profound worry are collapsing economy, loss of personal liberty, and what is going to happen in the immediate and long-term future.

One can almost physically feel the fear in the e-mails I receive daily. Worries over what the future holds fill the articles and, more to the point for this commentary, dominate the personal missives that search for answers that might provide some degree of comfort.

One of the more mildly fearful notes I received this week says in part:

> I watched the *Hal Lindsey Report* yesterday in which he said that he believes before the Rapture that Christians were going to be persecuted. After reading your "Nearing Midnight" article today I can see that Christians becoming more and more isolated for their support of Israel is just another sign that he is right. If Hal is right, with the Rapture being as close as it is, then persecution for Christians has to be very close. What is your take on this?

I listened to what Hal Lindsey had to say in that particular program, and he did paint a bleak picture for the immediate future. He correctly pointed to even more terrible times for the world a bit further out—during the Tribulation. I had so many urging me to watch Glenn Beck's program that I tuned in to that show on the several days he painted a frightening picture of what he says he believes George Soros and the New World Order minions have in mind for the world—particularly for the citizens of the United States.

Mr. Beck, like Hal Lindsey, gave as part of his view the prescription he thinks necessary to help cure the sickness from which the United States and the world suffer. It is interesting that both Lindsey and Beck—one Christian, the other secular (in that he is a *Fox News* pundit)—give faith turned toward God as a major part of any such remedy.

Now, I am aware Glenn Beck is a Mormon, and that this

fact makes the difference between the views of the two men and their recommendations quite distinct from one another. But the intensive urging of both to look more deeply into the crush of troubles weighing heavily on the minds of most everyone is more to the point. Both see what is happening in these strange times as emanating from dark, spiritual forces.

I know that Hal's analysis is correct because he realizes that the source against which humanity—particularly Christians—struggles is found in God's Word. I honestly don't know exactly what Glenn Beck sees as the chief opponent against which humanity must be protected. He points to George Soros and his ilk, but never seems to get to the root of the evil we face.

Lindsey knows—as do you and I who try to be attuned to God's Word in these prophetic times—that, according to the apostle Paul:

> We wrestle not against flesh and blood, but against principalities, against powers, against the rulers of the darkness of this world, against spiritual wickedness in high places. (Ephesians 6:12)

Paul wasn't writing about the George Soroses of the world. He was forewarning of the dark powers behind the earthly megalomaniacs who would be our masters. Maybe Mr. Beck sees those darker powers, too, but he can't bring himself about to cast God's light upon that unseen realm. Perhaps that is because he sees us, the American people, as the answer to our own spiritual problems. If we will just summon the same patriotic grit of the Founding Fathers, we can overcome the human diabolists like Soros. To aspire to vanquish "spiritual wickedness in high places"—the dark, satanic forces of the spiritual world—would not be possible. When all is said and done, Beck's viewpoint includes only the humanistic elements of the struggle mankind faces today. In this, sadly, he seems in lockstep with the world-order builders that God laughs sarcastically at as recorded in Psalms 2.

I won't go further about Glenn Beck concerning his acumen in pointing the way to overcoming in the struggle we face as the apocalyptic storm nears. His religion's prophetic beliefs dictate outcomes drastically different from those found in the Bible. Since he hasn't overtly introduced those to his audiences—at least, not yet—I won't address those here.

However, the biblical scenarios are the ones Hal Lindsey does introduce on a weekly basis to his audience. It is this view we will look at when thinking on the prospects we face, considering all of the bleak economic and societal news on the immediate horizon.

But, we've run out of column space for this week. We will begin scanning our darkening prophetic landscape through God's radar next week, God willing.

November 29, 2010
Scanning a Fearful Future: Part 2

Terrible times like no other in American history lurk somewhere in the future, according to Glenn Beck of *Fox News*. He is joined in his stated apprehension for what's coming by thousands of American citizens. Many of these are fear-filled Christians who look to Beck and others to inform them of the proposed terrors to come, and to tell them what to do about it. I continue to hear from some of these through e-mail on a weekly, even daily, basis.

November 2010

I would like to look briefly at developments across today's socioeconomic landscape, thus to examine as analytically and as fairly as possible the matters that give Beck and others fodder for their doomsday scenarios.

Economics-minded forecasters great and small watched the stock market bubble build during the days preceding the Lehman Brothers collapse of 2008, speculating wildly what the bubble's burst might bring. That financial aneurysm, they determined, would certainly rupture—and, of course, it did. Governmental insanity created by ultra-liberal politicians saw to it that people with champagne tastes and beer drinkers' budgets for years received home loans they didn't have much more than a prayer of ever repaying.

We are now familiar with the terms "Freddie Mac" and "Fannie Mae." We're equally acquainted with names such as Barney Frank, Charles Schumer, and others, who—in the name of "fairness" to those who couldn't afford housing like the more affluent—demanded these be given the loans anyway, despite the fact the recipients didn't have the income or collateral to support that level of debt.

Rather than govern the housing industry responsibly, the elected officials invested with the responsibility to oversee things, in concert with their Wall Street cohorts, foolishly threw caution to the fiscal winds. A banking crisis of unprecedented magnitude was thus created, with the housing bubble rupture setting in motion bank failures and threats of even greater crises.

Calls for massive bailouts to avert what the president of the United States and others in government and media speciously screamed would otherwise be world-rending calamity brought about the most devastating crisis of all. Trillions of dollars were, in effect, created out of thin air by the Federal Reserve Bank to save entities "too big to fail."

The totally irresponsible sleight-of-hand accomplished only the creation of an exploding national debt that most likely can never be repaid. Decisions made by some of the same people who helped create the problems strapped on the back of American citizens financial burdens that will weigh heavily on generations far into the future.

The resulting economic uncertainty deepened an abyss-like recession that more soundly thought-out measures would have surely lessened in severity. Jobs, as we know, are being lost; businesses are closing their doors; deflation or hyperinflation—the experts can't figure which—might collapse the American economy within a near-time frame (which the experts can't predict, either).

The stability of the global economy hangs in the balance, with the other nations and their monetary gurus wondering about the financial fate of the U.S. and its all-important dollar. And, make no mistake: Under present world economic structures, the fate of the American dollar is absolutely critical.

Enter Glenn Beck at the tip of the gloom iceberg. And "iceberg" is a viable term here because the things he and others are forewarning are indeed chilling. Statements the TV and radio show host make almost daily send shivers down the spine of many of his viewers. He says things like (I paraphrase), "Change is coming, and when it happens, you won't recognize your country. You will wake up next day, and it will no longer be America as you've known it. And, it will happen just that fast. I can't tell you when that transformation is coming, but it's coming."

Beck forecasts the same astonishing change for the entire

world in his proposed overnight transformational moment. His words sound almost out of the pages of Bible prophecy from the pretribulational view, don't they? But the change he predicts is tied almost exclusively to the earthly, not to the ethereal—almost, but not entirely, as we will soon find.

Economic collapse, thus societal rearrangements of apocalyptic dimension, is at the heart of his fearful forecast. He implies that we will, perhaps, awaken that morning to a monetary cataclysm—our dollar as worthless as the deutsche marks of the Weimar republic of Germany just before Hitler's meteoric rise to power in the 1930s. The Fox program host often raises the real probability, in his view, that inflation, which is on the rise, will skyrocket to astronomical levels when the great transformation he fears takes place.

He gives some key commodity future dollar amounts for what he claims the experts tell him will be exponential price rises. A small bag of sugar could be as much as $60 or $70. One ear of corn could be $11 or higher. A loaf of bread will likely be $24. Just under a pound of coffee could be $77. Fifteen ounces of orange juice will likely be $45, according to Beck's forecasters.

A Hershey chocolate bar, standard size, will cost $15.50, his experts say. Now, that is certainly a crisis in the making if it is an accurate prognostication. Chocolate lovers I know would probably join the rioters Beck believes will rage in the streets once cuts to federal government give-away programs have to be made.

Next week, we will think a bit on what a changed America might look like if truly effective remedies to deal with Mr. Beck's fearful vision of a new socioeconomic paradigm are ever implemented.

Terry James

December 2010

Scanning a Fearful Future

December 6, 2010

Scanning a Fearful Future: Part 3

The Federal Emergency Management Agency has internment compounds placed strategically around the United States. These will be used as concentration camps when anarchy reaches a critical point in America and the world. This sort of warning has been at the heart of fear-filled e-mails I've been receiving for the past seven years, at least.

Today, the trepidation concerning the likelihood of the collapse of America and the world issues daily from a populist mouthpiece. There are others, but Glenn Beck fills the role as chief forecaster of impending doom. He says frequently that we will awaken one morning and find that America has changed. We won't recognize the nation. It will happen just that swiftly, and the transformation will involve, among other things, probable hyperinflation that will make money valueless for most people in America. This means that the entire world will follow suit. Global depression, we infer, will be the plight of all but the ultra rich of the world—the George Soroses, etc.

Based upon Beck's dire suppositions, we consider things to

come. Just how far into the future all of this evil lurks, Beck doesn't know. However, based upon the rapid movement in economic uncertainties, it is likely, he implies, that it will happen sooner rather than later. That new dawning—or perhaps "nightfall" is the better term—will be bleak, he predicts. The dollar will have fallen as the reserve currency for most of the world's economies. Entire bank accounts will be wiped out, in that their contents likely won't be sufficient to feed a family for a day, much less for longer. Governments will be forced to cut social programs of every sort—completely eliminating them in most cases. Rioting will explode while those on the welfare roll and others used to government largesse will turn violent. The big inner cities will be particularly hard hit.

If the lessons learned from Hurricane Katrina in New Orleans can serve as example, looting and violence might well be the order of such changed way of life on that terrible day after the transformation forecast by Glenn Beck occurs. The sorts who looted during the devastating hurricane will almost certainly spill into the suburbs, then into the countryside, pillaging for food and anything else that strikes their fancy.

Riots in the streets of Greece, Spain, and most recently in London, brought about by governments imposing austerity measures on money spent on social programs, present a foreboding picture of how things in the U.S. might look within twenty-four hours of an economic collapse like the one Beck and others fear. In the United States, the very thought of what might take place when government handouts are cut off caused Indianapolis, Indiana, city officials to bring in greatly increased law enforcement when officials were about to announce that unemployment payments would not be extended.

So daunting are the prospects that even Beck stops short of delving too deeply into what such a changed world—catastrophically lacking in food, electricity, appropriate sewage treatment, and clean drinking water—would mean to Americans. But such change, he forewarns, is coming...and soon. It is coming, he says, because of the internationalist-elitists who want that transformed world through which to rule over the rest of us—a "New World Order," as George Soros, Henry Kissinger, Zbigniew Brzezinski, and even George H. W. Bush and other champions of globalism have termed it.

Presidents have for decades been leading America into the globalist economic arena. No chief executive has observably been more determined to meld the U.S. economy with the rest of the world than Barack Obama. He said in a speech in Mumbai, India, regarding his desire to take America into the global economic model:

> This will keep America on its toes. America is going to have to compete. There is going to be a tug-of-war within the U.S. between those who see globalization as a threat and those who accept we live in an open, integrated world, which has challenges and opportunities.[68]

Obama stated further that unemployment within the U.S. that might result from global economic integration is going to be the "new normal." It is just something we are all going to have to get used to.

Most every proponent of this move into globalism comprehends that the process of merging the American economy into the one-world configuration they desire will be painful for U.S. citizens. Wages will go down. America's living standard will fall, according to the globalists. Americans will face a struggle in the course that must be taken to reach parity for all of the world community. This is just a fact of life, according to those who know best. President Obama himself says that the nation's economy might not be fixed for quite some time.

Again, if I hear him right, Glenn Beck believes this change will be, for Americans, an instantaneous fall into an abyss of economic depression, not a slow slide into the poor house. He presents an almost fatalistic scenario, concerning our not being able to stop it from happening overnight. He urges all who will listen to prepare for the coming, contrived collapse of the American and world economies.

He says, at the same time, that he believes Americans have what it takes to thwart this drive toward New World Order—this effort to return to Babel. He indicates that he believes fervor for patriotism at the level of that of the Founding Fathers can reignite a foundational movement to restore sanity to government, economy, and culture/society.

At a rally in Washington D.C., he threw some spiritual/religious verbiage into the mix of his exhortation to take back America:

> Something beyond imagination is happening. America today begins to turn back to God. For too long, this country has wandered in darkness.[69]

Sounds like Beck is onto something there, doesn't it? Let's look more deeply into where that might be leading next time.

December 2010

December 13, 2010
Scanning a Fearful Future: Part 4

America is on the precipice of economic implosion, according to Glenn Beck and others. A sudden, catastrophic transformation will jolt us one morning upon awakening to the fact that the way of life we've known is gone. The *Fox News* host pronounces the nation's doom if his prescription for cure isn't followed.

If the cure is not taken, George Soros and his ilk, the New World Order titans, will march America's citizenry into global gulag—on the broad way back to Babel. There, all of mankind will, like John Lennon once sang, "be as one."

Beck's biblical allusions flow soothingly, once the dire diagnosis and prognosis for America's socioeconomic illness are firmly grasped by his audience. And, a growing number of people seem mesmerized by the host's descriptions, illustrations, and analyses.

The Lord God knew that being "as one" was a humanistic recipe for disaster, Beck pontificates. The Almighty rushed to the plains of Shinar—as recorded in Genesis 11—to spread humankind throughout all parts of the planet to avoid exactly what Soros and his buddies are again planning to foist upon earth dwellers. After laying out instructions and suggestions about how to survive some harsh, even terrifying, interim times just ahead by storing foods with long shelf lives and making other prudent preparations against the devastation the dollar's demise will assuredly bring, Beck shifts to spiritual counsel. He leads into this phase with his words at the rally, as mentioned earlier: "Something that is beyond imagination is happening. America today begins to turn back to God. For too long, this country has wandered in darkness."[70]

Almost tearful with emotion in his voice, Beck pleads for Americans to go to our knees and pray for the nation's salvation. Then, with a great inhalation of patriotic resolve like that of Washington, Adams, Jefferson, and other of America's founders, Beck, with Patton-like motivational rhetoric and steel in his voice, fortifies his troops for the battles ahead.

America will triumph through all the assaults against the republic, he declares with vigor, "because we are Americans." Americans always do whatever it takes to overcome evil.

Glenn Beck exhorts Americans to invoke God's name and help in the "take-back America" campaign. Good—so far as it goes.

With his next declaration, Beck frames his proclamation about the cure he envisions. He declares that the American people—those like the patriots in his audience—will do the necessary sacrificing and make the political and economic changes essential to set the U.S. ship of state back on course to a sound moral and socioeconomic mooring.

America will survive the great crash that is coming and, he implies, it will again become the greatest nation—although perhaps smaller, he adds—because of the goodness intrinsic within the American people. We are, he says, about to "witness miracles."

This is the point where emotionally hyped fervor and patriotic resolve—no matter how sincere—depart from truth that resides within the heart of God's prophetic Word. No matter how well constructed or intensive the efforts to implement it, Beck's blueprint—or any humanistic blueprint—for saving the republic is doomed to failure.

To this point, Hal Lindsey's view of Bible prophecy and

Glenn Beck's analyses and forecast for America's destiny have run relatively parallel. Both Lindsey and Beck see a time coming in the near term when America will suffer financial collapse. It will be, they each predict, a time of national and worldwide societal darkness worse than the bleakest years of the Great Depression. Based upon the staggering debt of the U.S. and of most every other major nation on earth, theirs is the only conclusion that can reasonably be reached using informed rationale.

Lindsey and Beck also envision a singular moment when America and the world will change forever. It will be an instant so calamitous that it will, in effect, eventuate in a totally transformed global order for every facet of human interaction.

This, however, is where similarities in their view of the future end. Now the views diverge as dramatically as the difference between the eternal places called Heaven and Hell.

As I wrote in the beginning of this series, Glenn Beck hasn't overtly interjected his Mormon beliefs into his foreboding predictions. Therefore, I won't address his pronouncements in regard to his religious beliefs—that is, except to again point out that the Mormon view of the end of human history differs greatly from what the Bible says about the consummation of all things encapsulated by this thing God created for man called time.

I feel justified in mentioning this because Beck himself more and more brings the name "God" and the need for the exercise of "faith" into his presentations. However, his consistently stated viewpoint makes it obvious that he believes the fate of us all will play out in an all-earthly scenario, with America winning the day, if we all follow his prescription for dealing with the coming calamity.

Hal Lindsey, like me and those who believe that Bible prophecy clearly speaks of what conditions will be like at the very end of the age, also sees America and the world headed into an economic morass. Unlike Glenn Beck, however, we are of the conviction that if indeed we are at the end of this dispensation—the Age of Grace (Church Age) as we believe is the case—this nation is beyond anything human intervention can do to save it. Next time we will look at what I'm convinced is God's view of things to come in the very near future.

December 20, 2010
Scanning a Fearful Future: Part 5

I must preface what follows by saying that I use Hal Lindsey in this look at the future because I and so many others hold him in high regard as the most widely recognized apologist for the pre-tribulation Rapture view of Bible prophecy. His book, *The Late, Great Planet Earth,* is of course the work that vaulted him into prominence. His continuing efforts over the decades to forewarn of things to come—with his current TV program serving as an excellent Bible prophecy platform—puts him at the top level of those who watch for Christ's return.

Lindsey has indicated on his television program, *The Hal Lindsey Report,* that he believes America and all other nations of the world are headed into the darkest of socioeconomic times. American Christians, he believes, face persecution unlike any that believers in the United States have experienced. He recommends, as does Glenn Beck, that people store food and make other preparations against possible hyper-inflated times to come.

While Lindsey advocates—as does Beck—that we strive to be good citizens and fight the staunch, patriotic fight through the ballot box in order to return the nation to one centered in morality and freedom, he says in practically the same breath that this world system is doomed. There is no hope, apart from the hope that is in Jesus Christ. His seeming dichotomy of thought evokes concerns that must be addressed.

We began looking into prospects for the near future by considering an e-mail I received from one such concerned Christian. Again, he wrote the following, in part:

> I watched *The Hal Lindsey Report* yesterday in which he said that he believes before the Rapture that Christians were going to be persecuted. After reading your "Nearing Midnight" article today, I can see that Christians becoming more and more isolated for their support of Israel is just another sign that he is right. If Hal is right, with the Rapture being as close as it is, then persecution for Christians has to be very close. What is your take on this?

This writer's perspectives carry much weight. It is Dr. Lindsey's view of things that impressed the e-mailer to write. Since I am asked for my "take" on Hal's position regarding severe persecution for believers being imminent, I must be true to my study of prophecy and risk going somewhat counter to his stated belief that Christians in America are necessarily going to suffer such intensive, satanically engendered travail.

I mean no disrespect for this man, certainly a special servant chosen for the Lord's prophetic ministry for these closing hours of the age. However, my assessment differs from his forecast to an extent that I sense it needs to be presented here.

Last-Days Diary

DECEMBER 2010

We have spent time thus far looking into the eerie, troubling changes taking place across the socioeconomic landscape of America and the world. Mostly, we've tried to get our brains around the apparent insanity of our leaders and why they have created crises then printed trillions of dollars to throw at those crises—all of this sleight-of-hand chicanery done to stave off supposed national and world cataclysm those leaders warned would otherwise destroy civilization as it has been known. Their supposed attempts to preempt economic Armageddon now threaten to bring about the collapse of every economy on the planet.

The foundation had to be laid thusly in order to begin answering the question so many people want to know. Our e-mailer framed well the fears of many who worry what the near future might hold. Since world conditions are in configuration that includes issues and events much like those for the Tribulation given in Bible prophecy, will Christians in America face severe persecution before Christ returns to this desperately wicked planet? That is among the most expressed concerns in e-mail correspondence I receive these days.

Hal Lindsey, like Glenn Beck, states that he believes there will be a cultural and societal breakdown due to an economic collapse that is surely about to take place in the United States. I infer from his strongly stated position that he believes Christians in America will face severe persecution as a part of the social and economic upheaval about to erupt in this nation.

In the final analysis, however, whether I accurately understand and expound upon Dr. Lindsey's thoughts in these matters is of minor consequence to the treatment at hand. The fact is that many Christians who do observe these times from a prophetic perspective need answers to questions like the one posed by the e-mailer. Trying to look at what lurks just ahead in the foreboding mist and haze of the coming days is the proposed objective of what follows.

Next time we will attempt to accomplish this, staying within the confines of what God's Word actually has to say about the very end of the age.

December 27, 2010
Scanning a Fearful Future: Part 6

There are so many ominous signals of stage-setting for fulfillment of Bible prophecy in every direction we look that even secular fascination with things to come is piqued. One such example is the History Channel's *Nostradamus Effect* series in which I was asked to participate. One of the most immediately troubling signals that threatens apocalyptic disruption of world stability is the very probable collapse of the global economy, which we've been examining. There is little doubt, using even a modicum of rationale, that monetary madness infects the entire planet. We will now peer through God's prophetic lenses into the portentous future nearest us.

The title I've chosen for this exploration, "Scanning a Fearful Future," envelops all of Glenn Beck and Hal Lindsey's thoughts about the dire immediate future for America and the world. If their extremely similar assessments of what this generation faces is truly about to take place, my answer to the recent question to the worried e-mail sender—representative of many such e-mailers—must be given quickly. The note writer, after prefacing his question by saying that Lindsey stated persecution is coming for Christians, said: "Persecution for Christians has to be very close," then asked, "What is your take on this?"

First, I must rephrase his question to get to the heart of what he and so many others are asking. The question they mean to ask is: "Persecution for *the church in America* has to be very close. What is your take on this?"

Believers in Jesus Christ—the born again (see John 3:3)—are being persecuted around the globe at this very moment. Many are suffering torture and martyrdom. Members of the true church of Jesus Christ have always suffered and died, and will do so right up until Christ's call, "Come up here!" (Revelation 4:2). So, what American Christians are concerned with is whether Christians in the United States will suffer the level of persecution endured by believers like those in, for example, the Sudan. For that matter, the question implies asking whether American believers will suffer to a major extent in any way whatever. Hal Lindsey expressed in several of his TV programs that he believed Christians in America will suffer persecutions, and, I infer, he was speaking of persecutions of the fearful sort—those that might include loss of life in martyrdom. This fearful future, again I infer, will likely be part of a severe societal/cultural breakdown brought about by economic cataclysm. This, as pointed out previously, is much like Glenn Beck's forecast for Americans in general.

My answer to the e-mailer and others who continue to ask similar questions is this: I don't believe Christians in America are prophetically scheduled for severe persecution like that being experienced by those in Sudan, China, and other such places around the globe.

Now I can almost hear the clicking of e-mails being typed. Some are already conjuring the questioning flames of retort:

"Do you think American Christians are too good to suffer persecution?"

DECEMBER 2010

"Do you think America is God's pet nation—that the U.S. doesn't deserve judgment?!"

Please...save your fingers the pain from the white-hot irritation shooting from your keyboard. I agree completely with you. American Christians are NOT too good to be persecuted. The U.S. does deserve judgment. There is no argument there. Now, please allow me to give my scripturally based reasoning in disagreeing with Dr. Lindsey on these matters.

I begin by inserting this caveat about my assertion that American Christians won't suffer persecution of the most heinous sort. My belief is predicated upon my prayerfully studied understanding that the world as we know it would have to first come tumbling down, then rearrange to be configured exactly as it is now in order to accommodate American Christians going into such persecution as feared by my e-mailer.

That world crash, then turnaround, just isn't going to happen. Everything is in place for Bible prophecy to unfold.

I believe that America will not suffer catastrophic collapse while Christians (true believers in Jesus Christ) remain on planet earth. You and I—whether believer or nonbeliever—are members of the most privileged generation in history. We are alive at the very end of this fascinating moment in human advancement. For believers, however, the privilege is magnified beyond imagination.

Believers in Jesus Christ are alive during this end of the Church Age for a divinely appointed purpose. We are witnesses to and participants in the very time the Lord Jesus Christ Himself prophesied would see Him revealed in spectacular fashion. The prospect is truly glorious.

While "Scanning a Fearful Future" is an accurate title for purposes of this examination of things to come, an equally appropriate title for those who are born again would have been "Scanning a Fabulous Future." We will look next week at specifically what I believe the near future holds for believers and nonbelievers alike.

JANUARY 2011

Scanning a Fearful Future (Conclusion)

January 3, 2011
Scanning a Fearful Future: Part 7

America and the nations of the world, as we have explored, are—according to Glenn Beck and Hal Lindsey—moving quickly down the road that leads to global socioeconomic cataclysm. I agree. Such a destiny lurks in the murkiness of the not-too-distant future. However, exactly how that destination will be reached and who among the planet's current population will suffer the disastrous fate predicted by Beck and Lindsey are matters for much closer scrutiny. Two questions we will try to address are in view as we look at the near future through the prism of Bible prophecy:

1) Will America and the world suffer Beck and Lindsey's feared versions of economic collapse, thus societal catastrophe?

2) Will Christians in America suffer severe persecution as part of any such catastrophic breakdown?

Now, here's where things can get quite confusing, if careful attention isn't paid to the thoughts I'm trying to convey. I am convinced that America and the world will suffer the predicted economic, thus societal, catastrophe. Persecution and martyrdom will coalesce to make life for believers even in the U.S. region hell on earth as a result of that immense calamity.

I am at the same time equally convinced that there will neither be national and worldwide economic and societal collapse nor severe persecution and martyrdom for American Christians. Lunacy? Not if one views things to come through Bible prophecy as it is truly given for us to understand.

God's ways are not our ways and His thoughts are not our thoughts (see Isaiah 55:8). Believe it or not, like it or not, God's Word demonstrates that He deals with mankind in dispensations—distinctive eras that He alone determines. This generation is part of the dispensation of grace—the Age of Grace, or the Church Age. This dispensation will morph into the Tribulation, a period of seven years of God's judgment and wrath also known as Daniel's seventieth week.

My seemingly irrational claims, viewed in light of dispensational truth, are on sound biblical footing. Please consider slowly and carefully. Putting forth that I believe America and the world both will experience and will not experience apocalyptic socioeconomic collapse makes sense from a dispensational perspective. Holding that American believers in Jesus Christ will not go through such persecution that includes martyrdom, all the while proclaiming that believers living in this nation will suffer persecution and martyrdom, is a biblically correct dispensational pronouncement.

These paradoxical proclamations are made understandable by the words of the greatest of all prophets—the Lord Jesus Christ. His astonishing prophecy about the end of this dispensation in which you and I are living addresses the two questions for which we seek answers.

Bible prophecy's answers to these are as follows, I'm firmly convinced:

1) Neither America nor the world will suffer societal and monetary catastrophe that will bring about apocalyptic collapse due to man-made accidental bungling or contrived manipulation. However, there will be a crash of the world's socioeconomic system, which will cause chaos of unfathomable scope, brought about by the God of Heaven in an instant of time.
2) Christians in America today will not face persecution of the sort suffered by martyrs in past ages and by believers in parts of the world at present. But, following God's next catastrophic intervention into earth's history, believers in North America—as well as all other believers in Jesus Christ—will suffer persecution even worse than that inflicted upon believers of previous times.

Most Relevant Prophecy

When thinking on prophecies that are stage-setting for the wind-up of history, we most often point to prophecies involving Israel being back in the land of promise as most key to where we stand on God's end-of-the-age timeline. The peace process and Jerusalem being at the center of the world's spotlight show precisely the lateness of the hour.

That said, no prophecy is more relevant for this moment than that given by Jesus Christ Himself, which encompasses not just the future of Israel and Jerusalem, but of the entire world:

> And as it was in the days of Noah, so shall it be also in the days of the Son of man.
>
> They did eat, they drank, they married wives, they were given in marriage, until the day that Noah entered into the ark, and the flood came, and destroyed them all.
>
> Also as it was in the days of Lot; they did eat, they drank, they bought, they sold, they planted, and they built;
>
> But the same day that Lot went out of Sodom, it rained fire and brimstone from heaven, and destroyed them all.
>
> Even thus shall it be in the day when the Son of man is revealed. (Luke 17:26–30)

This prophetic declaration by the Creator of all things is about the generation that will be alive at the dénouement of the age. Specifically, it refers to one catastrophic moment in the present dispensation when all of this world system will come crashing down. We will next look in-depth at the details wrapped up in Jesus' foretelling of planet earth's near future.

January 10, 2011
Scanning a Fearful Future: Part 8

Planet earth is on the brink of what both Glenn Beck and Hal Lindsey have stated they believe will be monetary and societal collapse of unprecedented magnitude. We also looked previously at a prophetic declaration by the Creator of all things, which is—I believe I can verify—about the generation that will be alive at the very end of the age.

Specifically, Jesus' prophecy in Luke 17:26–30 refers to one catastrophic moment in this present dispensation when all of this world system will come crashing down.

Are the two cataclysms—the one Beck and Lindsey talk about on their TV programs and the one Jesus foretells—related to each other? If so, how?

We will now try to answer the questions about world collapse, whether persecution for American Christians is imminent, and how it might all be tied together prophetically. We will do so by looking in depth at the details wrapped up in Jesus' forecast for earth's near future.

Jesus gave what I am convinced is the premiere end-of-the-Church-Age prophecy in Luke 17:26–30. He described in considerable detail world conditions and activities at the moment He will break in on things of this present age.

He tells in His prophecy just the opposite of what Glenn Beck says is on the brink of happening to the people of America and the world. That is, the Lord's description of how the worldwide catastrophe will happen differs greatly from the Fox host's prediction of the cause of the calamity he says is just around the corner.

Remember, Beck is predicting for the near future the direst of socioeconomic collapses. He recommends that we prepare for, quite likely, hyper-inflated times to come, at the very least. He indicates that he fears the collapse will touch off draconian governmental measures to quell the rioting that will occur when those millions who are given government handouts no longer receive the assistance. There is more than enough evidence of unchecked government today to prove Beck's fears are well founded. The phenomenal growth of federal intrusion into practically every facet of the citizen's life today portends grave consequences for liberty in the months and years just ahead. For example, bureaucratic regulation such as the move of the unelected Federal Communications Commission apparatchiks to invoke "net neutrality"—a Big Brother-like regulatory process that could establish dictatorial power over Internet use—threatens anyone who would express opinions counter to state-approved language. The current administration intends to implement this despite the fact that a federal appeals court has ruled the administration doesn't have the authority to do so.

Hal Lindsey sees the same cataclysm approaching, basically for the same reasons. He also recommends that we prepare for possible food shortages, and he says he believes Christians in this country will face severe persecution, which I infer to mean persecution of the sort suffered by martyrs for the cause of Christ. I agree with both of these gentlemen to some degree. And I disagree, also, with both—for differing reasons. But I reserve my thoughts in that regard for the biblically based logic I hope will make itself manifest as I analyze the words of the greatest of all prophets.

We now are familiar with what Glenn Beck and Hal Lindsey say about the two questions involving the probability of American and world socioeconomic collapse and, in Lindsey's case, about Christians in America facing imminent, severe persecution. Let's dissect carefully what Jesus predicts for the times just ahead. He prophesied in the Luke 17:26–30 passage that in the "days" He, the "Son of man," is about to break into earth's history, mankind will be doing certain things. It will be a time like the days of

Noah before the Flood and the days of Lot while he was still in Sodom.

People, the Lord said, will be eating, drinking, marrying, building, buying, selling, and planting. Things will be going along pretty much as normal for the time. The Lord indicates no catastrophic, worldwide, socioeconomic breakdown of any sort in this time immediately before "the Son of man is revealed" (Luke17:30)—the time He breaks into human history.

This time cannot be the Second Advent of Revelation 19:11. At the time, the Lord of lords and King of kings breaks through the planetary darkness of death and destruction at Armageddon, perhaps as many as three-fourths of all people on earth will have died as a result of wars, pestilence, and geophysical disasters brought about by God's judgment and wrath upon an incorrigibly wicked, unrepentant world.

In other words, living conditions at the time of Christ's return in power and glory at Armageddon will not be anything like those at the time He intervenes into human affairs as He describes in the days of Noah, days of Lot prophecy. At the end of the seven-year Tribulation period, it will be anything but business as usual. It will truly be hell on earth when Jesus comes to destroy all human government and the soul-rending carnage it has produced.

So, Jesus, in the Luke 17 account, was foretelling the days leading up to the time when He calls His church to Himself, known as the Rapture. To learn more about this stupendous event, read John 14:1–3, 1 Corinthians 15:51–55, 1 Thessalonians 4:13–18, and Revelation 4:1–2.

To repeat: Jesus was not describing His return to earth in the Luke 17:26–30 prophecy. He was telling about His coming to *above the planet* to receive His people—Christians—to Himself. Christians—the church—then will accompany Him back to the heavenly places He has prepared in the Father's house—Heaven.

Again, we have reached the limits of our space for this commentary. We will next further examine Jesus' telling us about this very hour in which you and I inhabit planet earth.

January 17, 2011
Scanning a Fearful Future: Part 9

Jesus Christ—God in the flesh—foretold that the time just before God's judgment and wrath befall rebellious mankind at the very end of the Church Age will be like it was in the days of Noah and of Lot. Although those times were wicked and all thoughts were focused continually on evil, people of the earth were carrying on with normal activities like eating, drinking, planting, building, marrying, buying, and selling.

In the days of Noah, people were carrying on business as usual right up until the moment that Noah entered the ark and all who were left on earth were swept away by the Flood. In the days of Lot, there was an air of civility, with Lot even serving as a judge at the city gates during the day. At night, however, the depravity ran rampant when homosexual lust turned to voracious, predatory assault. Lot and his family members were removed, and all people who were left behind in the city were consumed by the holocaust from Heaven.

Jesus said He will be revealed when conditions are like they were during those times. We have seen that the time when He intervenes into the affairs of mankind as described in Luke 17:26–30 will not be His Second Coming at Armageddon (Revelation

19:11). It will be another, earlier intervention—but catastrophic, nonetheless.

We have pointed out many times in these commentaries the strangeness of the dynamics of our times. Crises are building in many critical aspects of human interaction. We have wondered in amazement at the insanity of the dastardly mismanagement of economic matters by governments around the world. How, we puzzle over, have the economies of America and the world avoided crashing?

Why, despite threats of the destruction of Israel by the likes of Iranian President Mahmoud Ahmadinejad, has a preemptive attack on Iran's nuclear production facilities not occurred? Why, with the tremendous buildup of arms by the many Islamic Israel-haters in obvious preparation for an attack on the Jewish state, has there not been a major blow-up in the Middle East that would disrupt world stability?

Yet the anxieties about the world sitting on a number of powder kegs afflict only a few people, relatively speaking. Except for those who are unemployed in America, for example, it's business as usual. The majority of people just don't worry about the precarious position of the nation and the world. The masses are buying, selling, and marrying—even men with men and women with women, I might add. And building continues, despite the housing debacle and trillions of dollars of debt wrought by monetary madness such as that found in Fannie Mae and Freddie Mac.

Most troubling, the church in America is, for the most part, oblivious to world conditions that present strong evidence that we are on the brink of the prophesied apocalypse. This makes this generation of Christians precisely the one I believe Jesus was speaking to when He instructed us to, "be…ready; for in such an hour as ye think not the Son of man cometh" (Matthew 24:44).

But, as we have been examining, there are those who are scanning the fearful future. Glenn Beck, the *Fox News* program host, says he sees coming a man-contrived world economic collapse, hyperinflation, and societal collapse that only patriotic, sound-thinking, even spiritually inclined Americans can begin to fix. He doesn't know when it will happen, but he says it will happen almost overnight. We will awaken the next morning to a world totally different than what it was before we went to sleep.

Hal Lindsey, the author of *The Late, Great Planet Earth*, says much the same thing. He foresees, as a part of that feared socio-economic collapse, severe persecution for Christians in America at some point. Jesus' words, which I believe speak directly to this generation, present a different picture than Beck's forecast (and to some extent, than Lindsey's) regarding things about to break upon a mostly unsuspecting world. My own thoughts that follow are based upon what I believe is wrapped up in the Lord's fore-warning to our generation in Luke 17: 26–30.

Two statements are necessary at this point. First, it is God's staying hand that prevents the impending calamities outlined in this essay from collapsing America and the world into the worst times in history. Second, if things continue on their present course geopolitically and socioeconomically, and if God takes His hand of control off developments, the collapse feared by Beck, Lindsey, and many others will certainly come at some point. The longer the rebellion-engendered crises build, the more devastating will be the crash when it comes.

I begin my analysis of what lies just ahead in that fearful

future by applying Jesus' analogy in the "days of Noah, days of Lot" prophecy to the present generation. Jesus foretold that human activity will be going along in a business-as-usual manner. God, in one day, will take His family—believers—out of harm's way. That very day, His judgment and wrath will begin falling on those not taken. To reiterate because the point can't be overemphasized: If one accepts Christ's words as true, and as literal, as I do, one must agree that things must be going along as normal for the time when the sudden intervention happens. Jesus plainly says that the generation alive at the time of that divine intervention will be removed to safety before the devastating events of judgment take place.

Both Beck and Lindsey say they believe a world-rending socioeconomic collapse is imminent. Beck, at least, believes the crash and totally changed America and world will be brought about by the diabolical efforts of New-World-Order types like George Soros. Both Beck and Lindsey are recommending that we make preparations to survive that coming time of devastating collapse.

Yet Jesus tells us that it will be business as usual right up until the moment He removes believers from the planet. There is no man-made, worldwide catastrophe in Christ's prophecy. As a matter of fact, Jesus says all will be relatively normal, in terms of human activity, until that removal. Then He will be revealed by way of His cataclysmic judgment that begins to devastate planet earth. It is God who causes the cataclysm, not George Soros or any other human or other entity. Mankind's involvement in the whole matter is that of displaying total rebellion and refusing to repent of sin, thus bringing on God's righteous judgment. One era—the Church Age—comes to an end with the removal of believers. The next era then begins at some point with the confirming of the covenant with Israel, as given in Daniel 9:26–27. That period will be the seven years of Tribulation, the last three and one-half years about which Jesus said:

> For then shall be great tribulation, such as was not since the beginning of the world to this time, no, nor ever shall be. (Matthew 24:21)

Next we will look into the fearful future, specifically as it relates directly to America's near-term financial destiny and to whether believers will face deadly persecution.

January 24, 2011
Scanning a Fearful Future: Conclusion

My disagreement with Glenn Beck and Hal Lindsey regarding their belief that America is about to suffer economic, thus societal, collapse is only one of degree. There is absolutely no doubt that collapse is coming. It is how that implosion will eventuate and who will be caught in the carnage that are at the heart of my disagreement.

My divergence from Dr. Lindsey's fears about the immediate future for America and Christians is of the very mildest sort. I look to God using him in a mighty way during the past decades as validation of his mission being God-ordained. Thus confutation is entered with all due respect. That stated, I must give the reasons I believe Beck and Lindsey's fears for the immediate future are somewhat off the mark, as far as Bible prophecy is concerned.

Every signal across the geopolitical, socioeconomic, and religious spectrum—even signals involving the geophysical and astrophysical—scream through the sirens of forewarning. We are at the very end of the Church Age and are on the brink of the Tribulation. Yet most in America—including most believers in Jesus Christ—are going about business as usual. Except for the relatively few voices forewarning of the impending cataclysm, there is no recognition of or interest in the end-times storm warnings.

Jesus, as we have seen, said human activity will be like it is at present when He next breaks into earth's history like a thief in the night. This time, we look at the Lord's words in Matthew that parallel His words in Luke 17:26–30:

> But of that day and hour knoweth no man, no, not the angels of heaven, but my Father only.
>
> But as the days of Noah were, so shall also the coming of the Son of man be.
>
> For as in the days that were before the flood they were eating and drinking, marrying and giving in marriage, until the day that Noah entered the ark,
>
> And knew not until the flood came, and took them all away, so shall also the coming of the Son of man be.
>
> Then shall two be in the field; the one shall be taken, and the other left.
>
> Two women shall be grinding at the mill; the one shall be taken, and the other left.
>
> Watch, therefore; for ye know not what hour your Lord doth come. (Matthew 24:36–42)

As we have examined, this break-in upon mankind's history cannot be describing the Second Advent. It will not be business as usual at that time, when the planet is decimated by wars and God's judgment and wrath. Jesus is here speaking of the Rapture—His imminent, catastrophic break-in upon earth's history.

So, we come to our present hour. America is the apex nation of the world. That is, it is the most materially blessed nation and one of the most spiritually blessed nations ever to exist. This, despite the fact that it has degenerated in many ways to become perhaps the most wicked in human history. The United States is so blessed with material wealth that every nation on earth is inextricably linked to its economy in one way or another.

It is true that its dominance is under threat and is eroding quickly. The economic meltdown and unavoidable implosion of America's monetary hegemony is imminent. But everything of global financial significance still hinges on the health and fate of the American dollar. This is to the great consternation of the people Glenn Beck rails against as wanting to bring the dollar down so that a new monetary regime can be brought to bear on the hapless citizens of what they envision as a Babel-like, one-world order.

Despite incessant assaults, the American economy hasn't collapsed. It should have by now, but it hasn't. It is, despite ominous signs ahead, business as usual—just as Jesus said it would be at the end of the age. If America's economy crashes—as Beck says it will very shortly—the entire world will collapse to rubble. The business-as-usual element of Christ's prophecy would be out the proverbial window.

If the U.S. economy collapsed, taking the world's buying and selling capability into the darkest times in history, it would take years—if ever—for everything to recover so that things would again come into business-as-usual configuration. Yet the devastating, world-rending collapse is coming. It cannot be stopped. I completely agree with Glenn Beck and Hal Lindsey in seeing that coming economic catastrophe in the immediate future. However, I disagree that the folly of man or the deliberate manipulations of human diabolists will bring the fearful disaster. And the disaster will not happen until God's prophetic timing allows. It will continue to be business as usual despite increasing harbingers of economic calamity. Perhaps conditions will even look like they are improving. But if so, it will be smoke and mirrors—a sham "recovery." The damage is done. Recovery is impossible.

This all means that Jesus Christ is poised to do exactly what He foretold. The prophetic signals and conditions prevalent in America and the world should have the attention of every believer. Jesus is about to fulfill His glorious promise as recorded in John 14:1–3.

The Rapture, I believe Jesus is telling us, will be the sword of judgment that pierces the building, festering boil of humanistic rebellion. When the church is taken to Heaven, the minds of those left behind who want to control will no longer have restraint on their thoughts and ambitions. There will cease to be a governor on man's conscience, according to 2 Thessalonians 2:7–8, because the Holy Spirit will allow the evil within mankind to do its dastardly work.

This will be the time—during the chaos of the days immediately after the Rapture—that all of Mr. Beck's fears will come to fruition. Neither patriots nor anyone else will be able to save America and the world.

Now to try to answer my e-mailer concerning whether Christians in America will suffer severe, even deadly, persecution, as I infer Hal Lindsey believes. Christians of America in this pre-Rapture time certainly are not immune from persecution—even from the persecution like that suffered by the Christian martyrs of history. However, it would take a horrendous catastrophe—such as the one Beck predicts—for American society to totally turn its back on Christianity, thus to begin physically attacking Christians in the way Lindsey fears might happen.

The church, with the Restrainer resident within each believer, will continue to be salt and light—to exert influence over America's societal and cultural conditions. That influence, although becoming less and less effective, will be sufficient to prevent all-out, Nazi-like persecution against Christians in this nation.

When the Church-Age saints go to Christ upon His call to them (1 Thessalonians 4:16–17; Revelation 4:1–2), America and the world will be devoid of the church's buffering influence. Those who accept Christ during the Tribulation will undergo the most horrific persecution of human history.

Again, if a calamity like the one Beck forecasts were to befall this nation before Christ's foretold intervention into earth's history, such a collapse would take the U.S. and the world out of the time of business as usual Jesus said will be in place when He pays the earth that surprise visit.

Jesus was telling us in Luke 17:26–30 and Matthew 24:36–42 specifically about His coming for the church and the general time frame of that event. With all that is in alignment precisely as Jesus and the prophets described, I am convicted in my spirit that now is that time.

Those who haven't become part of God's family—believing in Jesus Christ for their personal salvation—face a fearful future indeed. They will be left behind in an instantly changed world gone mad with chaos infinitely worse than even Glenn Beck predicts.

There is still opportunity in this Church Age for the person who hasn't accepted the Lord Jesus as personal Savior to do so. But time is fleeting. The Rapture could take place at any moment.

Here is what God's Holy Word has to say to you, if you want to escape from this world that is soon to suffer God's righteous judgment. Truly follow these instructions from the heart of the God who loves you and wants you to be safe with Him forever. You will then be assured not of a fearful future, but of a future that is fabulous beyond description.

> That if thou shalt confess with thy mouth the Lord Jesus, and shalt believe in thine heart that God hath raised him from the dead, thou shalt be saved.
>
> For with the heart man believeth unto righteousness; and with the mouth confession is made unto salvation. (Romans 10:9–10)

January 31, 2011
End-Times Indigestion

A diagnosis of current, troubling realities in the Middle East leads to a disturbing prognosis. Indigestion is possibly the culprit that threatens to bring on the terminal condition that prophecy calls Armageddon. Okay, so maybe it's a bit of a stretch to liken what's going on in the most volatile part of the world to a human gastrointestinal condition. But it certainly seems that it is gas that is shaping up to be at least one incendiary ingredient that might ignite history's final holocaust.

JANUARY 2011

While the Mideast broils with vitriol against Israel, the one nation on earth specifically pointed out by Zechariah the prophet as being at the center of end-times hatred, a situation taking place in the belly of that geographical beast bears watching. Natural gas is emerging as a burning issue in that highly volatile region. Key prophetic players are at the center of the ongoing developments.

The European Union is at the heart of matters involving the recent discovery of natural gas in Iraq's Kurdish region. The EU has been striving to lessen dependence on Russia for supplying natural gas. Discoveries in Iraq open the possibility that the Europeans might be successful in accomplishing that independence. However, quickly rearranging relationships among nations surrounding the region of new gas discovery provoke some interesting thought, prophetically speaking.

The Nabucco consortium, a European group of oil and gas companies, hopes to construct a pipeline to southern Europe through Turkey. Nabucco is much more than just a commercial enterprise. It is an attempt to shift the balance of power in European energy politics, according to expert observers.

> If the 3,300-kilometer Nabucco is built, it will be the first major natural gas pipeline into central and eastern Europe that isn't controlled by Moscow. This is important because the EU fears Russian control of such a large chunk of its gas supply. Several EU member states have also suffered severe winter gas supply disruptions in recent years as Russia fought with its neighbor Ukraine over transit rights. So Nabucco has strong political backing from the European Commission, and is treated with disdain by the Kremlin.[71]

Europe's plans are far from being a done deal. The pipeline must go through both Iran (to an extent) and Turkey, as stated before. The Russians are almost certainly going to have a major objection to losing their monopoly on gas-supply operations in the region. And that country's influence is considerable. Russia has over the past several years made ever-tightening alliances with the two major nations with which the EU must deal in order to bring natural gas from the Kurdish gas fields. At the same time, those nations, Turkey and Iran, are continuing to solidify relations with each other. The three—Russia, Iran, and Turkey—have formed a triad of sorts. It is a fascinating arrangement in these strange days of quickly moving geopolitical realignments.

Russia and Turkey have just signed in Istanbul a strategic cooperation protocol for enhancing their bilateral relations. This was arranged by the Turkish-Russian Joint Strategic Planning Group, which is charged with carrying out preparatory work for the high-level Cooperation Council meeting in Moscow this March. Although the group didn't divulge any details of the strategic protocol, it is logical to presume that considerations regarding the proposed EU pipeline figure in the planning.

One source reports:

> Russian-Turkish ties have predominantly expanded on an economic basis, especially with energy deals. Projects in the energy sector such as Samsun-Ceyhan, South Stream and Nabucco will also be on the agenda of the preparatory talks. Turkey receives 70 percent of its energy resources, including gas and oil, from Russia. Turkey will also put into operation its first nuclear power plant with the cooperation of Russia.[72]

Russia no doubt intends to continue to exert hegemony over Middle East energy sources and supplies at all cost. Turkey, under its recently installed, antagonistic-to-Israel, Islamist regime, is firmly ensconced within the Russian-Iranian (Persian) camp. The EU will likely have to look elsewhere for its energy independence from the Russian Bear.

There is such a source to the south of Russia, Iran, and Turkey. Can you guess who that is?

> In 2009, a partnership that included Texas Based Noble Energy Inc. and Israeli oil companies discovered Tamar, an offshore gas field containing eight trillion cubic feet of natural gas. It was the largest gas find in the world in 2009 and the largest ever for Israel at the time.
>
> Last December, the company announced the discovery of the Leviathan field, which contains a whopping 16 trillion cubic feet of natural gas—enough to supply all of Israel's gas needs for 100 years—and promises to turn the once resource-starved country into a net energy exporter.[73]

There is talk of the EU contracting with Israel to provide the much-needed natural gas supply. It will be fascinating to watch developments, in consideration of the Gog-Magog prophecy of Ezekiel 38–39.

FEBRUARY 2011

Olivet Discourse Dissected

February 7, 2011
Olivet Observations

Distress, perplexity, seas, waves roaring—these are thoughts that came to mind in observing the past week's events that demanded attention above all others. Jesus' words in His Olivet Discourse about things that would be in view as His Second Advent nears seemed to leap from the hourly headlines.

With national and global economic distresses seething upon the surface of world interaction, the Middle East suddenly lit up in a series of perplexing developments for the autocratic governments of the region. Tunisia, Algeria, Egypt, Jordan, and Yemen erupted to one degree or another in demonstrations of protest. But petroleum flow, the lifeblood of world economic health, is directly affected by these uprisings, making it not just the problem of Egyptian President Hosni Mubarak's regime or the dilemma of the other regimes in the region. The whole planet is sucked into the Middle East vortex of turbulence. All of this is taking place at the same time that what is called the most violent storm in Australia's history, a cyclone said to be a category 5, approached that nation/continent.[74]

February 2011

The seas and waves of both the symbolic and the actual sorts are roaring in a way that can't be missed:

> And there shall be signs in the sun, and in the moon, and in the stars; and upon the earth distress of nations, with perplexity; the sea and the waves roaring. (Luke 21:25)

No other nation on earth is more at the center of all of this than Israel. Geographically—but more importantly, geopolitically—the Jewish state sits smack in the middle of that oil-saturated region. Even more crucially, Israel is spiritually at the very heart of the Middle East cauldron, just as Bible prophecy says it will be at the end of the age.

Many news pundits at this very moment are trying to understand the causes for the upheaval in the world today: Why the seemingly unsolvable monetary problems that threaten to bring every nation on earth to economic ruin? Why the irresolvable issues that portend war in the Middle East, which could result in nuclear Armageddon?

The talking heads, columnists, and bloggers take all of the distressing, perplexing matters under consideration from every conceivable perspective. They obsess on each intricate detail that seems to exacerbate inability to find resolution. They talk over each other to make their points in a frenzy of trying to find causes and solutions.

Except for very rarely referring to the biblically predicted war of Armageddon, the true source that can provide the answers they seek is never mentioned—and certainly never consulted. Radio talk show host Rush Limbaugh said on his radio program on Wednesday, February 2, that he has never believed anything of an apocalyptic nature when it comes to considering predictions involving world issues and events. He was talking about Paul Ehrlich's book, *The Population Bomb,* about the world being overpopulated by the year 2000, and how Ehrlich's "prophecy" had failed to materialize. Rush then said, "You don't even want to know what I think about the book of Revelation."

Well, I can tell you that I infer upon good authority that he has disdain for the book of Revelation, because I heard him in the mid-1990s when he told of how his father said that the book of Revelation should never have been placed into the canon of Scripture. Rush didn't want to elaborate then, either, because he said it just as his show was doing the familiar out-beep to an "obscene profit break," as he likes to jibe. He added just as the program went to commercial: "Now, what do you think about that?"

Because he will never let "religion" be discussed to any extent on his program, there has been no retort on air to his summarily dismissing God's prophetic Word that has the answers he and others are desperate to find. Well, El Rushbo, here's what that book you apparently disdain has to say, in part:

> For I testify unto every man that heareth the words of the prophecy of this book, If any man shall add unto these things, God shall add unto him the plagues that are written in this book;
>
> And if any man shall take away from the words of the book of this prophecy, God shall take away his part out of the book of life, and out of the holy city, and from the things which are written in this book. (Revelation 22:18–19)

If you will allow, Rush, I or others who believe God's Word has the answers about the distressing, perplexing problems pressing upon the world will welcome the opportunity to help you and your millions of listeners—on air or in private—understand what is going on and where it is all leading. Jesus Christ laid it out nearly two thousand years ago atop a promontory in the one city on earth where He will one day put an end to all conflict.

February 14, 2011
Temple Mount Tempest Mounts

It is the most incendiary spot on earth—the bull's eye in the cross hairs of Mideast rage. Focus on this singular point of earthly geography, however, doesn't come only from Jews, Christians, and Islamists. There is laser-like anger that burns far more intensely than that generated by ancient human involvements and animosities.

The Temple Mount—Mt. Moriah—in Jerusalem continues to draw the attention of seen and unseen, overtly obvious and clandestine, forces to the one place on this fallen sphere God chose as His touchstone for mankind. UFOs were recently reported by a number of sources to be hovering over as well as descending and ascending above the Dome of the Rock. Footage of video taken from various angles was reported to show strange, glowing orbs gyrating just above the Muslim shrine where the religion of Islam claims the prophet Mohammed one night rode on his horse from the now-covered stone into their version of Heaven. Things going on around the golden dome and its rock, however, are more often than not at the center of much more down-to-earth controversy.

This excerpt of a news item frames the most recent activity fueling the tempest atop Moriah:

> Muslim religious authorities are concluding a clandestine eight-month dig on the Temple Mount that is intended to erase traces of the Jewish Temple's Altar, Temple activists charge. The digs have been taking place under the Dome of the Chain, believed to have been built over thirteen years ago. For eight months, the dome—which has a diameter of fourteen meters—has been surrounded by a metal fence and black cloth, which hide whatever activity has been going on there from outside inspection. The Muslim Waqf religious authority has claimed the activity is simply a refurbishing of the structure, but refuses adamantly to let Jews or tourists near. Jewish activists made various attempts to enter the Dome, but met with no success....
>
> *Our Temple Mount* [a news outlet] notes that according to Jewish tradition, the place where the Dome of the Chain is located is the spot upon which the sacrificial Altar stood in Temple times. Temple activists said that the Muslim digs are intended to erase the Jewish connection to the Temple Mount.[75]

The digs are a decades-long part of efforts by the Islamists to remove artifacts that might prove Israel's link to the Temple Mount. There are worries by some Israeli engineers that so much digging and tunneling has been done beneath some sections of Moriah that part of the mount could collapse. Should that take place, and the Dome of the Rock or other shrines considered sacred by Muslims be damaged, fears are that such an occurrence could provide a reason for blaming the Jews. Thus a rallying point for instigating yet another war by a joint Arab coalition could be established.

Strange circumstances have always surrounded this promontory where the Jewish temples sat housing the Holy of Holies and the Ark of the Covenant. It is the very center—geographically speaking—of God's salvation process for mankind. The Holy of Holies was the fifteen-foot cubed room where the heavy veil that separated God's presence from fallen human beings was ripped from top to bottom by the hand of the Almighty at the moment when Christ cried "It is finished!" and gave up His Spirit to death as the supreme sacrifice for the sins of all mankind. Because of reason behind that tearing of the veil, all people now have direct access to God through His Son, Jesus.

The second Temple, known as Herod's Temple by some, was destroyed in AD 70 when the Romans destroyed Jerusalem and razed the building to extract every jewel and precious metal they could find from the ruins. The Muslims claimed the Mount centuries later and erected their shrines, claiming it for Allah based upon Mohammed's supposed adventures—the night flight to Heaven from the large, flat stone that the Dome of the Rock now covers.

Israeli General Moshe Dayan, for reasons that are still a mystery, gave Jerusalem's religious leaders of Islam the right to act as overseers of the Temple Mount, following the Israeli victory over Arab military forces in the 1967 Six-Day War. The tensions over access to the Mount have increased ever since, with the Muslim factions digging—it has been established—to try to remove all evidence that the temples ever stood there.

Behind the building tempest is God's most vicious enemy. He seethes with contempt for the Creator of all things. He hates everything associated with Jesus Christ, who died just outside the Temple area so that human beings—whom he hates, also—can be redeemed and reconciled to God, the Heavenly Father. Bible prophecy foretells that during the time of Jacob's trouble (Jeremiah 30:7), Satan will bring his man, Antichrist, to sit in a rebuilt Temple atop the Temple Mount (2 Thessalonians 2:4). That "man of sin" will declare himself to be God and demand worship on penalty of death to those refusing to comply. All will have to obey by accepting the beast's (Antichrist's) number and mark, or be beheaded—or no doubt die in other ways even more horrendous.

The Temple Mount is the one place on earth most coveted by Lucifer the fallen one, known now as the devil. Satan—as he is also known—couldn't usurp the throne of God in Heaven, and is determined to usurp God's earthly throne, where God has promised that His Son, Jesus Christ, will one day rule and reign over the millennial earth.

The Temple Mount tempest continues to mount. Israel, Jerusalem, the Temple Mount, and the ongoing attempt by the diplomats of earth to try to force a false peace covenant upon God's chosen people, the Jews, should be at the center of attention of every Bible-believing observer of these troubling although exciting times.

February 21, 2011
Blueprint for End-Times Monetary System

International Monetary Fund (IMF) officials recently let it be known the direction of their thinking for solving the growing economic crises facing the nations of earth. Their cogitations, it is no surprise to those of us who view ongoing developments from the perspective of Bible prophecy, include two basic elements: 1) They want a single monetary unit; and 2) they want to make it electronic currency. Special drawing rights—SDR—represents a synthetic electronic basket of currencies. This system has been around for many years, but now, enhanced by tremendous advances in technology, is viewed by the powers that be as representing a genuine device to take down the American dollar and establish a monetary device that can power the much-desired New World Order.

The proposed currency unit of the IMF's blueprint—the electronic monetary unit we in this column have consistently written about as likely part of an end-times economic regime—is termed "special drawing rights." Lack of confidence in the U.S. dollar as the world's reserve currency is purportedly at the center of the IMF's increased insistence that the world be moved to a new single world currency unit. The organization, in issuing a report entitled "Enhancing International Monetary Stability—A Role for the SDR?" sees the SDR as an embryo out of which a truly one-world economic system can grow.

The powers that be, according to the report, see SDR as a transitional monetary device—a seed for bringing into being something far more effective. The report states:

> In the even longer run, if there were political willingness to do so, these securities [currencies wrapped in the SDR] could constitute an embryo of global currency.[76]

The SDR, as stated previously, has been around for many years. But, it has, with the advances in technology, reached the point the globalists believe it can be used to oust the dollar and institute a fiscal entity capable of giving them more control, thus increased power over world economy. It is widely reported that the SDR is a hybrid—comprised in decreasing proportions of the dollar, the euro, the yen, and the pound.

Russia's once-and-future president, Vladimir Putin, for one, is unhappy with the arrangement of SDR structure as it currently exists. China, with its burgeoning economic power, certainly objects to that structure. The SDR will doubtless undergo dynamic changes in coming months, if indeed it will be at the center of a new global order as IMF titans envision.

I've written in this column numerous times that I believe the mark-and-numbering system of the Tribulation era—Antichrist's economic system of control—will involve electronic funds transfer. Again, the prophecy of that final humanistic system that will be controlled by Satan's man of sin foretells the following:

> And he causeth all, both small and great, rich and poor, free and bond, to receive a mark in their right hand, or in their foreheads,
>
> And that no man might buy or sell, save he that had the mark, or the name of the beast, or the number of his name.
>
> Here is wisdom. Let him that hath understanding count the number of the beast; for it is the number of a man; and his number is six hundred threescore and six. (Revelation 13:16–18)

The Internet, no doubt enhanced through advancing technological means, will provide the person-to-person linkage throughout the world that will make possible the enslavement indicated by the prophecy. Buying and selling, using the hybrid Internet and some form of SDR, will enable Antichrist to exert the control about which God's Word forewarns.

One can imagine how such an electronic linkage might be touted by a deceptive, cunning beast regime, promising a true democracy for the first time in human history. Each person would, the regime's propagandists might proclaim, be able to have individual votes cast and instantly tallied with all other votes. One man, one vote, as the Roman Empire promised—but never fully delivered—to its citizenry. Such a promise would, of course, be a sham even worse than the many promises by politicians and political parties today in America. Antichrist will manipulate and use the satanically inspired system to produce the results he will demand.

Like so many developments for fulfillment of Bible prophecy coming at this generation from every conceivable direction, the IMF's determination to implement a global monetary system of its own making is a signal of the lateness of the hour.

February 28, 2011
Pastors Forewarned

One of the most-mentioned laments among those of us who have Bible prophecy as our calling is that seminaries are not teaching prophecy and pastors are not preaching and teaching prophecy today. We refer to the majority of the seminary instructors and preachers who otherwise preach and teach God's Word as inerrant truth.

Those who view the Bible as merely a book with good suggestions for how to live, but don't consider it the literal Word of God, can't be expected to understand the crucial necessity of preaching and teaching the whole Word of God. These pick and choose verses, applicable or not, to put forth their ear-tickling homilies, which by their very nature avoid doctrinal truth. So, we aren't pointing a finger of admonishment at these.

Sadly, however, this description fits a growing number of seminaries and their graduates. It is getting harder to tell the genuine from the pretenders. More and more the words are sugar-coated, the points supposedly made trailing off into the ether of mumbo-jumbo irrelevance. When one gently probes one or the other of the Bible-believing/preaching pastors with the question: "Do you preach prophecy?" the answers are along the same line. It's my experience and that of others who ask the question that 95 percent of those asked say something akin to the following:

"Prophecy is just too hard for people to understand."

"I just don't know about the subject, because we just barely touched on it in seminary."

"Teaching people how to live as a Christians is more pressing."

"It scares people, so I just don't want to worry them unnecessarily."

"People have been saying the Second Coming is here for years, and we are still here. We need to deal with the here and now, not pie in the sky."

And my personal favorite:

"Some preachers are premillennial, some postmillennial, or whatever. I'm 'pan'-millennial. I believe it will just all 'pan' out in the end."

I have to tell you—confess, I guess—that this last one always presents a personal test of my temperament. Whenever I hear it, I see red, even though I've been as physically blind as the proverbial bat since 1993. Some of these preachers—a few—become a bit defensive and get rather exercised, launching into tirades, arguing that we prophecy types read far too much into the headlines as they might relate to biblical prophecy. And I readily admit that this has and continues to happen more often than it should.

The many episodes of date-settings for the Rapture over the years, for example, have done disservice to God's prophetic Word. Too often I receive formulas from all sorts of angles and configurations that claim to give the precise time of Christ's coming in the Rapture, or that propose to have the answers to other prophetic events.

Despite the fact that there are those who are overly speculative in their views of Bible prophecy, the following must be said. To the pastors of America who claim the Bible as the inspired, inerrant Word of the Living God but callously ignore its prophetic content—be forewarned. Your excuses/arguments won't stand the test at the judgment seat of Christ. You will be held accountable by the very Lord you proclaim you love so much—the same Lord about whom the angel told John: "For the testimony of Jesus is the spirit of prophecy" (Revelation 19:10b).

That same Jesus gave us the Olivet Discourse, during which He laid out general and specific things to come. The Gospel accounts give Christ's commandment of what to do about the many prophesied things He had just foretold: "Watch" (Mark 13:37). Prophecy makes up at least 27 percent of the Bible. Half of that 27 percent has been fulfilled, with half yet to be fulfilled. Anyone with spiritual ears to hear and spiritual eyes to see is capable of following the Lord's command to "look up" when seeing the things He foretold "begin to come to pass" (Luke 21: 28).

Certainly, if God calls people to be pastors—shepherds of His flock—He equips them to feed the flock His whole Word, not just the parts the pastor selects as important, while summarily dismissing the other parts of God's Word. Jesus said to "watch" for prophetic developments. And, spiritually attuned eyes and ears—a condition all pastors should seek to appropriate and maintain—can hear and see that we are at the very end of the Church Age.

Just this week, the entire world, not just the Middle East, exploded with rage. From Cairo and the capitals of Tunisia, Yemen, Jordan, Libya, Bahrain, and Iran to the U.S. capital emulating the austerity cuts tumult in Europe, the seas and waves of humanity are roaring with distress and perplexity. From Juarez, Mexico, and the deadly drug wars to the seas off Somalia and the murderous pirates who prey on their victims, violence fills the whole earth.

Israel stands alone in the global spotlight as the most-hated nation on planet earth. The world is in economic chaos, headed for total collapse. All the while, technology is progressing geometrically in ways that will one day provide earth's last tyrant with the satanically endowed ability to enslave most all people on this fallen sphere.

Yet many pastors of America are into building bigger, more beautiful edifices in order to more spectacularly entertain their audiences. They make claims that they are telling of God's love. But, they are stressing how to tap into that love in order to gain favor for acquiring material things; they are not teaching how to share the message that Jesus' love is shown in that He died to save us from our sins. Too many pastors are moving farther from teaching doctrinal truth. One such truth being assiduously avoided is that of Christ's Second Coming.

Thankfully, this Laodicean model doesn't apply to all mega churches in America today. Some genuinely preach and teach truth from the Bible, although most, I'm sorry to have to say, continue to push aside Bible prophecy in favor of sticking exclusively to life-lesson theology. The responsibility to "watch" must, by the Bible's very definition of the word "preacher," fall first and foremost on those who are called to shepherd God's people. The Word of God warns specifically about keeping the flock informed, and about those commissioned to do so who fail in that responsibility:

> My people are destroyed for lack of knowledge; because thou hast rejected knowledge, I will also reject thee, that thou shalt be no priest to me. (Hosea 4:6)

Paul's admonition applies to pastors and teachers even more, perhaps, than to those whom they shepherd and instruct.

> Study to shew thyself approved unto God, a workman that needeth not to be ashamed, rightly dividing the word of truth. (2 Timothy 2:15)

These are perilous times, dear pastors and teachers. Bible prophecy at this juncture in human history isn't frivolous or an elective to be chosen according to the pastor's whim. The hour is late, and God's people haven't a clue. It is critical that you begin giving them biblically prophetic nourishment.

The End-Times Bottom Line

March 7, 2011
End Times—The Bottom Line

Global economic chaos is driving the distress and perplexity of the nations of planet earth. The words of the greatest of all prophets, Jesus Christ, echo in cavernous reverberation with each succeeding news report from the capitals of earth's monetary centers.

> And there shall be…upon the earth distress of nations, with perplexity; the sea and the waves roaring.
> (Luke 21:25b)

Jesus' Olivet Discourse spoke to conditions exponentially moved beyond norms. In other words, the "distress" and "perplexity" that nations will be experiencing as His Second Coming nears will be beyond any ever known by people of earth. And, in biblical terms, "seas and waves" refer to the masses of peoples. Jesus said that because there will be unprecedented distress and perplexity among the nations, the peoples populating those nations will be "roaring."

All one must do to understand that the roots of the upheaval rocking America and the world at this very moment involve economics is to think on the acceleration of events in the headlines since September 11, 2001. It has been a decade of powerful disturbances beyond any experienced before.

America launched retaliatory action against those in the Middle East deemed complicit in the attacks in New York City and Washington D.C. Iraq was "liberated," and Saddam Hussein paid for his tortures and murders. But, from that action—which seems to be at least the beginning of fulfillment of Zechariah 5—has come the unleashing of worldwide jihad.

The U.S. economic engine, which has made the nation the most productive industrial power in history, runs on the petroleum most easily accessible in the regions surrounding Saudi Arabia. Manipulative money brokers, in my mind, have managed to, for reasons of their own, prevent drilling and refining of this nation's reserves, making America vulnerable to the economic danger we now face.

Compounding the dangers, some of our "leaders" have engaged in financial skullduggery. By damaging U.S. infrastructure through the banking debacle and politically engineering the trillions of dollars run up in debt—while selling the nation by offering Treasury bonds to perhaps America's most dangerous enemy, the Chinese—they move America ever more swiftly toward third-world status.

The explosion of revolution throughout the, for the most part, oil-rich nations surrounding Israel paints the end-times picture. That incendiary anarchy that has ignited fires of unrest in the U.S. and in various capitals of Europe shows the world to be "in distress...with perplexity; the sea and the waves roaring."

It is true that the twentieth century was one of tremendous

turbulence. World Wars I and II brought death, destruction, pestilence, and starvation of monumental proportion. The economic abyss that was the Great Depression certainly was preached by ministers as akin to the biblically prophesied apocalypse—and it was even claimed to be so by many pundits of the times.

However, the crashing of the World Trade Center towers to the streets of New York City on that terrible Tuesday morning seemed to have unleashed demons that continue to cause destruction more violent than that wrought during the entire previous century. That cascading avalanche is increasing with destructive force while it roars through our time with each hour that passes.

The toll in loss of human life thus far in the twenty-first century hasn't come anywhere near the death-dealing inflicted in the previous century. But, so far as the humanistic powers that be are concerned, the potential for apocalyptic-like carnage has reached near critical mass. To the money masters—the economic titans—the bottom line is not the human toll, but the fiscal Armageddon to be avoided while controlling the ongoing economic avalanche and using it to best effect for their own nefarious purposes.

Concern over the great monetary upheaval overrides all else with the globalists elite. The seas of human populations must be maneuvered in puppet fashion to bring in their idea of how the world system should run.

All of the above is to say that, in my view, Jesus' words point precisely to the world conditions developing around this generation at this very hour. It is oil and the wealth it represents that Satan is obviously using to try to bring about the destruction of the human race. That destruction is Satan's bottom line (1 Peter 5: 8).

But, of course, it will never happen, because Jesus said of the final seven years of this earth age, the Tribulation:

> And except those days should be shortened, there should no flesh be saved; but for the elect's sake those days shall be shortened. (Matthew 24:22)

I've mentioned the bottom line for the humanists who want to control the world through manipulation of economics. I've mentioned Satan's bottom line—his desire to destroy all of mankind. Now we look at God's bottom line, for this is the one destined to be achieved for all who will accept His Son as the only cure for the deadly soul disease from which they suffer.

God wants the souls of all people to be saved out of their lost condition, thus from His judgment and wrath that must fall upon earthly wickedness. This is why Christ hasn't yet come for His church in the Rapture. About this, the apostle Peter writes:

> The Lord is not slack concerning his promise, as some men count slackness, but is longsuffering toward us, not willing that any should perish, but that all should come to repentance. (2 Peter 3:9)

Sadly, not all will accept God's offer of rescue from the coming seven years of horror we term the Tribulation, or from the lake of fire for all of eternity. However, it isn't our worry to know who will and won't believe. It is the duty of each who calls Christ Lord to make sure the message is proclaimed that Jesus died, was buried, and resurrected so that all who believe in Him will have everlasting life. We must let the lost world hear the message that Christ might come at any moment for His own in the Rapture!

That's the Christian's bottom line for these end times.

MARCH 2011

March 14, 2011
Israel's Standing Is America's Hope

With America slipping precipitously in morality, economy, and most every other category one can think of, it does the patriotic heart good to find an area where the nation seems to be holding firm in the positive sense. At least a majority of its citizens, if not its current presidential administration, is holding firm.

The category is a most important one. As a matter of fact, in terms of God's opinion, it is all-important to the health of individuals or national entities.

If one listens to the mainstream news these days—or over the past several decades, for that matter—one continues to hear that Israel is the chief cause of unrest in the Middle East, that the Jewish state is one of the main causes of hatred for America around the world. The impression is conveyed that the people of the U.S. thus have turned their collective sympathy away from Israel and toward the people supposedly represented by the Palestinian Authority (PA).

The diatribes by mainstream media against Israel have been relentless under the guise of news reporting. Each succeeding hit piece adds to the picture designed to convince Americans to view the Jewish nation as an illegitimate and cruel occupier of lands belonging to the "Palestinians." That's why it is so heartening to get truth, for a change, that paints a different picture. That picture shows that the people of this country aren't buying the lies. Americans overwhelmingly see Israel as the good guy, not the bad guy, of the Middle East.

By a margin of 63 percent to 17 percent, the annual Gallup Poll indicates that support for Israel over the land-protest causes of the PA is overwhelming. This percentage is nearly as high as it has ever been. It is currently only 1 percentage point less than its highest point, reached in 1991. The poll was first taken in 1988, and at that time 37 percent favored Israel while 15 percent favored the PA. The percentages changed drastically (to 64 percent in Israel's favor) during the Persian Gulf War of 1991, and have remained strongly in Israel's favor since that time.

The picture is much different, however, on a worldwide basis. The BBC reports that Israel loses by 49 percent to 28 percent in a global poll of Israel versus the PA. Israel finished twenty-fourth out of twenty-seven in a worldwide, online poll against nations whose popularity was measured. The Jewish state came in barely ahead of Pakistan, North Korea, and Iran. The poll shows that Israel's standing globally continues to decline.

There are two primary reasons Israel's standing in the U.S. continues to remain high despite mainstream media efforts to turn opinion against that nation. One of the primary reasons is the loss of virtual monopoly suffered by the networks ABC, CBS, and NBC and those one-time broadcast giants' declining ability to collude with the major newspapers of the country and their dissipating readership.

The rise of the individual citizen's ready access to numerous news sources that are independent of the networks, newspapers, and wire services have allowed truth about the real troublemakers in the Middle East to shine brightly. Cable, Internet, and the blogosphere now give instant enlightenment to events as they unfold around the world. Digital cameras in cell phones now record video of breaking news events. Such news events in 1988 had to be filtered through network news cameras.

The old media was a dictatorship of sorts—a type of tyranny

about which the once and future Israeli prime minister once spoke. Benjamin Netanyahu, in a speech at an event honoring Ronald Reagan on February 17, 2001, made the following astute observations:

> The greatest service that dictatorships have received in the twentieth century was this thing, the microphone. And the microphone would give a single dictator the ability to control the minds and hearts of millions of people, to tell them who is the enemy, who are the well poisoners of the earth, who are the cancer that has to be excised. That's how Israel was referred to in the Middle East. That's how the Jewish people were referred to in the heart of Europe by the Nazis. It is the power of the microphone, the power of mass communications, controlled from above, that was the greatest threat to freedom in the twentieth century....
>
> We are witnessing the breakup of that monolithic control. Because you now have, or very soon will have, millions of people, tens of millions, hundreds of millions of people, ultimately billions of people, who can access networks of information and communication from below, who can become their own broadcasters, or narrowcasters and that is fundamentally eroding the power of dictatorships.[77]

The second reason for Israel's continued high standing in American public opinion can be attributed to a considerable extent to Christians who recognize God's plan for that people. Actually, it is the most important reason Israel is receiving high approval ratings in America. It is also the reason America has been so blessed for so many years. The biblical prescription for an individual or a nation having favor in God's view of things involving His chosen people is made crystal clear by the Almighty's own words to Abraham, father of the patriarchs of Israel:

> And I will make of thee a great nation, and I will bless thee, and make thy name great; and thou shalt be a blessing.
>
> And I will bless them that bless thee, and curse him that curseth thee: and in thee shall all families of the earth be blessed. (Genesis 12:2–3)

March 21, 2011
"World Now in the Tribulation!"

E-mail assaults my inbox these days, informing me that we are now in the Tribulation. The messages come not only from the usual Rapture antagonists, but from those who claim they have always held the pretribulational Rapture position, but now it is obvious to them that the world has entered that last seven years of God's wrath and judgment. We have been wrong about the Rapture's timing, as witnessed by things going on in our minute-by-minute, breaking-news reports.

Disdain for any mention of Rapture lies at the heart of the more-often-than-not caustic rhetoric.

I will serve up for your consumption some thoughts of one of the more irritable e-mailers. The writer has as the subject line: "The Japanese earthquake." The e-mail reads in part:

> [The signing of the Daniel 9:27 covenant]...happened last year in Cancun Mexico under the guise of a Climate Change treaty. Therefore, the pretribulation theory of the Rapture is over and done with; it is as dead in the water as the birds falling out of the sky recently. The Antichrist has confirmed that covenant just as the Bible said would be the instance, but don't take any notice of what he says; initially, he was acting under the directives of the Bilderberg group and that is why he always appears to be speaking in riddles, saying something at one time, and then later on completely reneging on what he had said earlier at a later date.
>
> [This is] just as the Bible describes him as being: a master of intrigue. That was his position to begin with, but I am not too sure if that initial position may have changed dramatically and that he is now acting under the directives of Satan, who is more than likely sitting on his right shoulder, is whispering in his ear, and telling him what to say and do. There is one point, though, I must concur with, and that is the obvious popularity of the pre-tribulation theory which can very easily be put down to the false self-worth of some who are of the mindset that as the Lord has saved them he is never going to let them go through the worst time in the history of the world. How false the doctrine and mindset of those individuals who follow the Rapture cult is.

I presume President Barack Obama is the person to whom this writer refers as filling the bill for being Antichrist. If so, this is not an unusual designation by those who declare that the pretrib view is in error at best, and is a cultic abomination at worst.

Certainly with the constant stream of bad news coming from Japan, it is made to seem that we have entered apocalyptic times. The several nuclear reactors damaged by the 9.0 earthquake-spawned tsunami are fodder for those who offer evidence that the pretrib Rapture view is in error—or is heresy—and we now should look for Antichrist to begin working his dark, Tribulation magic. There is little doubt from this quarter that the son of perdition will have a full plate to deal with once he steps into the end-times spotlight. A cursory scan of what these troubling times have already served up makes the point.

The world is in financial meltdown as portentous as the melting-down nuclear reactors on the island of Japan. The Middle East is in an uproar that is almost assuredly a precursor to alignment for the wrap-up of history leading to Christ's Second Advent. Israel is being forced by the world of nations into a position of accepting the deadly covenant of false peace our anti-Rapturist e-mailer declares to already be a done deal. Despite some scientists with blinders on declaring that nothing is unusual about the mega-magnitude earthquakes and other episodes of nature, it is obvious to the most casual observer that something is up with the frequency and intensity of the geophysical upheavals.

Nonetheless, in the literary spirit of the Ides of March just past, friends, reviving empire Romans, and countrymen—lend me your ears...the church of the Lord Jesus Christ is still here on planet earth, serving as salt and light. God the Holy Spirit continues to restrain the growing evil of this fallen sphere. He will do so until the church—all who are born again (John 3:3)—

departs when Christ calls that body to Himself (John 14:1–3; 1 Corinthians 15:51–55; 1 Thessalonians 4:13–18; Revelation 4:1–2).

I leave you with the same reassurance the apostle Paul imparted to the Thessalonians of his day, when they thought they were now in the Day of the Lord (Tribulation):

> Now we beseech you, brethren, by the coming of our Lord Jesus Christ, and by our gathering together unto him,
>
> That ye be not soon shaken in mind, or be troubled, neither by spirit, nor by word, nor by letter as from us, as that the day of Christ is at hand.
>
> Let no man deceive you by any means; for that day shall not come, except there come a falling away first, and that man of sin be revealed, the son of perdition,
>
> Who opposeth and exalteth himself above all that is called God, or that is worshipped, so that he, as God, sitteth in the temple of God, showing himself that he is God. (2 Thessalonians 2:1–4)

March 28, 2011
Church Called into Heaven!

It is a headline of all headlines: "Church Called into Heaven!" I say it "is" a headline of all headlines, because it is as good as already accomplished. We have God's Word on it.

Paul the apostle and prophet wrote it this way, as recorded in his letter to the Corinthians:

March 2011

For the Lord himself shall descend from heaven with a shout, with the voice of the archangel, and with the trump of God; and the dead in Christ shall rise first;

Then we who are alive and remain shall be caught up together with them in the clouds, to meet the Lord in the air; and so shall we ever be with the Lord.

(1 Thessalonians 4:16–17)

It is a thrilling prospect, considering all of the uncertainty created by upheavals taking place in the world today, that Christ will one day, perhaps very soon, call His church—all Christians—to Himself, for the glorious trip to Heaven.

Let not your heart be troubled; ye believe in God, believe also in me.

In my Father's house are many mansions; if it were not so, I would have told you. I go to prepare a place for you.

And if I go and prepare a place for you, I will come again, and receive you unto myself; that where I am, there ye may be also. (John 14:1–3)

This past Tuesday, March 22, 2011, at 11:30 a.m. CDT, the Lord fulfilled part of that magnificent prophecy. He called into Heaven a tremendous warrior for His great cause—the putting forth of the gospel message. Jesus called a stalwart member of the church, whose name ironically reflects that immense body of believers destined to go to Christ in the Rapture.

Dr. J. R. Church was called into God's eternal realm following a valiant battle with colon cancer. Certainly there wasn't a greater champion for the pretribulational Rapture view of Bible prophecy than Dr. Church. His trademark sign-off for the *Prophecy in the News* television program was "Keep looking up!"—the reference taken from Jesus' words recorded in Luke 21: 28.

The half-hour program, which will now be carried on by his long-time ministry partner and friend, Gary Stearman, reaches millions of viewers in America and around the world by broadcast, cable, satellite, and Internet (www.prophecyinthenews.com). The show covers issues and events taking place around the world, always dissecting those matters with faithful adherence to truth given by Scripture involving prophecy presented in the Bible.

Linda Church, Dr. Church's wife of fifty-two years and close confidante in ministry matters for many years, will continue to work as director of the ministry.

Prophecy in the News is among the most remarkable such ministries, in my opinion. The research and in-depth analysis are served up for the reader/view from a perspective that always challenges one to dig deeper. And, like I find the Bible itself, I find the depths to which their material can be mined are deep indeed.

J. R. Church obviously had a vision for what God prescribed for these troubling although exciting days near the end of the age. His many books and other writings—like those found in the monthly magazine, *Prophecy in the News*—point with broadly encompassing, yet precisely directed focus to the most pertinent aspects of things to come. He was a noted lecturer and was often invited to speak at prophecy conferences and within other venues across America and in other parts of the world.

Gary Stearman, an immensely talented writer and researcher, is cut from the same eschatological cloth, instilling confidence that the Lord's work will continue to shine prophetic truth in the stormy geopolitical and socioeconomic times that are almost certainly ahead.

On a personal level, J. R. was a friend who never failed to say "yes" when I asked him to join in one of my book projects that included a number of authors. He trusted me—without question—to maintain unwavering fidelity to truth from God's Word while we prepared the compilations for publication. That spirit of trust he imparted remains a stabilizing ingredient within the foundation of everything I consider when trying to discern what God wants next from me in the hours, days, and months He has allotted for me in this brief lifetime.

J. R. Church's own time on this fallen planet was all too brief, from the vantage of those of us who benefited so much from his teaching and counsel—those of us who admired and held him close as brother and friend. But, his call into Heaven was from a vantage point infinitely more knowledgeable than ours. When Christ's call comes for those of us who name the name of Jesus, all will be made understandable—whether at the end of life, or at the Rapture of the church. *Keep looking up!*

April 2011

Israelicide—Nations' Self-Destruction

April 4, 2011
Israelicide

Forewarning of the fate that the nations of earth face leaps from Bible prophecy. Those who make Jerusalem and Israel the object of hatred will pay a terrible price. And make no mistake, the city and nation (Jewish people) are inextricably linked:

> And in that day will I make Jerusalem a burdensome stone for all peoples; all that burden themselves with it shall be cut in pieces, though all the people of the earth be gathered together against it. (Zechariah 12:3)

To "burden themselves" with Jerusalem and with Israel (Judah) in this case means to come against the city and people in a hostile sense. God is saying through Zechariah that at the end of the age, near the consummation of His dealing with this earth system, all nations of earth will make Jerusalem and His chosen people the center of their anger and aggression. The aggressors against God's city (Jerusalem, the apple of his eye—see Zechariah 2:8) and the Jewish people will result in devastation for those attackers.

Perhaps it's just the old advertising guy in me, but I want to coin a new word—"Israelicide"—for what the nations of the world are in process of doing. The word means two things in my thinking: 1) To commit satanically inspired genocide against the Jewish race; and 2) The collective suicide of Israel's enemies whose coalescing unity of mind curses Israel.

It doesn't take a historian's knowledge to understand that the Jewish race—the nation of Israel—has been hated and harassed as no other people throughout the millennia. Although some—like Iran's dictator, Mahmoud Ahmadinejad—claim that the Holocaust perpetrated by the Nazis against the Jews never happened, that it's all fabrication by the hated Zionists, the world knows the horrific truth about genocide against God's chosen people.

The record of the demise of those who made the Jews the object of their hate was made manifest before the eyes of the peoples of all nations. Germany was completely defeated and divided. The remains of Hitler and his henchmen lie strewn in ignominy, their memories detested by all but those of like heinous anti-Semitic hatred. They committed Israelicide, in both meanings of my term.

The promise to Israel's patriarch, Abraham, remains in effect: "And I will bless them that bless thee, and curse him that curseth thee" (Genesis 12:3a). Nations of earth are in the process of committing Israelicide, in my view, collectively insisting that Israel is the central problem in the Middle East. It is the Jewish state that in the opinion of most of the diplomatic world is holding up progress in the "Roadmap for Peace."

Those same diplomats, along with their mainstream news media cohorts, point accusatory fingers at Israel upon each retaliatory strike they make to try to keep their enemies at bay. At the same time, the murder of an innocent Jewish family—the Fogel family, including their three-month-old baby—by Israel's enemies is hardly mentioned by the diplomatic community or the mainstream journalists of the world.

Prophesied events are being set up on an hour-by-hour basis. The Islamist countries are in incendiary turmoil, as the headlines continually remind us. These nations have Israel encircled on all sides except on the side of the Mediterranean—the sea into which a number of the leaders of Arab states plus Iran's Ahmadinejad have vowed to push the Jewish state. There is good reason to believe that all of this upheaval is being orchestrated by various elements in cahoots with the Muslim Brotherhood, in preparation for an ultimate effort to erase Israel from the earth.

Some are convinced this will all play out in a war they believe is predicted by a prayer recorded in Psalms 83. Certainly, one can't deny there are powerful dynamics moving and shaking in the land around which end-times Bible prophecy is centered.

The militant Islamists of the Arab nations and Iran are bent on committing Israelicide, there is no doubt. They have declared their intention loudly and for a long time. The Bible says Israel's enemies will do just that, but in the sense of the second meaning of my newly coined word, not in the sense of the first definition. They will commit Israelicide.

Someday, such an attack will be their final death knell. For certain, Israel's Middle East and northern enemies will pay the price for their hatred as recorded by the prophet Ezekiel:

Last-Days Diary
April 2011

Thou shalt fall upon the mountains of Israel, thou, and all thy bands, and the peoples that are with thee; I will give thee unto the ravenous birds of every sort, and to the beasts of the field to be devoured.

Thou shalt fall upon the open field; for I have spoken it, saith the Lord God. (Ezekiel 39:4–5)

April 11, 2011
It's the Economy, Not-So Stupid!

Many of us remember the slogan the Bill Clinton political machine bombarded us with during Clinton's 1992 presidential bid: "It's the economy, stupid!" The mainstream media took the slogan and used it like a shillelagh to beat George H. W. Bush and secure for Clinton his first term. The slogan's meaning was that all other considerations were secondary, or didn't matter at all. People were to think how economically bad it had been under George Bush 41.

Well, in my view, the slogan was at that time a sham, to use another Irish term. It was a phony charge—a political tool without merit. I say that, because looking back at the time of the closing days of Bush's one term, the economy was like a boom cycle as compared to the ominous bust time the national and world economy faces at present.

People were to be considered "stupid" who didn't agree that Bill Clinton was the answer to the supposed money woes Democrat Party campaigners claimed voters of that pre-Clinton presidency faced. The Obama administration has brought America a national debt that currently stands at $14.2 trillion, with a real unemployment rate which is at, some experts say, 13 percent or so and about to rise drastically.

Members of each party can be faulted for much of what we face economically. But, it is primarily the party Mr. Obama now leads that has been responsible for running up spending totals with entitlement programs that have bankrupted the U.S. That party has been almost exclusively responsible for increasing America's debt by trillions in the first two years of this president's administration. The housing bubble that burst was a creation by that party for the most part. Barney Frank, Charles Schumer, and others like them, passed legislation, then had oversight for administrating a scam of monumental magnitude. In order to secure votes for their party—again, in my perception of the matters involved—these and their ilk saw to it that thousands upon thousands of people who couldn't afford much more than the lowest rents available got mortgage loans for houses that only the affluent can in reality afford. This, all in the name of "fairness" in the woolly minds of those who, it seems after all, are the "stupid" ones among us.

But they aren't stupid. Rather, they are clever and conniving in their understanding of how the American political process works. Now, as Mr. Obama's former pastor, Jeremiah Wright, has said about America deserving the 9/11 attack by the Muslims, "The chickens have come home to roost." Now the price must be paid for the insanity perpetrated by the super-colossal debacles that were Fanny Mae and Freddie Mac, and the stimulus bailouts of companies and institutions "too big to fail."

In considering what's important in making decisions politically, personally, spiritually, and in every other way, the central issue is unmistakable. In the current season of unprecedented fiscal storms, the problems are in our face. It is the economy, to all who are not "stupid." If we don't make wise decisions this time around, there might not be any more times around for the American way as we've known it.

All who come to www.raptureready.com on a regular basis know that we first and foremost put forward Jesus Christ as the answer to all problems. God's plan for His creation called man is the only antidote to the evil that bombards and penetrates our daily lives. The love of money, as we know, is the root of all kinds of evil (1 Timothy 6:10). So, the foundational problems at the very core of life upon this fallen planet involve monetary matters—the economy.

April 18, 2011
Global Monetary Masters Surround Israel

We have watched over the past months while Israel's Islamist neighbors have ignited in revolutionary fervor. They surround that tiny country, their dictatorial governments in chaos. Because they have been in a constant rage against Israel since its rebirth into modernity in 1948, blood-vowed to erase that nation from the earth, the sudden pyrotechnics within their ranks makes the Middle East the true powder keg it has been designated since the end of World War II. Diplomatic powers that be are focused on the region as intensely as ever in history.

Great concern for petroleum interests has thrust those in high places into the fray in ways only they can intervene. The global monetary masters have begun to surround the beleaguered Jewish state much in the way that Israel's hate-filled Arab enemies surround that country. Their cordon consists of economic strength—not as overtly threatening as the collective military machinery of the nations that have combined to come against them in 1948, 1956, 1967, and 1973, but threatening nonetheless.

Two institutions representing the global economic hierarchy have weighed in on the matter most pressing with regard to what I will term "Israel vs. the world." I'm referring to the potential violence wrapped up in the so-called "two-state solution" controversy. I believe that the monetary factors at the heart of the pressures now being exerted make up the nucleus of Zechariah's prophecy. It is a prophecy we have looked at often:

> The burden of the word of the LORD for Israel, saith the LORD, who stretcheth forth the heavens, and layeth the foundation of the earth, and formeth the spirit of man within him.
>
> Behold, I will make Jerusalem a cup of trembling unto all the peoples round about, when they shall be in the siege both against Judah and against Jerusalem.
>
> And in that day will I make Jerusalem a burdensome stone for all peoples; all that burden themselves with it shall be cut in pieces, though all the people of the earth be gathered together against it. (Zechariah 12:1–3)

The international community, in the form of what is called the Quartet, has for years been pressuring other Israeli governments and now the Benjamin Netanyahu government to discontinue building settlements in the areas of contention around Jerusalem. The U.S., the United Nations, the European Union, and Russia continue to insist that Israel come to the table of peace on terms favorable to the Palestinian Authority (PA).

The "Roadmap to Peace" is in reality a blueprint for bringing down Israel's guard against an ever-tightening semicircle of hostile Islamist governments that want to push all Israeli Jews into the Mediterranean. That semicircle is now made more portentous by the fall of Egypt to Israel's south, Egypt now likely to fall into the hands of the Muslim Brotherhood.

The two institutions that give the international community its true power and authority as the Quartet and others join in tightening the circle against Israel are the International Monetary Fund (IMF) and the World Bank. Global economic authority is the real power behind the power. These have made their intentions known.

The World Bank has strongly supported the recognition of an independent Palestinian state following the backing by the IMF. In a Thursday report, the World Bank compared core Palestinian institutions favorably with those in established countries.

> The PA announced that it intends to work on the recognition of an independent Palestinian state at the UN General Assembly this September.
>
> More than one hundred countries have so far officially recognized Palestine as a state based on the 1967 borders, boundaries that existed before Israel captured East al-Quds (Jerusalem), the West Bank, and the Gaza Strip.[78]

Israel insists that unless issues concerning borders and security are settled, there can be no Palestinian state. The PA is threatening to apply for Palestinian statehood with the UN, the organization filled with representative nations heavily against Israel and in favor of Islamist causes.

Such an approval by that world body—creating a Palestinian state without Israel's participation in the process—would put the Jewish nation in direct conflict with the great majority of countries of the world if Israel refused to allow the new Palestinian state to take over territory Israel considers its own. Some—including this writer—believe that part of the recent intervention by nations against the Libyan regime of Moammar Gadhafi was designed to create precedence for a future such international community intervention. Such an action against Israel thus might be considered justifiable in the minds of the globalist monetary masters wanting to create a Palestinian state so as to control Middle East petroleum assets. Zechariah's prophecy continues to take shape.

April 25, 2011
Quartet Singing Deadly Song

Homer's protagonist in *The Odyssey* and the adventures through which the unknown author moved him are brought to mind with the many voices from the diplomatic world singing the same refrain without ceasing—even though egregiously out of tune. These days, I am reminded of how deadly such allurement can be.

Odysseus, the wandering Greek hero, is given instructions for how to safely negotiate his return home. One of the chief obstacles he is told that he will face on his voyage is that of passing by the island of lovely Sirens, the half-human, half-bird female creatures that lure mariners to their death on the island's rocky shoals with their irresistible song, promising to reveal the future.

Odysseus follows his instructions and has his crew aboard the ship plug their ears with bee's wax. He tells them to tie him to the ship's mast and instructs them not to loosen the restraints, no matter what.

Odysseus is the only one who can hear the Sirens' song, and he is driven mad with desire to be set free to go to them. But, his faithful crew just ties him all the more securely to the mast, and they move safely past the island to face the obstacles of the rest of their journey.

Israeli Prime Minister Benjamin Netanyahu is on a voyage perhaps not as Homeric, but certainly one through which he must negotiate his way with extreme care, if he is not to run the Jewish ship of state aground on some very deadly shoals. He is hearing the not-so-lovely "Sirens" from many directions calling for his government to give into international pressure—thus to assure a future of peace for all concerned. So far, he has remained securely lashed to the mast, and his government has kept the bee's wax in their discerning ears of better sensibility.

The lyrics of the song the geopolitical Sirens sing are confusing, to apply the most generous description of their attempts at allurement. But the fact that the chorus spews insanity in its efforts to seduce Netanyahu to throw caution to the wind is the most realistic assessment of the attempt at seduction. The latest of the alluring words come from the leader of the Palestinian Authority.

> The Palestinian president says he is opposed to another armed uprising against Israel, even if faltering peace efforts fail altogether. Mahmoud Abbas told reporters in Tunisia on Wednesday that he remains committed to a US-backed target of reaching a negotiated peace agreement with Israel by September.[79]

The same leader has in recent weeks declared he will go to the UN, bypassing Israeli input regarding the two-state solution process, to declare Palestinian statehood. His tune has changed for the moment, and one has to wonder what to make of this particular alteration in the siren call to Benjamin Netanyahu and his crew while they try to negotiate some of the most treacherous Mideast waters in history.

This is indeed a strange turn of attitude, since the PA has just received the promise of financial backing from the World Bank and International Monetary Fund, as reported in this column last week. Now—after Secretary of State Hillary Clinton has just told the PA and others who seek to declare a Palestinian state without Israel's participation that the U.S. rejects such a plan—yet another stanza is added to the Siren call that further confuses. The Quartet is singing a deadly refrain in a not-so-veiled threat to the Netanyahu government:

> Foreign diplomats warn that if Netanyahu fails to present new peace plan soon, superpowers may officially endorse Palestinian state in 1967 border, with east Jerusalem as its capital.
>
> American and European diplomats warned that if Prime Minister Benjamin Netanyahu fails to present a new peace initiative soon, the Quartet [U.S., United Nations, European Union, and Russia] may be compelled to recognize a Palestinian State in the 1967 borders, with East Jerusalem as its capital, the *Los Angeles Times* reported on Tuesday.[80]

It should be considered truly a miracle of biblical proportion if our Odysseus—Mr. Netanyahu, strapped to that mast while the Israeli ship of state plows through the turbulence—doesn't go stark-raving mad while listening to the cacophony coming from the beckoning Sirens who want to usurp what little land Israel possesses.

It seems to me that the wild-eyed beckoning by supposedly the brightest planet earth has to offer—the diplomatic elite—makes the case that they, themselves, suffer from madness of the sort that drove the mariners of Homer's tales onto the rocks of destruction. Their wailing is enough to drive anyone crazy.

These are hearing the seductive words of the one being who, since iniquity was found in him, has wanted to usurp anything that belongs to the God of Heaven. It is a deadly song they are listening to. It is a deadly song they are singing to God's chosen people. It is a Siren call that will bring all nations of earth to Armageddon.

May 2011

Rumors of My Death (Not So) Exaggerated

May 2, 2011
The Shortness of Time
By Todd Strandberg

Terry has been a part of Rapture Ready for over a decade now. I met him at the annual Pre-Trib Study Group conference in Dallas. We have worked together on several book projects, and our combined effort is responsible for adding dozens of articles to the site. Our partnership almost came to an abrupt end last Friday as Terry suffered a massive heart attack.

I know Terry is writing about his experience in his section on this page, so I will just mention the basic facts. I had just arrived home when his wife, Margaret, called me over, saying that Terry was having chest pains. Since he had just worked out, I thought that he had just strained himself. We called an ambulance, and they came within about ten minutes.

My expectation was that they would take him to the emergency room and spend the next hour running tests to see what was causing the pain. I was totally shocked when Margaret called me, saying that Terry's heart had stopped three times, and the doctors had to shock him back to life each time.

What I take away from Terry's brush with death is the realization that his nearly two decades of prophetic work almost ended. His latest book would still come out in June, but that would be it. The physical dying part doesn't bother me. What causes me distress is the sudden interruption. I fully understand the rules of life, but I still want to shout, "Hey wait, we still had plans here!"

Years ago, when I first started working on RR, I dreaded the idea of the Rapture occurring before I could finish some key sections of the site. Now that RR has become a massive wealth of information, I'm open to the possibility of the Lord taking us home to glory.

Christopher Hitchens is a well-known atheist who is dying from esophageal cancer.[81] He is now at the point at which he can no longer speak. Before cancer stole his voice, he said his about his pending death, "You're at a party and you're tapped on the shoulder and told you have to leave. The party is still going on but it's going on without you."[82] Since Mr. Hitchens has decided to reaffirm his atheism in the face of certain death, I think being booted from a party is the least of his troubles.

A few days ago, David Wilkerson died in a car crash. He was the pastor of Times Square Church in one of New York City's most gang-infested districts, and he founded the highly successful, faith-based Teen Challenge drug treatment and Christian mentoring program. Wilkerson also wrote the book, *The Cross and the Switchblade,* which has sold more than 30 million copies. I'm sure Wilkerson had more productive things on his mind than dying, but unlike Hitchens, he had good reason to look forward to the afterlife.

There is an old saying, "Death is nature's way of telling you to slow down." It's only true if you are the one who is coming down with a bad case of rigor mortis. For the living, death is nature's way of giving you a motivational kick in the pants. Our time on earth is limited, and we should make the best of it.

Terry doesn't need any motivation. Within two days of returning from the hospital, he had written his usual article for this page, and we had recorded a session for our "Rapture Talk" blog radio program. He is now making preparations for the release of the book *Demonomics.* His attitude is as long as the Lord wants him on earth, he will do everything he can to promote the end-time message.

I encourage Christians reading this article to be mindful of our place in the kingdom of God. We are racing against two clocks—the biological clock and the one that is counting down to the Rapture. I believe that the Lord has given every person at least one gift. Don't let life pass without having your gift opened.

> I have fought a good fight, I have finished my course, I have kept the faith:
>
> Henceforth there is laid up for me a crown of righteousness, which the Lord, the righteous judge, shall give me at that day: and not to me only, but unto all them also that love his appearing. (2 Timothy 4:7–8)

May 2011

Been Dying to Write This...

By Terry James

Please bear with me in this week's commentary. I don't like to get "up close and personal," as ABC sportscasters used to say in announcing an interview with one athlete or the other. It's just not professional, in my view, for purposes of communicating in forums such as ours. But, personal I am going to get for this one. Hope you don't mind.

Staying with the ABC sports analogy, I was doing my three- or four-times-per-week workout on Good Friday just past. I had done the warm-ups for the usual fifteen minutes or so, and then I had done the barbells (ugh!). Done were the push-ups—seventy of them, except very cheap ones (fooling myself, mostly, that I was doing them right). Then were accomplished the knee-lifts while lying on my back for five minutes. Doing the Body by Jake sit-up machine next had completed that part of the workout.

Then it was time for aerobics. I have this rowing machine with one hundred pounds on the back of it that is an excellent leg-press device, which is also used to do some upper-body stuff. I did all this in the usual fashion, the workout now flowing toward its one-hour and twenty-minute conclusion. I decided to skip the treadmill and go straight for the recumbent bike—to just sort of chill out, or cool off, or however one chooses to term one's winding-down regimen.

A burning pressure began, then, just behind my sixty-eight-year old sternum. It was a pain I had felt slightly three days earlier while just sitting around working on something on the computer. At that time it had been mild, and I had thought of it as a case of a little more than usual heartburn—indigestion. I think I even popped a Tums or something.

This time, however, the pain worsened by the second, until it was a severe pressure gnawing at my chest, as if something wanted out of there.

I walked around, just knowing it would shortly ease. But it didn't.

"Think you better call 911," I said to my wife. She took one look at me, knowing that that was the very last thing I would ever do—want an ambulance. It almost was…

The medics arrived ten minutes later, I was told. I was conscious and answered their questions, even as in pain and as out of breath as I was. This, even though they tried feverishly to find a pulse.

"Can't find one," one of the guys said to the other, who joined him in frantically searching.

Meantime, I'm thinking, "No pulse…what does that mean? One is dead when there is no pulse."

They strapped yours truly to the gurney and we were off, the pain in my chest becoming excruciating. One of the rescuers put some nitroglycerin beneath my tongue, while saying to the dispatcher, "Think we have a coronary going."

The ride was rough. Ambulances of that sort aren't built for the patient's comfort; they just want to get you there. I felt every bump in the brief ride of ten minutes at most. I felt us stop, heard the door open, felt them jerking the gurney forward. I heard a high-pitched noise that sounded like a transition from one function to another within some sort of computerized system. Sort of like a *blip*.

I saw them, then. I was with them, and they were all beautiful young people in their twenties, it seems in retrospect. They were smiling brightly. Their faces glowed effulgently—not like something ghostly, but with the fresh glow of youth of those in perfect health. They beckoned me to join them.

I wanted to just be with them—to talk and enjoy that ambience. I had no thought of what had gone on before—the pain, the ride. This was real. It was real, and I loved it, and I could feel the love of these young people as we faced each other.

Then I remember thinking,"Wait!" There was something going on. I was in a nightmare. I was being transported with chest pains. I felt my bare chest with my fingertips, thinking, "Oh, no. I am on this gurney. I'm not in that beautiful—real—place. I was back in this nightmare—only this was reality.

People were working at high speed. They said I came back talking. I don't remember what I said; neither did they.

One guy said, "We hit him with the paddles." I questioned that remark. "Paddles?"

"Yes, your heart stopped," he said.

The pressure again began building, agonizing—a fire thrusting to get out from behind the sternum.

Suddenly there was again the computer-like prompt. I was with the beautiful, young people, whose smiles were brighter than any ever displayed in toothpaste commercials.

Again there was regret, as I found myself on the table where they prepared the angiogram to find out the position of the blockage.

Then, I was with those youngsters again, only this time the memory becomes fuzzy, but I do know I was among them, talking with them in a serenely joyful place.

Back to the ER and the flurry to save my life. I had been hit with the defibrillator for the third time. My heart had completely stopped on three occasions, but now I sensed the medics had things under control.

A doctor, one of the most highly regarded interventionist cardiologists in the state, just happened to be down from the Arkansas Heart Hospital, which is twenty minutes away in Little Rock. He was only one room away, and was on my case and finished with the procedure within forty-five minutes.

I was told by this doctor that 50 percent of all who have the sort of heart attack I had die before getting to the emergency room. Most that do get to the hospital don't make it. The attack was in an artery that is the most crucial. They call the blockage the "widow maker."

Now, what do we make of this? What do we do with it?

Well, "the Lord will bring you to Himself when He chooses" is one lesson reconfirmed within my own faith. He wants something else to be done through me. Certainly, I believe writing this commentary is one of those things.

Was I in Heaven? I don't know. To be absent from the body is to be present with the Lord, Paul the apostle tells us. I didn't see Jesus, and He is my Lord.

But, we are all one in Christ, the Lord Himself tells us in John 17. So, in one sense, I could have been with the Lord by being with those people who appeared to be in the full bloom of youth. And, I sensed the absolute peace and joy their demeanor—collectively—projected. Christ is within us and we are one.

But, there's another side to this reality that seemed more real than the earthly nightmare to which I returned three times. The Lord didn't show me that other side (the hellish side), but the thought pulses strongly within my spirit as I write this. Just as Heaven is a place to be longed for with great anticipation, Hell is just as real, and a place to be shunned at all cost. (Read Jesus' own words on the subject in Mark 9:43–48.)

The choice of whether to accept Jesus Christ as Savior is your choice. The time of death is not yours to make. Even if by suicide, the death will not have taken God by surprise. Believe in Him today with every fiber of your being. Heaven is real. So is Hell. Only accepting God's love gift of His Son's shed blood on Calvary can cleanse you or me from sin—the soul-destroying thing God cannot permit to come into His holy, majestic presence.

Jesus is the only way to Heaven (John 14:6). You and I must come to Him in order to ever be a heavenly citizen. The alternative is the nightmare world about which Jesus forewarned.

Here's the only formula for going to Heaven when you die or at the Rapture of the church:

> That if thou shalt confess with thy mouth the Lord Jesus, and shalt believe in thine heart that God hath raised him from the dead, thou shalt be saved.
>
> For with the heart man believeth unto righteousness; and with the mouth confession is made unto salvation. (Romans 10:9–10)

May 9, 2011
Osama's Death and Christian Reaction

Many Americans broke out in celebration when Al Qaeda mastermind Osama Bin Laden's death was announced Sunday night, May 1. The demonstrations of glee weren't nearly as wild as the scenes from almost every Muslim nation the day the twin towers in New York fell. There was no firing of AK-47 weaponry into the air, but it was ebullient demonstration nonetheless.

May 2011

President Obama was said to have turned to an aide and remarked: "We got him!"

How did you react when you heard the news? My only reaction was to think that now Osama faces not the seventy-two virgins promised to all Muslim men faithful to Allah once they assume room temperature, but that he confronts something far different. His death gave no pleasure, no sense of retribution or vengeance—but neither did I then or now have regrets that he is gone from this world.

Had I lost a family member or dear friend in the World Trade Center Towers, the Pentagon, or the crash of the airplane in Pennsylvania that day, perhaps I would be satisfied to the point of elation at the news of his death. But, I don't think so.

The satisfaction I receive is that of knowing that Bin Laden can no longer add his demented thought processes to those of his fellow Islamist madmen. To me, there is no joy in the demise of anyone, except in knowing that, in this case, he won't be in on planning future murders in the name of Allah. This is indeed a significant volley in the war declared on terror by George W. Bush following September 11, 2001. Killing Osama Bin Laden, however, can't change the fact that he and his henchmen murdered nearly three thousand people that fateful day. It can't alter the fact that thousands of U.S. service men and women have died or been wounded in pursuit of dealing with the evil Bin Laden perpetrated and his fellow terrorists continue to carry out.

Bin Laden's death doesn't stop the $1.28-trillion-and-counting cost of the military action against radical Islam the U.S. has and is footing. In this, he has been successful—helping achieve his vow to bring the great Satan to its knees, economically speaking.

So, his being killed isn't reason to declare victory, even though it is obviously a cause for celebration by those who are so inclined.

There are thousands, even millions, to take his place. There is little time to spend reveling in this one, demonically driven man's death. His assassination is that sort of violence on which the jihadists feed. Violence feeds Islamist war makers like the warm Gulf waters feed a hurricane.

Am I saying that Osama Bin Laden should not have been dispatched in this raid by the Navy SEALs? Of course not. I am saying that to vigorously celebrate his being killed should not be allowed to become, either individually or collectively within the American psyche, a visceral bloodlust to render evil for evil. Especially, this should not be the mindset of the Christian, in my view. Such action should be taken only in order to try to make civilized society safe from such beastly activity as carried out by Bin Laden and his ilk. The Bible condones such action by duly authorized governments because this is a sinful, murderous world, and such killers must be stopped to promote the general safety of peace-loving people.

Hypocrisy and worse are front and center in all of this taking down of Osama Bin Laden, while the mainstream media takes no notice. The present American president operates within a political philosophy that disdains capital punishment, no matter the crime—primarily, I believe, because he thus wins the hearts, minds, and votes of minorities who view themselves as victims of injustice. Yet he and his political associates see nothing wrong with the taking out of Bin Laden, because it was the politically expedient thing to do. Executing a man—within the American judicial system, for murdering a person—is something the liberal mindset considers barbarism. They slap each other's backs, however, for the good fortune—or well-executed plan—in sending Osama Bin Laden on his eternal journey. Their poll numbers might benefit from the action taken.

Such duality of thought shows a trend toward the same sort of madness carried on by the fanatic Islamists. Fanatic Muslims see nothing wrong with killing when it serves the best interest of their cause and is sanctioned by their holy book, the Koran. It is justice of a grossly perverted sort by which that self-indulgent mindset operates.

So, those who name the name of Christ should not find carnal enjoyment in the death of Osama Bin Laden or anyone else. He is gone, and I am glad. He was a danger to those I love, as well as to everyone who might fall under his unalloyed evil plotting. But, I take no pleasure in his death—only a degree of solace. The Lord of Heaven Himself has set the example for what should be the Christian's attitude in such matters:

> As I live, saith the Lord GOD, I have no pleasure in the death of the wicked, but that the wicked turn from his way and live; Turn ye, turn from your evil ways.
> (Ezekiel 33:11)

May 16, 2011
Recognizing Israel

Hamas leadership has just let it be known that it will accept a Palestinian state set within the 1967 borders as those borders stood before the Six-Day War of that year. This they will accept, dropping their demands that a Palestinian state must encompass a much broader territory.

The Hamas top strong man, Mahmoud al-Zahar, told the Palestinian news agency Ma'an that he would be willing to accept the installing of a Palestinian state "on any part of Palestine," rather than holding to the group's previous demand that such a state be formed from "the [Jordan] river to the [Mediterranean] sea."[83]

However, he proclaimed that they will never "recognize Israel" as a legitimate state, because to do so would be to take away the right of future Palestinians to liberate all of the land from Israeli control—i.e., the war against the hated Jewish enemy must continue, regardless of whether a territory is granted and a Palestinian state established.[84]

The only recognition Israel receives in these troubled times is in the form of recognition of the nation being an interloper in the Middle East—an oppressor of the Palestinian people. It is a generally accepted truth that almost all nations that make up the United Nations view Israel as the culprit in fomenting war-like rumblings in the Middle East.

The Obama administration, with Secretary of State Hillary Clinton heading the State Department, has done little in the way of supporting Israel in opposition to such hatred and vitriol that spews from the UN on practically every occasion of the Israeli-Palestinian question coming to the forefront for debate. As a matter of fact, the record of the Obama administration and this era of the State Department has been dismal from the standpoint of standing by the Jewish nation while it is diplomatically assaulted from every angle possible.

We have learned time after time of the U.S. State Department and this president pressuring Israel to stop building housing units in its own territory—territory hard earned and won with blood after being attacked by vicious enemies in a number of wars since Israel's birth into modernity in 1948. The American policy with regard to Israel—as part of the "Quartet" policy—these days is to consistently try to twist the arm of Prime Minister Benjamin Netanyahu and the Israeli government into giving up this land so the "Roadmap to Peace" can proceed to the satisfaction of the surrounding Muslim nations.

Now, the terrorist Islamists who have an overwhelming influence on the Palestinian Authority demand yet another concession by the world community. They demand that they be given the territory they seek, but declare also that their blood feud against Israel will never end until Israel is no longer an entity in the Middle East. Like Iran's crazed president, Mahmoud Ahmadinejad, they prefer that all Jews be drowned in the Mediterranean.

The duplicity of the Israel haters surrounding that nation are understood from double think/double talk issued from the current mouth in charge of the terrorist leadership.

Speaking to Ma'an on Wednesday, Zahar, hinting at the possible political line of a future Palestinian unity cabinet, said that the truce with Israel was "part of the resistance not its rejection," adding that "a truce is not peace."[85]

Israel's enemies will never recognize Israel as the legitimate owner of the vast land God gave that people. The hatred is satanic, and will continue right up until the Lord Himself puts an end to the hatred. Sadly, most of the church of Jesus Christ also doesn't recognize Israel as the legitimate owner of that land, the land God calls His own.

Replacement theology runs rampant among the pulpits and pews in America, either tacitly or outrightly declaring that the church has replaced Israel in God's prophetic plans.

Nothing could be farther from truth found in God's Word. The very fact that Israel is recognized only in the most hateful way by the world and is front and center of controversy in that region many term the "Holy Land" should alert the Bible-believing child of God that recognizing Israel at this late hour is all important. That nation is the key to where this generation stands upon God's prophetic timeline.

Israel is the clear signal that Christ's shout, "Come up here," must be very near indeed.

May 23, 2011
God's Definition of Genius

Reports are that Christopher Hitchens, the well-known atheist, has told friends and the press that if he were to make a last-minute deathbed conversion, they should not believe it. It would be his delirium, not his rational mind, doing the converting.

Reports are, too, that the deathbed is now his fate, as he lies dying of complications due to advanced throat cancer. He remains unrepentant and apparently unafraid of whatever comes next.[86]

Hitchens has long prided himself in his ability to debate, debunk, and debase all claims of religion in regard to the afterlife. He particularly has seemed to take enjoyment from intellectually dismantling the Bible and Christianity. There is no God, he has consistently claimed, lacing much of his confutation with acerbic wit intended to dissect Christianity with a laser-like argumentation scalpel. He seemed to delight in humiliating his debate opponents with ridicule. Many people—Christians whose God the British, self-styled intellectual has denied—have prayed for him. The prayers were that he be healed both physically and spiritually.

A special day of prayer for him was arranged, which he summarily dismissed:

> Author and outspoken atheist Christopher Hitchens, undergoing chemotherapy for cancer, skipped Everybody Pray for Hitchens Day Monday. "I shall not be participating," said Hitchens, author of the book *God is Not Great: How Religion Poisons Everything.* "[Incantations,] I don't think, have any effect on the material world."[87]

Hitchens' fellow Brit, also an intellectual known for his derogatory views on religion, talks about the afterlife from the view of one who has lived at death's door for many years:

> "Heaven is a fairy story for people afraid of the dark," the eminent British theoretical physicist Stephen Hawking said in an interview published on Monday.
>
> Hawking, 69, was expected to die within a few years of being diagnosed with degenerative motor neurone disease at the age of twenty-one, but became one of the world's most famous scientists with the publication of his 1988 book, *A Brief History of Time.*
>
> "I have lived with the prospect of an early death for the last forty-nine years. I'm not afraid of death, but I'm in no hurry to die. I have so much I want to do first," he told the *Guardian* newspaper. "I regard the brain as

> a computer which will stop working when its components fail. There is no heaven or afterlife for broken down computers; that is a fairy story for people afraid of the dark."[88]

Both men are looked upon by the world as possessing genius. This is particularly true of Hawking, who is held up by some as almost the equal of Albert Einstein in terms of his cerebral brilliance. In his book, *The Grand Design,* published in 2010, Hawking stirred controversy among some religious leaders. The physicist declared in the book that there was no need for a divine force to explain the creation of the universe. God, in other words, isn't relevant. As a matter of fact, in the minds of many of the world's scientific "geniuses," there is no god. Evolution is their religion, and man, himself, is god.

The Lord of Heaven says the following about all of this:

> The fool hath said in his heart, There is no God. Corrupt are they, and have done abominable iniquity; there is none that doeth good. (Psalms 53:1)

The world when David penned those words was likely almost tame compared to the lawlessness of our time. The intellectuals of these end-of-the-age days are at the head of the line of rebellious humanity. God's words through David more nearly reflect this generation than they do David's:

> God looked down from heaven upon the children of men, to see if there were any that did understand, that did seek God.

> Every one of them is gone back; they are altogether become filthy. There is none that doeth good, no, not one.
>
> Have the workers of iniquity no knowledge, who eat up my people as they eat bread? They have not called upon God. (Psalms 53:2–4)

The genius of this world is but condemned foolishness in the eyes of God. His view of wisdom is all that matters.

> The fear of the LORD is the beginning of wisdom: and the knowledge of the holy is understanding. (Proverbs 9:10)

May 30, 2011
"Rapture" at Center of End-Times Storm

The couple of weeks just past bring in focus—for me, at least—stark reminders of the times in which we find ourselves, in relationship to Bible prophecy. Geophysical disturbances wreaking death tolls in the central United States are part of events engendering the sense of the lateness of the hour, prophetically speaking. The tornado that tore apart Joplin, Missouri, killing more than one hundred people and injuring hundreds of others, certainly adds to the sense of this being a prophetic hour. Studies show that records for devastating storms, earthquakes, and other such phenomena seem to be falling with each month that passes.

I personally had my life touched by the most recent outbreak near Oklahoma City, when one of my closest friends in ministry lost everything he owns, while, thankfully, he, his wife, and neighbors were safe in a storm shelter. We have written many times in these commentaries—and others have written in their commentaries—about the frequency and intensity with which so many things that appear to be end-times indicators are storming upon a world ripe for God's judgment. The birth-pang convulsions are front and center of our daily, even hourly, headlines.

World economic crises continue to mount, but are pushed to the back burner as far as headlines are concerned, because things of more immediate import crowd them out for the moment. Still, the global economic meltdown continues. The U.S. is in a position out of which it looks impossible to ever emerge. The rest of the world, particularly Europe, is in even worse fiscal condition. The powers that be, the global monetary gurus, seem to have become calloused to the truly monumental seriousness of the situation. It is as if they believe they can indefinitely delay the inevitable payments coming due.

The monetary manipulators have their eyes set on a completely changed economic order as the solution, no doubt. They need a crisis of major magnitude in order to galvanize all of their elements of aspiration into rearrangements which they can completely put under their collective, controlling thumb.

At the same time, things are heating up that involve the U.S. and the world dealing with the nation Israel. There is no more profound signal of where this generation stands on God's prophetic timeline than things going on in this arena of geopolitical activity.

The American administration speaks out of both sides of its mouth, in one breath betraying Israel in doing things like selling arms to Israel's enemy Arab states, but denying arms sales to the Jewish state.

Over the last year, the United States refused to approve any major Israeli weapons requests. Government sources asserted that the refusal represented a White House policy to link most arms sales to Israel to progress in the U.S. plan to establish a Palestinian state in the West Bank.

At the same time, Obama has approved more than $10 billion worth of arms sales to Arab League states, including Egypt, Kuwait, Jordan, Morocco, Saudi Arabia, and the United Arab Emirates.[89]

In the next breath, President Obama demands the impossible of Israeli Prime Minister Benjamin Netanyahu. Then, after receiving so much negative backlash, he backtracks on his declaration that Israel must give the Palestinians land so the 1967 borders can be reestablished—claiming the U.S. is an unmovable friend of the Jewish nation.

Israel's being at the center of the vital issues of peace and security for that Jewish state and for the world cannot be overemphasized. This is the number-one signal that we are bumping up against the very end of this dispensation—the Age of Grace.

This fact and all of the other things of prophetic significance we write about week after week are overwhelming in the weight of evidence they present, telling the discerning student of Bible prophecy and observer of the times that Christ's shout "Come up here!" must be near indeed.

And, this brings me to the interesting thing I would like to point out at this most crucial hour. Thanks to Harold Camping, I believe the world has moved forward a significant notch in the matter of nearing the end of the age. One news media scoffer reported the following:

> When the world did not end at precisely 6 p.m. yesterday, Doomsday prophet Robert Fitzpatrick's fragile grasp on reality crumbled.
>
> "I don't understand why nothing is happening," said Fitzpatrick, flipping through his Bible for clues to why Rapture failed to show up on time. "It's not a mistake. I did what I had to do. I did what the Bible said," he said, looking increasingly disheveled and confused as he stood in Times Square before mocking crowds.
>
> Fitzpatrick is a follower of Harold Camping, 89, an Oakland, Calif., evangelist who promised that on Judgment Day the righteous would be sucked up to heaven while sinners—even children—were to rot among fires, earthquakes and tsunamis engulfing the Earth.[90]

Now, I said above that, thanks to Harold Camping, I believe the world has moved forward a significant notch in the matter of nearing the end of the age. The scoffers are fully out of the woodwork, that's for certain. Camping's failed prediction brings 2 Peter 3:3–4 into focus as never before:

> Knowing this first, that there shall come in the last days scoffers, walking after their own lusts,
>
> And saying, Where is the promise of his coming? For since the fathers fell asleep, all things continue as they were from the beginning of the creation.

Todd and I have received some proof of this on an up-close-and-personal basis via e-mail. Here are but a few examples.

- "How is it up in heaven?"
- "We're enjoying hour after hour laughing our [posteriors] off at the great stuff you have on your website (on our off time, of course). Keep up the great work...what a bunch of kooks!"
- "You don't really actually believe in this garbage do you? Well I guess we can just all wait and see soon that you are all crazy and full of crap. LOL! What a crock! Aaaahahah ahahahahahahahahah huuuuuuuuuuuh AAAaaaahahaha hahahahahahaha Now will you get a life?"
- "Really—are you retarded? Did you experience brain damage in an accident? You idiots.... Taking money from common people.... You will roast if there is a god."
- "You are all idiots, really.... Congratulations on the brilliant predictions. You are retarded, you are a moron. You should be poor and homeless soon. Happy rapture day—you [expletive deleted]."

Well, you get the drift of the comments that make Mr. Camping's failed prediction of Rapture out to be ours as well.

Yes, 2 Peter 3:3–4 is most assuredly in the process of being fulfilled. But, that's nothing new. We have seen such scoffing for...well, decades.

Here is the thing I want you to see that I find so fascinating. With all of the obvious prophetic indicators in play every hour of every day at present, we now have the word "Rapture" in the middle of it all! People now know what the Rapture is by definition, at least to some extent.

Whereas the "Left Behind" series by Tim LaHaye and Jerry Jenkins made some aware of the word "rapture," Camping, through demonstrable media hatred for anything truly Christian, has made the word practically a household term. Mocking or not, the ubiquitous use of the term has left most within the U.S. and much of Europe, at least, without excuse.

The Lord of Heaven never brings His judgment and wrath without sufficient warning. The world is hearing the sirens…

Evil End-of-Days Behavior

June 6, 2011
End-Times Violence in View

Memorial Day 2011, the holiday this year to remember those who have died fighting to keep American liberty alive, turned violent across the nation, the youthful, lawless bands making a mockery of our free society. In so doing, yet another prophetic signal of the end of the age crawled to the forefront of our headlines.

A few of the episodes of evil assaulting law and order comes from one report. The event known as "Urban Weekend" spawned many such displays of lawlessness. In Miami, even one gay organization head called for a restoration of civility.

> [Herb] Sosa, president of Unity Coalition, Miami-Dade County's leading Hispanic gay-rights group, said he's concerned some people have called him racist, after he demanded an end to Urban Weekend.
>
> "It has nothing to do with racism," said Sosa, who lives near 9th Street in South Beach. "It's a lack of respect

> for the city they're visiting. It's as simple as that. This morning, there were six cars parked on my block with their mirrors ripped off, their antennas ripped off."[91]

Reports of violent gang activity and intrusions into private Memorial Day gatherings caused anger among Miami residents. Sosa was but one who let his ire be known to the mayor.

Far to the north, the violence was even more pronounced.

> Fights broke out among rival gang members on Carson Beach in South Boston yesterday and spilled out across the city, triggering a massive law enforcement response from at least five agencies to stem the violence.
>
> Police said the gang members are part of a group of more than one thousand youths who have used social media sites like Facebook to plan unruly gatherings on the beach on three of the past four nights.
>
> The groups have been larger and rowdier than even veteran South Boston troopers remember.
>
> "Veteran troopers assigned to the State Police barracks for a couple of decades have never seen as large a volume of kids that were there tonight," [a police spokesman] said.[92]

While fights started spontaneously over the city of Boston, requiring that mob-control law enforcement get involved en masse, things in Charlotte, North Carolina, exploded in violence as well. A Memorial Day-related festival turned into the rage of youthful gangs in that city, and one man reported:

> "There were two female traffic officers and one male officer, and they were, like, taking cover because they didn't know what was going on," [Andy] David says. David says he was running with a crowd, "and then we looked to our right, and there was a guy just laying there and blood was pouring from him."
>
> One man died, another was injured, and it all led to one of the city's largest mass arrests.[93]

These outbreaks were not isolated to Miami, Boston, and Charlotte. Similar acts of rage in the streets spanned the country over the holiday period. The availability of Internet is pointed to as helping those responsible for organizing the violence.

Like with the "days of rage" we hear about that are planned for the Middle East and the many violent displays in Europe exploding over economic turmoil, America is beginning to reap the violence of refusal to discipline ourselves in every way discipline should have for decades been applied. This neglect now means the chickens are coming home to roost, as President Obama's America-hating former pastor, Jeremiah Wright, said of our nation deserving being attacked on September 11, 2001.

And, no, I'm not agreeing with Wright that America deserves such attacks. I'm simply trying to point out that our failure to tend properly to matters of morality, law, and order now is causing the nation to inherit the whirlwind of consequences. For example, the violent intrusions from across our borders to the south, with American ranchers, border patrol officers, and illegal aliens trying to find a better life for themselves are being butchered by the drug cartel thugs, because the U.S. Constitution about governing immigration has been ignored by this administration.

This neglect is particularly manifest within the nation's youth gangs. The dumbing down in education of the black and Hispanic—and, yes, the dumbing down of Caucasian youths, too—and the ever-expanding welfare rolls destroy incentive to improve the individual. Lawmakers making every effort in 1963 to kick the God of Heaven out of America's public classrooms lies at the heart of the tragedy.

We have written on many occasions that the perilous times Paul the apostle warned about are upon this fallen world. He wrote in prophetic terms that people in the days just before Christ returns will be "fierce." Jesus Himself foretold that it would be in that day "as it was in the days of Noah."

Violence filled the whole earth in the days before the Flood of Noah's time. Daniel the prophet said the end would be with a flood. Violence is surely an ever more observable part of that end-times tsunami about to swallow this generation.

June 13, 2011
The U.S.-Kings of the East Connection

A most interesting bit of news jumped out at me. It wasn't something I hadn't thought of; I've written about it and spoken about it in interviews. But, here it was, acknowledged in a secular news forum that—to me, at least—confirms a prophetic reality.

> President Obama has declared that an economic catastrophe will result if the U.S. debt ceiling isn't raised within a matter of weeks in order to meet the nation's payment obligations. Raising the debt ceiling is something a significant number of Republican members of Congress, in

> particular, don't want to do without cuts of $1.5–$2.5 trillion in future federal spending.
>
> To many global economic analysts, America defaulting is unthinkable.
>
> Li Daokui, an adviser to the People's Bank of China, said a default could undermine the U.S. dollar, and Beijing needed to dissuade Washington from pursuing this course of action.... "I think there is a risk that the U.S. debt default may happen," Li told reporters on the sidelines of a forum in Beijing. "The result will be very serious and I really hope that they would stop playing with fire." Interviews with government officials and investors show they consider a default such a grim—and remote—possibility that it was nearly impossible to imagine. "How can the U.S. be allowed to default?" said an official at India's central bank. "We don't think this is a possibility because this could then create huge panic globally."[94]

Here is the singular thought from the experts in this story that confirmed for me my own thinking over the years of observing U.S. positioning, as juxtaposed against other world powers. It comes from someone within Oman, who speaks for the sultanate and its Persian Gulf neighbors:

> "Our economies are substantially tied up with the U.S. financial developments," said a senior central bank official, who spoke on condition of anonymity.[95]

The bottom line is that if the United States economy suffers catastrophic meltdown, the whole world will come crashing down as well. The entire world—including the growing behemoth, China—is inextricably linked to the financial influence America exerts.

This is not a boast; it is fact. And this is why there is such distress and perplexity among the world's nations, fiscally speaking. The other national entities can't simply cut themselves loose from U.S. influence and survive. That is why, despite all of the complaining and posturing by the Chinese government, the leaders of the newfound capitalistic mega power have to accept America's indebtedness to them, no matter how slow-paying the U.S. might be. The Chinese are, after all, the most patient of all people.

And this is where I believe the prophetic picture begins to form with regard to this king of the kings of the East nations of Revelation 16:12.

The inscrutable Chinese powerbrokers need the U.S. to continue building its burgeoning economic base. They siphon America's economic lifeblood hourly the way Count Dracula suctions his victims' blood in the vampire movies. They will neither call in America's indebtedness, nor engage in major military troublemaking that would stanch the flow into their coffers.

Those coffers are being filled for one purpose, and it is prophetic. For years—during the days of the Cold War and before—China has had the ability to raise a force of 200 million troops. That number, according to Revelation 9:16, is the number that the kinds of the East will bring across the dried-up Euphrates.

However, such a force, which prophecy indicates will destroy one-third of all humanity, could not be equipped with military assets that could do the job. There wasn't enough funding to underwrite such a force. America's wealth is what is helping to prepare the way for the kings of the East. We are funding, thus fueling, its military ambitions for the dastardly, decimating job it will do in fulfillment of its biblically prophetic destiny.

The oil fields of the Middle East lie on the other side of the Euphrates River from China, a voracious consumer of energy.

> A new report says that China has overtaken the United States as the world's biggest consumer of energy. Oil company BP said Wednesday that China moved to the top in 2010 with 20.3 percent of global demand, ahead of the United States at 19 percent. The report says China's consumption rose by 11.2 percent last year compared with 3.7 percent in the United States. China's surge led a 5.6 percent increase in global energy demand, the biggest one-year jump since 1973.[96]

It is the American dollar—as anemic as it seems these days—that is filling the Chinese coffers, thus funding its military. The leadership of the great dragon nation is still bent on world domination, make no mistake.

June 20, 2011
End-Times Signals

Two end-of-the-age signals in particular punctuate the news this week. Both portend dire things to come. Each, at the same time, provides comfort to those who are looking for Christ's Second Coming.

While prophetic indicators are in every direction one looks, one signal I find especially fascinating as well as portentous is the tightening noose of government around our lives. Such intrusion is threatening for the obvious reasons. My fascination stems from the fact that it is being carried out with such ease. Those doing the intruding are able to make a seemingly legitimate case for tightening the noose—a case against which it's hard to argue.

We don't have to search out the Washington D.C. basements of conspiracy theorists or the deep, caligionous cabals of the Bilderbergers to find evidence of the strangling of freedom. We have only to consider what's going on in good ol' hometown USA.

> CEDAR FALLS, Iowa—The government of a Midwest college town is now requiring the city's businesses and apartment buildings to post their keys outside, so authorities can enter the properties "in case of emergency." According to the Cedar Falls City Council, the plan to require property owners to post keys in designated lockboxes—that city officials can open with a master key—is a justified way to allow the fire department and other authority's access without breaking down doors, especially in cases of false alarms. To many Cedar Falls citizens, however, giving the city keys to their businesses and homes is a gross violation of the Fourth Amendment's private property rights and a plan fraught with potential for abuse.[97]

This is not a conspiracy "theory," but a local government already putting legal shoe-leather to their intentions of "helping" the citizenry of a small city within the Hawkeye caucus state. The mind leaps backward in time, from what such government "concern" might mean in the future for small-town America to a news item from the same organization almost two years ago:

JUNE 2011

> A newly released Rand Corporation report proposes the federal government create a rapid deployment "Stabilization Police Force" that would be tasked with "shaping an environment before a conflict" and restoring order in times of war, natural disaster or national emergency. But civil libertarians are worried just exactly what the force would do, domestically or overseas. Page 16 of the 213-page report says the new elite unit's purpose depends on where it is and who would be in command.
>
> "The answer to this question (about its purpose) depends on the situation into which an SPF might be inserted. The SPF could be used for missions such as: shaping an environment before a conflict; law enforcement duties in an active conflict environment; or security, stability, transition and reconstruction (SSTR) operations after a conflict. It could operate as an independent entity under a U.S. ambassador or a UN Senior Representative to the Secretary General (SRSG), or as a force element reporting to a Joint Task Force (JTF) commander," the report states. The purpose statement doesn't say where the new unit would be deployed.[98]

That report from a year and a half ago went on to suggest that such a force would almost certainly be used in the U.S. to supplement martial law enforcement in case of civil chaos.

One expert in the study of government control of civilians during times of unrest said the report leads him to believe the goal is power, and that a major springboard for such a power grab comes from the economy:

> Conditions have been intentionally created within the United States which makes some kind of chaotic catastrophe very likely. This event could be anything the mind of man can dream up due to the overwhelming public debt and huge deficit which is budgeted to grow by trillions over the next few years.[99]

Keep in mind that statement was made nearly two years ago. We are seeing the beginning of unrest from just such a building economic threat. It is unclear where the proposed domestic civilian control force stands, but those who seek ever-increasing power and authority never let up in their quest. The lust for power is built, it seems, into the fallen nature of man.

Perhaps the next arena we can look for in which a power grab will emerge is that of the Internet. The current cyberspace chaos created by the hackers is bound to bring out the controllers.

> WASHINGTON—A shadowy group of hackers behind a string of recent cyberattacks claimed to have breached the U.S. Senate website and taken internal data.
>
> The Senate Sergeant at Arms, responsible for congressional security, confirmed there had been an intrusion into the server hosting the public website, [www.senate.gov], but said no sensitive information was compromised.
>
> The hacker group, which goes by the name of "Lulz Security," published files online at [www.lulzsecurity.com] said to have been swiped from [www.senate.gov].
>
> "This is a small, just-for-kicks release of some internal data from [www.senate.gov]—is this an act of war, gentlemen?" Lulz Security said in a statement.

> "We don't like the US government very much," the group added. "Their sites aren't very secure."[100]

All business transactions—meaning the world economy—is headed toward a paperless, cashless, and unified means of monetary transaction. Additionally, governments desperately desire to invoke taxes to relieve the chaos that shortfalls are creating and will create in the near future.

There is no doubt, in my thinking, that the Internet is about to have some heavy cyberspace chains attached in very short order. Ultimately, Antichrist's regime will be a hybrid Internet, with a form of electronic funds transfer governing in some way that will give the beast absolute control of all buying and selling (Revelation 13:16–18).

The second news topic, and one of even more important to the end-times picture than that of growing governmental intrusion in America, is the European Union inserting itself more heavily into Israel's business. The news story cuts to the heart of the end of the age from the perspective of Bible prophecy.

> Following a French initiative to restart negotiations between Israel and the Palestinian Authority by convening a Middle East peace conference in Paris, the European Union is now advocating an international peace plan as an alternative to a unilateral Palestinian plan to secure state recognition at the UN in September.
>
> In a letter to U.S. Secretary of State Hillary Clinton, UN Secretary-General Ban Ki-moon and Russian Foreign Minister Sergei Lavrov, the EU's foreign policy chief, Catherine Ashton, called for the urgent convening of the

> Middle East Quartet. The Quartet—the U.S., EU, UN, and Russia—would gather as a precursor for support for a peace [based upon President Barack Obama's 1967 borders suggestion].[101]

Many Bible prophecy students have long believed that Europe is the reviving Roman Empire out of which will emerge "the prince that shall come" (Daniel 9:26–27). The beast, as Antichrist is called, will confirm a covenant of peace for seven years with Israel, and, in effect, with the other nations of the world, according to the prophet Daniel. The EU and Israel being at the center of this drive to institute a humanistic peace plan is the number-one signal that Christ is now at the door, readying to shout "come up here!" (Revelation 4:1).

June 27, 2011
Pastors' Powerlessness

A power vacuum exists today that was foretold almost two thousand years ago. Its effects on this generation and beyond are profound, and are destined to make an even more deleterious impact on America and the world in the days just ahead. The apostle Paul prophesied the following:

> This know, also, that in the last days perilous times shall come. For men shall be…having a form of godliness, but denying the power of it. (2 Timothy 3:1, 5a)

Many pastors within Christianity today, I am sorry to have to say, are complicit in helping fulfill this prophecy on an hourly basis.

First, let's define the term "Christian pastors." Within the context of Paul's prophecy that I wish to examine here, I refer to those pastors who truly preach and teach that Jesus Christ is the only way to redemption, to reconciliation with God the Father. All others who claim to be clergy within Christianity I completely disregard, because God's Word discounts them as false prophets, as defined by the following Scripture, to give but one example:

> But there were false prophets also among the people, even as there shall be false teachers among you, who privily shall bring in damnable heresies, even denying the Lord that bought them, and bring upon themselves swift destruction.
>
> And many shall follow their pernicious ways; by reason of whom the way of truth shall be evil spoken of.
>
> And through covetousness shall they, with feigned words, make merchandise of you; whose judgment now for a long time lingereth not, and their damnation slumbereth not. (2 Peter 2:1–3)

Again, to be clear, when I say "Christian pastors," I'm referring to genuine pastors: Bible-believing preachers who lift up Christ as the only way to salvation.

Some will say that Paul's "perilous times" warning of men who would display the end-times characteristic of "having a form of godliness, but denying the power of it" applies to the false teachers of Peter's prophecy, not to true preachers called by God to be shepherds of His flock. I agree that Paul's 2 Timothy prophecy applies to those interlopers who deny Jesus Christ as the only way to redemption.

However, the accusation against those who have a form of godliness, but deny the power of it" can apply as well to God's true shepherds. The condemnation is in some ways even more to the point than when leveled at the false preachers and teachers. It's my contention that Christian pastors today—and, sadly, I believe this includes the majority of them—deny the power of God when they deliberately cast aside prophecy given in the Bible that is for time yet future.

We have written in these commentaries, and many others have written and spoken on the fact that God's Word, the Bible, consists of at least 27 percent prophecy. Half of that prophecy has been fulfilled; half is yet to be fulfilled. Although it can be proven through study of the Scripture and by examining history that the Bible is always accurate in putting forth prophecy in past instances, pastors—preachers and teachers—consistently and persistently ignore preaching and teaching things to come.

By this willful disregard for presenting this vast body of scriptural truth, men of God—called and anointed by the Lord as guardians of His truth and shepherds of His flocks—deny the great power wrapped up in the astonishing reality that our God is the only one who knows the end from the beginning—and in excruciating detail, might I add.

For the most part, preachers of today seemingly avoid the prophetic Word at any cost. And, in God's holy economy, the cost must be astronomical. These shepherds of God's precious people are denying those people the assurance of the hope that He promises. Jesus Christ, their Lord and Savior, is the fruition of God's magnificent plan for their journey into forever. With the knowledge of Christ's return plainly given as imminent in God's love letter to mankind, the born again should be living victoriously, not with cringing fear or, even worse, in almost complete apathy.

The prophetic Word says:

> Teaching us that, denying ungodliness and worldly lusts, we should live soberly, righteously, and godly, in this present world,
>
> Looking for that blessed hope, and the glorious appearing of the great God and our Savior Jesus Christ,
>
> Who gave himself for us, that he might redeem us from all iniquity, and purify unto himself a peculiar people, zealous of good works. (Titus 2:12–14)

The majority of those who aren't informed about what's going to happen next in this judgment-bound world, or who are totally unconcerned about things of God, are fed pabulum rather than meat for living life in the way the Lord intended. These are as often as not force-fed the prosperity, name-it-and-claim-it false teaching that is anathema to truth from the Word of God. The only ones accumulating wealth are the preachers of such spirit-dulling poison.

To the pastors and teachers who do in fact teach doctrine and sound biblical principles, may the Lord bless you to the extent to which you remain faithful to break the Bread of Life in the way it should be fed to your flocks. But, if you don't include prophecy as an important and generous part of your messages—that Jesus is coming again, and might come at any moment—you are falling far short of deserving full commendation. You are denying the true power of God. You are exhibiting only a form of godliness.

Respectfully, please pay attention, you who are the truth-bearing pastors of our Holy God. These are the times to which all of Bible prophecy has pointed for millennia. These are perilous times. Signals are rampant that this generation is the generation that will almost certainly see the Lord's return in power and glory. Israel and the peace process, with all nations beginning to turn against that state, dear pastors, is the number-one signal that we are bumping up against the very end of this swiftly fleeting age. Christ's shout, "Come up here," is imminent!

You will be held accountable at the judgment seat of Christ for how you treat His whole Word in feeding your flock. Jesus spoke to the great power and importance resident within prophecy while addressing the churches. John recorded what the resurrected Lord directed him to write:

> The Revelation of Jesus Christ, which God gave unto him, to show unto his servants things which must shortly come to pass; and he sent and signified it by his angel unto his servant, John,
>
> Who bore record of the word of God, and of the testimony of Jesus Christ, and of all things that he saw....
>
> Behold, he cometh with clouds, and every eye shall see him, and they also who pierced him; and all kindreds of the earth shall wail because of him. Even so, Amen.
>
> I am Alpha and Omega, the beginning and the ending, saith the Lord, who is, and who was, and who is to come, the Almighty. (Revelation 1:1–2; 7–8)

Terry James

July 2011

Restrainer of Evil in Wicked Times

July 4, 2011
Restraining Evil

When looking at the black-and-white films the Allies shot within the Nazi death camps following victory over Hitler's Germany in World War II, it is difficult to comprehend that evil had the tethers of restraint during the time of that horrendous regime. The images of walking skeletons that were the Jewish "survivors" of those camps remain etched in the memory of anyone who has seen those videos.

The same level of pictorial record doesn't exist for the genocidal rampages inflicted on their own people by Joseph Stalin, Mao Tse-tung, Pol Pot, Idi Amin, and the murderers of the other despotic regimes in modern times. However, eyewitness accounts and some photographic evidence make it hard to fathom that those beastly tyrants were restrained in their butchery.

The Bible nonetheless bears witness that God the Holy Spirit governs the consciences of human beings. In biblically prophetic terms, this truth is most evident in Paul's second epistle to the Thessalonians:

> For the mystery of iniquity doth already work; only he who now letteth will let, until he be taken out of the way.
>
> And then shall that wicked one be revealed, whom the Lord shall consume with the spirit of his mouth, and shall destroy with the brightness of his coming. (2 Thessalonians 2:7–8)

Paul the apostle was saying in this prophecy that evil was at work in a big way even at the time he was writing the letter. Still, the Holy Spirit would continue to restrain that evil until the Holy Spirit removes as restrainer of evil. Then all Hell will break loose as the Antichrist is revealed. The spirit of Antichrist is already present in the world—and was manifest even during John's day (read 1 John 4:1–3). The mystery of iniquity about which Paul prophesied and this spirit of Antichrist are intertwined and interlinked in the ancient web of lawlessness we call evil.

Jesus foretold what will happen once the restrainer (the Holy Spirit) removes from governing the wickedness that is in the hearts and minds of people of the post-Rapture world:

> For then shall be great tribulation, such as was not since the beginning of the world to this time, no, nor ever shall be. (Matthew 24:21)

The Lord prophesied just how bad things would become:

> And except those days should be shortened, there should no flesh be saved; but for the elect's sake those days shall be shortened. (Matthew 24:22)

July 2011

God will shorten the days of that time of Great Tribulation, because if He let things go on to their ultimate conclusion, without the return of Christ, every being of flesh and blood on the planet would be destroyed. Such is the mystery of iniquity that exists today, and will become exponentially worse once the restraint on evil is no longer in place. Then, the ultimately evolved man—as evolution would have it—will step to the forefront of fallen human history. Antichrist will inflict horrors on the people of earth in ways Hitler, Stalin, Mao, and the rest of history's madmen could not have even imagined. His regime will be the most bloodthirsty of all time.

Lawlessness is everywhere we look today. Whether considering the Middle East and the riotous rebellions, the unions of Greece who threaten to destroy all civility because of the austerity measures being voted, or thinking on America and the unbridled thievery of youth groups known now as flash mobs, the evil the Bible deems the mystery of iniquity is swelling like a great caldera that is about to explode across the world.

A large number of youths attacked pedestrians in an area of Philadelphia on Saturday, July 25, sending people to the hospital with broken limbs and other injuries. Such is becoming the way of many youth gangs in the larger cities around America.

In some cities, the new lawless group activity is something called mob snatching or mob grabbing, in which the youngsters, ages eleven to nineteen, first organize their next hit online, then quickly rendezvous near their next victim-merchant. They rush into the store, begin grabbing anything they can, and bolt out the door before any of the hapless store personnel know what has hit them.

The youth, particularly within the inner cities, have been

taught by cultural inculcation that they have been held down by the affluent, so their actions are justified. It is no more than simply—the inference is—Robin Hood robbing the evil sheriff of Nottingham.

Can there be much doubt that if they will commit such bold acts now, when the Holy Spirit is no longer restraining such evil thinking and actions, America will quickly become a hellish existence in which anything goes? There are growing concerns that a breakdown of society within the U.S. is inevitable. Such concerns were voiced earlier this year by—of all sources—a Russian diplomat. Imagine! The Russians are worried about America becoming a tyrant state because of the signs of coming anarchy.

Former CIA official Philip Giraldi said the following about a law that the Obama administration is trying to get through Congress to combat people who oppose government, or who act in terroristic ways, such as is the case of the "flash mob-ocracy" that is developing.

> The mainstream media has made no effort to inform the public of the impending Violent Radicalization and Home-grown Terrorism Prevention Act. The Act, which was sponsored by Congresswoman Jane Harman of California, was passed in the House by an overwhelming 405 to 6 vote on October 24 and is now awaiting approval by the Senate Homeland Security Committee, which is headed by Senator Joseph Lieberman of Connecticut.
>
> Harman's bill contends that the United States will soon have to deal with home grown terrorists and that something must be done to anticipate and neutralize the problem.... Harman's bill does not spell out terrorist

> behavior and leaves it up to the Commission [which will govern the implementation of the bill] itself to identify what is terrorism and what isn't.[102]

It is almost as if the U.S. federal governmental powers that be have taken Paul's 2 Thessalonians 2:7–8 passage to heart. It seems they anticipate a time when draconian measures will become necessary to restrain the evil that is coming. Antichrist's restraint will be even more draconian, but his own evil will far surpass all other iniquity of history, the Bible foretells.

July 11, 2011
Turkey's Magog Moment

It seems at least forty years ago that I read Salem Kirban's novel, *666*. A major portion of the fictional account of the times at the end of the Church Age dealt with the Ezekiel 38-39 Gog-Magog attack into the Middle East by Russia and all of the nations the prophecy foretells will storm toward Israel to destroy that nation and plunder the land.

Ezekiel prophesied a vicious coalition of anti-God, Israel-hating hordes that will rage in full fury, taking peace from the earth. Among the chief people mentioned who are to be part of that assault is "the house of Togarmah of the north quarters, and all its bands" (Ezekiel 38:6b).

Author Kirban portrayed with powerful imagery, I thought, the warlord the Bible calls "Gog" and many of the other characters God's Word forewarns will attempt to inflict murderous damage on the chosen nation and on the world. His account was particularly interesting, in retrospect, because he seems to have been somewhat prescient with his fictional presentation that the attack would be undertaken with ancient, not modern, weaponry—i.e., Kirban's novel account had the Gog-Magog forces storming over the land using the literal war-making tools Ezekiel reported in his vision of that future invasion.

> And the word of the LORD came unto me, saying,
>
> Son of man, set thy face against Gog, of the land of Magog, the chief prince of Meshech and Tubal, and prophesy against him,
>
> And say, Thus saith the Lord GOD: Behold, I am against thee, O Gog, the chief prince of Meshech and Tubal,
>
> And I will turn thee back, and put hooks into thy jaws, and I will bring thee forth, and all thine army, horses, and horsemen, all of them clothed with all sorts of armor, even a great company with bucklers and shields, all of them handling swords. (Ezekiel 38:1–3)

I say Kirban was seemingly prescient, because his novelistic scenario included a technological breakthrough, as I recall, that had neutered conventional weaponry. The engines of modern warfare—as the author would have it—could no longer be employed. It was something along the lines of what has come to be known as electromagnetic pulse (EMP) technology—a weapon touted to have the capability of frying the electronic circuitry of modern machinery.

So, in the author's story, Gog led his forces down toward Israel, where, of course, the evil ones met their complete destruction when the Lord intervened, as the prophecy says He will do when the actual attack occurs.

Turkey's history is replete with accounts of its cavalry exploits. Its armies are famous—or in some cases infamous—for their use of horses in warfare. Its horsemen are legendary in, for example, firing arrows while at full gallop. Even today, some of the finest horseflesh is found in the region Ezekiel calls Togarmah.

While I find fascinating the fact that Kirban could look a bit into the future to anticipate progression of modern weaponry, I'm still of the opinion that the weaponry Ezekiel saw in the vision God gave him was the weaponry of today, not actual horses and accoutrements. As a matter of fact, I'm not fully convinced that EMP truly is capable of doing what I've read time after time in e-mails it will one day do to, for example, America's power grids and its sophisticated tools of war.

Such "warnings" have been issued as attacks about to strike for decades. I'm not saying some such things can't happen, but it's becoming akin to the little boy who cried wolf. It is incumbent upon us who are watchmen to weigh carefully things that are shaping that will likely be prophetic in nature—then report with responsible accuracy.

Certainly, Turkey has the history and the ability to raise a cavalry that could do battle if modern war machinery was rendered useless. Does that scenario look to be the likely unfolding of Bible prophecy regarding the Gog-Magog assault? I, at least, don't think so. The world is facing a truly massive event as given in the Ezekiel 38–39 prophecy. Any threat horseflesh might present seems puny in comparison to the horrendous carnage described.

One development that should be most mesmerizing to the observer of things taking place for the wind-up of this present dispensation does involve Turkey, the region Ezekiel called Togarmah. Until very recently, Turkey was one of a few of Israel's friends in or around the Middle East. The relationship has changed in ways that can only be described as portentous. A report by Joel Richardson begins as follows:

> With Prime Minister Erdogan's Islamist AK party having seized its third landslide election victory in Turkey, many throughout the international community have been watching to see what will be next on the Turkish agenda.
>
> Now there are strong indicators in the Turkish media that Turkey is planning on literally doubling the size of its army—this coming from the nation that already has the largest army in Middle East and the second-largest army in NATO, second only to the United States. Presently, Turkey's army has over five hundred thousand troops. Its army is larger than France, Germany, and England combined. And now Turkish media are reporting that they are planning on adding another five hundred thousand paid soldiers.[103]

It is a legitimate question to ask: Is Turkey in the process of preparing for the fulfillment of its Magog moment?

July 18, 2011
Rome's Place in Prophecy

Economic emergencies in the news turned my thoughts to Rome and its place in the final unfolding of Bible prophecy. Following the trail of great world empires to today's news headlines leads inescapably to the conclusion that the birthplace of the Caesars figures to be at the very center of end-times turbulence.

Terry James

JULY 2011

Daniel the prophet gave a sweeping panorama of the major empires that would appear in the time of Babylonian King Nebuchadnezzar and conclude with the world system of government being broken to dust (Daniel 2:26–45). This prophecy of humanistic dominion over the world and its dramatic end came through Daniel's interpretation of the king's night vision about a gigantic, metallic man-image.

Those who have studied the appearing, dominion, and destruction of each succeeding kingdom within the prophecy almost without exception believe the iron legs of Nebuchadnezzar's man-image to represent the Roman Empire. That powerful empire divided into the two legs—the western leg, with Rome as capital, and the eastern leg, with the capital being Constantinople (now known as Istanbul).

Rome is most important to think upon in Daniel's overall prophetic unveiling because it is the "people" out of whom the one called "the prince that shall come" will emerge to step onto the stage of history as dictator of earth's final human government (Daniel 9:26–27). This brings us to some logical conclusions, I think. Since most all other indicators are now on stage for human history's final act, should Rome not be front and center as the end-times spotlight illuminates?

To set that stage again—as we have done so many times in these columns—here are some of the main signals that we are near the end of the end times:

The Kings of the East—Revelation 9 and 16. China and the powers of Asia are on the rise as potentially earth's most powerful entities.

Gog-Magog—Ezekiel 8–39. Russia, Iran, Turkey, and others have formed alliances that continue to grow in strength.

The European Union (EU)—Daniel 9. The EU is forming the revived Roman Empire.

The United Nations—Psalms 2. This personifies mankind's globalist desire to throw off God's restraints.

Israel—Zechariah 12–14. Israel is at the center of hatred, both its Arab neighbors and the UN as a whole seeking to destroy God's chosen nation.

Cries for Peace—1 Thessalonians 5:3. These cries are coming from the international community, which is attempting to impose peace on Israel that would divide the land God gave the children of Abraham, Isaac, and Jacob.

Many more specific signposts indicate that the present world is at the end of the Age of Grace (Church Age). So, with all of the stage-setting for Christ's return in view, should Rome, the geographical as well as historical system that will produce the world's last and most terrible tyrant, not be front and center?

The answer of course, is yes, it must—and that geographical entity just happens to be at the center of one of the great end-times indicators not mentioned above, but most important to consider.

The love of money is the root of all evil (1 Timothy 6:10). This world system, whose would-be masters love the power wealth can generate, is caught up in what I believe is the catalyst for bringing Antichrist's regime to its prophesied position of satanic control. Most who believe they are destined to control the world don't have a clue that the great upheaval in economics they are struggling with is the result of the master manipulator—Satan himself—fomenting the tumult. The only way to ever reestablish any degree of control from this point is for there to take place a complete rearrangement of all matters monetary.

This rearrangement can't happen as long as national sovereignties exist—as long as there is relative liberty left on the planet. Therefore, it will take a crisis of monstrous proportion to bring everyone into compliance with controls of a completely changed world—a new economic world order.

Rome is at the very center of the great economic storm, as the following news excerpt reports:

> Italy's Unicredit bank fell by 20 percent last week and the decline continued today. Some blue chips such as Fiat had trading suspended due to the gravity of losses.
>
> Italy's citizens are generally frugal and pay by cash rather than by credit card (also to dodge taxation). The big debt problem in Italy is government debt. The country's debt amounts to $1.8 trillion, of which 26 percent must be refinanced in 2011 and 2012.
>
> As Italy has displayed stagnant growth for the past decade, impervious to governments of the left or the right, has a low degree of competitiveness and a low birth rate, analysts are questioning how Italy will be able to service its debts.
>
> This in turn creates a vicious cycle: The greater the pessimism that Italy cannot repay its debts the higher the cost of borrowing becomes fueling further pessimism until an explosion occurs.[104]

I firmly believe that the Rapture of the church is the crisis that will convince the world—the Western world, at least—to forfeit what little freedom there might be left, and give power and authority to the beast. Antichrist, son of Rome, Satan's ultimate dictator, will derive his power and control through a perverted economic system as foretold in Revelation 13:16–18.

Rome's place in prophecy is taking shape before the eyes of God's watchmen on the wall.

July 25, 2011
Sobering Scenario

As one who has at times dallied a bit in fiction writing from the biblically prophetic perspective, my novelistic interest was piqued this past week. A self-designated regular Rapture Ready visitor sent his speculations that have the bite of prophetic truth.

The writer struck a chord. Redistribution of wealth is the thing that his sobering scenario conjured in my mind. Rarely, if ever, and certainly not in great depth, has thinking of the catastrophic ramifications the Rapture will entail with regard to redistribution of wealth been forthcoming. Redistribution of wealth, of course, is a major pillar that supports the framework the devilish brains of the liberal ilk have constructed in foisting on all of us their thus far very successfully destructive social/cultural model.

Those who demand the American taxpayer fund a leisurely lifestyle for those who are capable of working, but won't, according to the scenario offered by our friend, would, on the surface, seem to have the perfect answer to their long-pursued dream of taking from the haves and giving to the have-nots: the Rapture!

Here's what Matthew wrote:

> I have been following Rapture Ready for years and have read hundreds of articles, but I don't think I have heard this theory yet:

Immediately after the Rapture, the world descends into a financial meltdown due to the current financial crisis coupled with the shock of the missing believers. A healthy portion of the missing people leave behind large sums of physical and liquid assets including bank accounts and property such as real estate, vehicles, weapons...you name it.

With the Holy Spirit removed, neighbors will be pillaging neighbors to hoard as much property from the missing people as possible. After the easy stuff is gone, identity thieves go wild and begin attacking bank accounts and stocks via computer.

Governments will do what they always do—eager to seize the assets of the missing people, they are faced with a problem: knowing whose assets are available to seize. It won't be as easy as searching the church directory, because many so-called Christians and church members will be left behind. Additionally many will be killed in the chaos, and others will use the Rapture as a smokescreen to flee from their financial and legal obligations.

In order to stop the losses brought about by identity thieves, the world will need to conduct a modern census of sorts. First, all electronic commerce will be frozen. Then everyone is required to "register" in order to buy and sell once again. During the registry process, some type of biometric or RFID [radio frequency identification] is applied to each person. Only those who register will be able to participate in commerce once again. After a reasonable period of registration, governments world-

> wide will immediately seize the assets of all those who failed to register.
>
> The pretext of the "mark of the beast" [will be] the need to stop the theft and looting. Only a "criminal" would refuse to register. In actuality, the government achieves the vehicle for a single currency and becomes the biggest looter of all.

Such a scenario isn't beyond the pale. At the very least, immediately following that great, imminent event, there will be confusion and fear that will cause the thin veneer of civility, law, and order to quickly shred.

Considering the rioting and other acts of ugly displays of discontent among the masses in current times, such a maddening thing as millions suddenly disappearing will be catalyst for creating mob rule of almost inconceivable proportion. The aftermath will make Hurricane Katrina's effects on New Orleans' ne'er-do-well looters seem tame by comparison.

The Holy Spirit's influence as restrainer will be missing, according to 2 Thessalonians 2. The truly beastly nature of lost mankind will emerge when the consciences of people left behind are no longer governed by the Creator of all things. Especially because of the material wealth left behind in this nation, America will be set up for incendiary ignition in much the way decades of decaying underbrush in a great forest acts as kindling for a great forest fire.

We have for some time written that we believe the Rapture will be the event that will pop the surreal bubble of economic insanity that we have watched grow for months. It is a bubble that has been built, in large part, by the very liberal social engineers mentioned earlier.

It is more than ironic that those same destructive would-be builders of a humanist utopia might finally have their crisis that is too good to waste. They will even be able to continue to build their political base by redistributing the wealth left behind. At least, that's the quite plausible conclusion implied by Matthew's post-Rapture scenario.

But the real result of such a scenario would be the New World Order builders achieving the power, the control after which they have always lusted. And the masses, frightened out of their wits, will, when such a scenario eventuates, willingly give that power and authority to any regime, to any dictator, who offers hope.

There is only one True Hope—the blessed hope of Titus 2:13. His Name is Jesus. If you haven't yet done so, receive Him now as your Savior. Don't be left behind.

Last-Days Diary
AUGUST 2011

The God-Haters Are Here

August 1, 2011
God's Irrelevance Becoming Prophetically Relevant

Todd Strandberg, my ever-inquisitive partner—we consider him our genius family member—reported last week on his probe of the atheists gathered in Las Vegas. A Rapture Ready friend who visits the site regularly sent a note pointing to a particular observation Todd made in his article. Todd wrote: "If they don't believe in a 'Guy up in the sky,' I don't understand why they would make such a fuss over Him."

That is a brilliant observation/question proving the Shakespearian maxim, "Brevity is the soul of wit." But the statement does much more than validate the thought from Hamlet. It shines the light of truth on the madness of the people of the planet more and more attempting to push the Almighty into irrelevance. Nowhere within the dynamic interactions of mankind is this determination to push God aside more manifest than in the Israeli/Palestinian confrontation in regards to the two-state controversy. The growing global mindset to make God's promises to the chosen people irrelevant is profoundly significant in terms of end-of-the-age Bible prophecy.

The following news item helps explain:

> The Bible is an "ancient holy book" that is irrelevant to the Palestinian Authority's aim to take over all of Judea and Samaria from the Jews, a PA activist said in a rare debate last week with a "settler" in a Washington synagogue.
>
> The Bible is full of "medieval" traditions that should not be considered or influence decisions on whether or not to create the Palestinian Authority as an independent state within Israel's borders, Dr. Hussein Ibish, Senior Fellow at the American Task Force on Palestine, said in the debate with David Ha'Ivri, director of the Shomron (Samaria) Liaison Office....
>
> Ibish's comments were in answer to Ha'Ivri's statement that Jerusalem is mentioned over eight hundred times in the Bible and not at all in the Koran and that most of the Biblical narrative relates to events in Judea and Samaria.
>
> The live debate on the subject "Palestinian State or Jewish Homeland?" came less than two months before the Arab League is expected to ask the United Nations to recognize "Palestine" as an independent country based on the Arab world's territorial and political demands, which deny recognizing Israel as a "Jewish" state....
>
> Ibish, born in Lebanon and a self-described agnostic, has campaigned on American campuses as executive director of the American Task Force for Palestine.[105]

God is deemed irrelevant by the movers and shakers in geopolitics, most of whom are agnostic or atheist in their worldviews.

AUGUST 2011

Bible prophecy is immeasurably moved forward in setting the stage for fulfillment with developing matters involving the push for a Palestinian state. Satanic tendrils can be sensed snaking through proceedings and enmeshing in spider-web fashion at the highest diplomatic levels.

Anti-Semitism is on the rise as strongly as in pre-Nazi Germany. Israel is the target of the God despisers while the world moves ever closer to Armageddon.

We returned this week from the Future Congress in Branson, where I spoke Sunday in a Power Point presentation I called "Omega Signs: Unmistakable Pointers to Christ's Any-Moment Intervention." A number of world leaders were shown in video clips at the beginning of the presentation, giving their opinions on the crises shaping up to be a catastrophic future for planet earth if the New World Order builders don't get their way. One key video clip that struck me as particularly telling of the satanic rage against Israel, thus against the God who made promises to the heirs of Abraham, Isaac, and Jacob, contained the answer to a question posed to Secretary-General of the United Nations, Ban Ki-moon.

The UN secretary-general was asked by the interviewer: "So, is there any doubt in your mind, as Secretary of the United Nations, that east Jerusalem, in particular, is occupied territory—that should not even be discussed in negotiations [about] the status of it as occupied territory, or do you have another perspective of it?"

Ki-moon answered: "The United Nations has made it quite clear that this is the occupied territory, and thus will treat it as such."

This statement by the man the United States government—

you and I—help support by funding the UN with far more billions of dollars than any nation, seethes with the collective rage of most member states of the UN body against God's chosen nation.

That world body is working maliciously and furiously to bring about the Palestinian state without Israel having any say in the matter. And that, of course, means that they think God has no say in the matter, either. One report says the following:

> Israeli officials believe that the Palestinians will avoid the UN Security Council and will appeal to the General Assembly to avoid an almost certain US veto. A Palestinian independent state is expected to gain the support of more than 140 countries of UN members.
>
> The PNA [Palestinian National Authority] is tirelessly working on the preparations ahead of the UN meeting in September, where a meeting on the final draft of the UN resolution would be held in Doha of Qatar on August 4.
>
> "We are in the final stages of discussion on the best possible mechanism. We will evaluate appealing directly to the UN or going to the UN Security Council even with the possibility of UN Veto," [a top PNA official] said. "The Palestinian plan would call on the world body to recognize an independent Palestinian state on the 1967 borders," he said.[106]

It is this very action—dividing Jerusalem—that will bring all nations to Armageddon, according to Joel 3:2. The attempt to make irrelevant the God of Heaven—the only God there is—is an act of collective suicide for the one world order builders. The

Lord has the final word on the foolhardy machinations of these neo-Babel architects:

> The kings of the earth set themselves, and the rulers take counsel together, against the LORD, and against his anointed, saying,
>
> Let us break their bands asunder, and cast away their cords from us.
>
> He who sitteth in the heavens shall laugh; the Lord shall have them in derision.
>
> Then shall he speak unto them in his wrath, and vex them in his sore displeasure.
>
> Yet have I set my king upon my holy hill of Zion.
>
> I will declare the decree: the LORD hath said unto me, Thou art my Son; this day have I begotten thee.
>
> Ask of me, and I shall give thee the heathen for thine inheritance, and the uttermost parts of the earth for thy possession.
>
> Thou shalt break them with a rod of iron; thou shalt dash them in pieces like a potter's vessel. (Psalms 2:2–9)

August 8, 2011
Prepping for the Crash

The Dow Jones Index fell more than 500 points on Thursday just past. Panicked European markets started the slide, and it is uncertain where the plunge will end. Fear is on the rise that a Great Depression-type economic crash is coming. Even the normally optimistic talk-show host Rush Limbaugh, who pontificates from his radio-bully pulpit about America's resilience against cyclical damage to the economy by liberal presidential administrations, is heard these days grumbling in undertones of trepidation. He worries about America's chances of survival with regard to the current debt crisis and the government's refusal or inability to stop the profligate spending.

No sooner had President Obama signed the just-passed legislation to raise the nation's debt ceiling, thus averting U.S. financial default, than monetary markets around the globe began reacting negatively. Wall Street stocks fell more than 2 percent. Japan's Nikkei fell approximately the same amount. Standard & Poor's economic outlook presented a bleak assessment; Moody's ratings service placed Washington's AAA credit score under a "negative outlook." Dagong, China's credit agency, downgraded America's credit from A+ to A. The S&P downgraded U.S. credit rating on debt over the weekend to AA.

No matter whether there is a temporary eventual uptick from these negative reactions, it is obvious that America's influence on the world's financial markets is profound, just as we have said in these columns time after time. The monetary moguls of planet earth are not favorably impressed with this nation's printing of more money to cover debts. No other nation in history has long been able to sustain such economic madness without collapse. Now is different from any other threatened collapse because America's crash would bring the entire world imploding to unprecedented depression.

The intricately linked ties every nation has to this economically crippled colossus called America finds the fiscal movers and shakers of the world doing much the same things many lesser mortals are doing these days as they cast their wary glances at the bleak outlook. While many average Joes are buying silver, gold, and other tangible commodities, and some are storing food and preparing to survive what they see as a coming world economic collapse, the power brokers at the top are prepping in their own special ways. They have been doing so for some time.

The monetary masters of the world have known for some time that the current way of money manipulation is unsustainable. Things have got to give at some point. As Todd and I have many times discussed, it is utterly amazing that America's, thus the world's, economy hasn't long since come crashing down. It is my contention that it is not these economic gurus at the top that have been able to prevent such a collapse, but the very hand of God that is holding things together—allowing the massive bubble of pseudo prosperity to build.

For whatever the reason the fall hasn't come, the financial finaglers are more than aware that a crisis could bring cataclysm in terms of economic destruction. These are using the phenomenal technologies that have developed over recent years to prepare for such catastrophe, on a much grander scale than are the average Joes who are prepping for bad times ahead.

The collapse is coming; of that they are certain. The key in their prepping, I believe, is control. They want above all else to maintain control as things tumble. They want to be sure things are in place to bring the economic structure of their world down in a somewhat orderly manner so the framework and substance of their wealth aren't scattered and far-flung. They want to have all materials within easy reach so as to be able to begin immediately reconstructing their kingdom to their liking.

It is interesting that the mindset of such planning encompasses the entire political spectrum, left to right. As a matter of fact, it is a conservative initiative that is at the nucleus of one such element to help control monetary matters at the basic consumer level through advanced technology.

> Internet providers would be forced to keep logs of their customers' activities for one year—in case police want to review them in the future—under legislation that a U.S. House of Representatives committee approved today.
>
> The 19-to-10 vote represents a victory for conservative Republicans, who made data retention their first major technology initiative after last fall's elections, and the Justice Department officials who have quietly lobbied for the sweeping new requirements....
>
> A last-minute rewrite of the bill expands the information that commercial Internet providers are required to store to include customers' names, addresses, phone numbers, credit card numbers, bank account numbers, and temporarily-assigned IP addresses, some committee members suggested. By a 7-16 vote, the panel rejected an amendment that would have clarified that only IP addresses must be stored.
>
> It represents "a data bank of every digital act by every American" that would "let us find out where every single American visited websites," said Rep. Zoe Lofgren of California.[107]

The intrusion into the lives of and control of the American consumer has long been in development. Computers and the public's ever-increasing integration with the Internet through commercial transaction is one of many technological wonders that will give the would-be masters the control they believe they need to affect a manageable collapse of the U.S. and global economies, when such a fall eventuates.

The prepping continues apace, and the technologies for economic bondage are progressing geometrically. However, God's prophetic Word foretells a different scenario for the ultimate system of control that will come from present planning by the globalist elitists—the Antichrist system of Revelation 13:16–18. Daniel the prophet was given the prophecy through God's angel, who interpreted for him Babylonian King Nebuchadnezzar's dream involving history's world geopolitical/socioeconomic kingdoms. In foretelling what would become of man's attempt to establish a one-world government that excludes Almighty God, Daniel was told to prophesy the following:

> Thou, O king, sawest, and behold a great image. This great image, whose brightness was excellent, stood before thee; and the form of it was terrible.
>
> This image's head was of fine gold, its breast and its arms of silver, its belly and its thighs of brass,
>
> Its legs of iron, his feet part of iron and part of clay.
>
> Thou sawest till that a stone was cut out without hands, which smote the image upon his feet that were of iron and clay, and broke them to pieces.
>
> Then was the iron, the clay, the brass, the silver, and the gold, broken to pieces together, and became like the chaff of the summer threshing floors; and the wind carried them away, that no place was found for them; and the stone that smote the image became a great mountain, and filled the whole earth. (Daniel 2:31–35)

AUGUST 2011

All the prepping done by the would-be world architects who plan to bring about a new economic order from the coming collapse is destined for failure. Their attempt at rebuilding, leaving God out of their plans, will be crushed by the returning King of all kings—the Lord Jesus Christ. The only prepping that can assure a safe, secure future is the preparation already accomplished by Jesus Christ. He did it all on the cross at Calvary nearly two thousand years ago. He is the Ark that will provide shelter from the destruction that is coming.

August 15, 2011
Post-Rapture Rumblings

Middle Eastern madness has always boiled and bubbled to the surface throughout history. Such has been the case in recent times with rioting fomented, almost certainly, it is thought, by the Muslim Brotherhood.

The rioting has brought down the likes of Egyptian President-Dictator Hosni Mubarak and threatens the Syrian tyrant Bashar al-Assad's brutal regime. The Mideast cauldron is synopsized from the following report:

> The Arab Spring, literally the Arabic Rebellions or the Arab Revolutions, is a revolutionary wave of demonstrations and protests occurring in the Arab world. Since 18 December 2010 there have been revolutions in Tunisia and Egypt; a civil war in Libya; civil uprisings in Bahrain, Syria, and Yemen; major protests in Algeria, Iraq, Jordan, Morocco, and Oman, as well as on the borders of Israel, and minor protests in Kuwait, Lebanon, Mauritania, Saudi Arabia, Sudan, and Western Sahara.[108]

Most leaders of the nations mentioned have either resigned or have promised not to seek reelection when their terms are up. It is a region that pulses with rumors of war, as the much-hated Israel sits at the center of the tumult. The rioting is like a spreading disease across the skin of the land where man's final war will conclude. But it is not a rash that can be kept localized. Europe has been experiencing hot spots that are jumping the Atlantic to pop up even in the United States.

Anger over governmental economic chicanery and/or mismanagement, as well as perceived racial biases, is the driving force behind each and every instance of the rioting that keeps breaking out. Lawlessness is intensifying in the UK.

> David Cameron recalled Parliament from its summer vacation as police arrested 525 people following the worst rioting in Britain since the 1980s. London saw a third night of violence and unrest spread to other cities.
>
> The prime minister, speaking outside his Downing Street office in London after a meeting with ministers and security chiefs, said the House of Commons will hold a one-day emergency session on Aug. 11. Police leave has been cancelled and Metropolitan Police Deputy Assistant Commissioner Stephen Kavanagh said the London force is preparing for "mass disorder again tonight."
>
> "I'm determined, the government is determined, that justice will be done," Cameron said. "This is criminality pure and simple, and it has to be confronted and defeated."[109]

Gasoline bombs have been thrown at vehicles and businesses have been set on fire in the current outbreak of violence. It began

August 6, following the shooting of a man in the northwest section of London, Tottenham, when a man of Afro-Caribbean origin was killed in a shootout with police. Tottenham has a heavy concentration of people of Afro-Caribbean origin.

Prime Minister Cameron hasn't yet called out the military to control the rioters, but word is that British armed forces could be called upon, should rioting spread and become unmanageable. The British rioting comes on the heels of upheavals over austerity cuts on social largesse in nations across Europe. Greece, Portugal, and others such as Ireland have seen outbreaks of destructive rioting.

We remember the recent mobs in Wisconsin when the governor worked within the legislative process to limit government union power in order to bring sanity to state budgetary spending. Civility was not found when many of the protesters—who were riotous by any definition of the term—didn't get their way.

One is left only to imagine the nightmarish goings-on in the large cities like Detroit, Chicago, Los Angeles, and others in the aftermath that will follow the Rapture. The Holy Spirit (the Restrainer) will withdraw from His office as governor on the consciences of mankind, we are told in 2 Thessalonians 2:6–8. Then evil will be unleashed to make life hell on earth for all of those left behind to face God's wrath and judgment.

Jesus foretold that as part of the end-of-the-age signs, nation will rise against nation (Luke 21:10a). The word for "nation" in Greek translates to "ethnos" or "ethnic" in English. Jesus was saying that racial strife—as well as economic, unsolvable turmoil—will be at the center of the nations in distress with perplexity (Luke 21:25b).

Based upon things going on in the Middle East, Europe, and now the U.S., with mobs beginning to do what is right in their own eyes, it seems to me that post-Rapture rumblings can be heard on the prophetic horizon.

August 22, 2011
Fiscal Fluctuations Foreshadow Final Führer

Sorry about the alliteration—just couldn't resist it…

Great Britain, France, and Germany, Europe's nucleus nations, are in economic flux not experienced since the powerful foundational gyrations of the European Union. This past week's regional dynamics put into focus, in my estimation, the scope of the monetary mania that has gripped the global financial markets, particularly since the crisis of 2008.

There has suddenly matured, it seems to me, the ongoing plan to make Europe into a single state, fiscally and geographically. I'm not saying that this conforms, necessarily, to what Bible prophecy foretells, because that end-times entity (found in Daniel 2, as one scriptural example) seems to imply something more along the lines of a pared-down EU—i.e., Bible prophecy seems to have Antichrist's power base and launching pad to be a kingdom that is partly strong and partly broken, much like the constantly bickering group of European states as they presently exist—these prophetically reduced to only a group of ten or so.

The final führer will, I infer from God's prophetic Word, have to take over this group by offing three of the "kings" (Daniel 7 and Revelation 17). So, I'm not saying that Europe will soon be one nation, as are the states in America. What I wish to point out is the swift and vigorous movement of things at this moment in the geopolitical arena that is second in importance only to Israel, in terms of Bible prophecy.

The British are caught up in turmoil like at no other time in their history. Besides the rioting and threats of societal breakdown, they are confronted by European pressures to embrace EU efforts at total union.

> David Cameron [British prime minister] was under mounting pressure last night to hold a referendum on EU membership amid claims that the Coalition is paving the way for full eurozone financial integration.
>
> Tory and Labour MPs believe that Chancellor George Osborne's hopes for a single eurozone tax system will lead to the EU becoming a fundamentally different organisation to the one the UK joined in 1973.
>
> Many also fear that Britain will come under intense pressure to adapt its tax and regulatory policies to conform more closely with the eurozone once fiscal union is under way, even if the UK remains outside the single currency. Steve Baker, Tory MP for Wycombe, said: "It is very clear that the EU is heading at full speed towards being one country."[110]

The leaders of the continent's two major member-states are heading the call for bringing the EU into total unification. Worldwide monetary upheaval is providing the impetus for the drive toward one European nation superstate.

> PARIS—the leaders of France and Germany called Tuesday for greater economic discipline and unity among European nations but declined to take the expensive

financial measures seen by many investors as the only way to halt the continent's spiraling debt crisis.

The Dow Jones industrial average fell, the euro slid against the dollar and key European markets edged down in off-hour trading after Chancellor Angela Merkel of Germany and French President Nicolas Sarkozy announced the results of their emergency talks in Paris.

Sarkozy called for a "new economic government" for Europe that would meet at least twice a year with European Union President Herman Van Rompuy as its head....

The two leaders also proposed a Europe-wide tax on financial transactions and pledged to harmonize their countries' corporate taxes in a move aimed at showing the eurozone's largest members are "marching in lockstep" to protect the euro.[111]

The EU's key leaders have talked just the past week about the need for a strong singular economic government, at the head of which should be the current EU President Herman Van Rompuy. While this is fascinating, considering the fact that we believe the "prince that shall come" (Daniel 9:26) will come from a revived Roman Empire, which this effort certainly seems to portend, I don't believe Van Rompuy is that "prince."

The reason I can say this with a sense of confidence is that: 1) Europe is still quite a way off from becoming that revived Roman Empire—economically, at least; and 2) The church is still here, and Paul prophesies in 2 Thessalonians 2 that the man of sin—Antichrist—won't be revealed until the Holy Spirit removes as restrainer of evil.

This also cannot happen while the church is here. The Holy Spirit resides within each living believer of the Church Age (Age of Grace). When the church leaves, the Holy Spirit resident in each member of the church will interact with mankind (those not taken in the Rapture) in other ways. History's final führer will then make his presence known. We see the foreshadowing of his appearance within the moving and shaking of the economic earthquake taking place today.

August 29, 2011
Quaking in D.C. a Forewarning

Mr. President, tear down this wall…

What wall? The wall your administration has erected between the American people and the nation Israel.

The Gallup Poll most recently told you—told the world—that by a wide margin, we the people of the United States believe Israel is not the problem in the Middle East, or anywhere else. By a margin of 63 percent, we have made it known that we want America to continue to embrace the Jewish state as a close friend and ally—the only true ally we have in that violent part of the world. Yet, you and those you send as interlocutors in that one-sided, so-called peace process consistently lock arms with Israel's blood-vowed enemies to try to bully that nation to give in to demands that will never end as long as Israel exists.

Israel's enemies—and that list includes every Arab state to one degree or another—want Israel eradicated. The 5.8 shaking your present mansion received while you were enjoying the golfing, luxury, and beauty of Martha's Vineyard, Mr. President, is a not-so-gentle reminder that the God of Israel will never let that happen.

You have touched the apple of the Almighty's eye, and continue to do so as the threatened September date of Israel's assault by the UN against God's chosen nation draws nearer. By refusing to state firmly and emphatically that the U.S. will exercise the Security Council veto power in any attempt to create a Palestinian state with the bullying tactics of Ban Ki-moon and the Islamist-controlled delegations of that organization, you directly dare the God of Heaven to do anything about your obdurate stance against Him. The quaking in the nation's capital is a mild forewarning of what is to come, if your actions, and lack of action, continue on the course you have chosen with regard to Israel.

We are not currently witnessing God's judgment and wrath with this earthquake, or with Hurricane Irene that is assaulting the East Coast of the nation. When His wrath—His judgment—does fall, it will be, Jesus prophesied, a time more terrible than any that has ever existed on planet earth (Matthew 24:21). But, God is warning yet again, I'm convinced, that dealing with Israel is a deadly serious matter in His interaction with mankind. The closer the time of Christ's return, the more intense His forewarnings will become.

America has been Israel's friend—her protector, in human terms. America has, therefore, been blessed of God beyond any nation in history, with material wealth and godly moorings of Christianity at our very foundation. But, the tide is turning, as anyone with eyes to see and ears to hear can discern.

Economic catastrophe looms on the national horizon to such a degree that this great nation's fall will literally bring the entire world down when it crashes. And, it's not a matter of *if* that will happen, but *when.* We have been experiencing an economic earthquake for months—even years—and the shaking is getting worse. Now the geophysical quaking is shaking the very foundation of Washington D.C.

But, the earthquake is mild—very mild, my spirit tells me—compared to the shaking that is coming upon this country and world. Much of the quaking—socioeconomic and geophysical—is a direct result of the way America and the world are dealing with the nation that the God of Heaven has, in His absolute authority, determined cannot be destroyed. Satanic forces are ratcheting up everything possible to keep God's promises to Israel from being fulfilled. There is bound to be such titanic shaking as we are presently experiencing while the biblically prophesied battle between what secularists call good and evil takes place. Be assured—the outcome of that battle is already determined.

Knowing that this request isn't likely to produce the desired answer, ultimately, I still must make the plea as one given the commission to forewarn during these prophetic times. Mr. President, please do all within your power to see to it that America comes down on the winning side. Regardless, Israel will be the winner. The Creator of all that is has made the following promise:

> Thus saith the LORD, who giveth the sun for a light by day, and the ordinances of the moon and of the stars for a light by night, who divideth the sea when its waves roar; The LORD of hosts is his name:
>
> If those ordinances depart from before me, saith the LORD, then the see of Israel also shall cease from being a nation before me forever. (Jeremiah 31:35–36)

Last-Days Diary

SEPTEMBER 2011

Jerusalem in the Crosshairs with Anti-Semitism as Trigger

September 5, 2011

The Jerusalem Obsession

A perhaps not-so-shocking, but certainly attention-getting, news item points to the ugly head of anti-Semitism arising in not-so-jolly old England these days. The stark growth of Israel and Jew-hating is front and center in the kin of a prominent British leader you will recognize.

> Laura Booth, sister-in-law of Quartet envoy Tony Blair, has called on "Lebanon, Jordan and Egypt liberate Al-Quds [Jerusalem]." The former British prime minister's family member has previously sailed illegally to Gaza on a flotilla boat....
>
> During last week's demonstration, Booth went on another rant against Israel. "We say here today to you, Israel , we see your crimes and we loathe your crimes. And to us your nation does not exist, because it is a criminal injustice against humanity. We want to see Lebanon,

Jordan and Egypt go to the borders and stop this now. Liberate Al Quds! March to Al Quds!"[112]

Current issues and events that look to be harbingers of the biblically prophesied apocalypse bombard this generation of earth's inhabitants. Jesus' Olivet Discourse prophecies, foretelling things to come in the time of "great tribulation," seem to leap from news reports that are becoming so routine that they no longer shock. No signal is more prophetically significant than present circumstances involving the city where Jesus was crucified nearly twenty centuries ago.

Jerusalem is at the center of satanic rage, and the rage is bursting forth at the center of supposedly civilized Europe, where Islam is in the process of taking over. This is as the Old and New Testament prophets said it will be just before Christ returns to a planet that is home to a world of rebels against God. That rebellion is scheduled, the prophets forewarn, to culminate in history's final and most destructive war. Armageddon will be triggered because of both Satan and fallen mankind's determination to install themselves upon the single spot on earth dearest to the heart of God.

Mt. Moriah sits at the southern end of the ancient city, crested by a golden dome that represents 1.5 billion people whose religion demands of its adherents blood-vowed opposition to God's chosen nation, Israel. This is the place God picked to have His temple on earth constructed. It is the precise location where the Third Temple will sit—the Temple that will be desecrated by Antichrist, earth's last and most beastly tyrant.

Even more importantly, the Temple Mount will be the home of Christ's millennial temple. Moriah, then to be known as Zion, will be supernaturally elevated by the tremendous topographical changes caused when the Lord's foot touches the Mount of Olives at His return.

Diplomats of the world have, for the past four decades, engaged in effort after effort to bring stability to the region, at whose heart the city of Jerusalem sits. We remember the many jettings to and from Washington D.C., Jerusalem, and other capitals of the Mideast. From Henry Kissinger, Zbigniew Brzezinski, James Baker, Madeleine Albright, Colin Powell, and Condoleezza Rice to, now, Hillary Clinton and even Barack Obama—America's secretaries of state and a most strangely assertive president have burned many gallons of jet fuel trying to find the formula for peace that would defuse the Armageddon bomb.

All of that diplomatic shuffling is mere prelude to the fretting that is about to take place over this, the most important, thus most volatile, city on planet earth. Zechariah the prophet foretold the end-time anxiety that we believe is now on the precipice of gripping the international community.

> The burden of the word of the LORD for Israel, saith the LORD, who stretcheth forth the heavens, and layeth the foundation of the earth, and formeth the spirit of man within him.
>
> Behold, I will make Jerusalem a cup of trembling unto all the people round about, when they shall be in the siege both against Judah and against Jerusalem.
>
> And in that day will I make Jerusalem a burdensome stone for all peoples; all that burden themselves with it shall be cut in pieces, though all the people of the earth be gathered together against it. (Zechariah 12:1–3)

There is good reason for the building anxiety. Israel's terrorist-sponsoring neighbors to the north strive mightily to develop nuclear bombs and missiles that will deliver them. No one doubts in which direction these missiles will be pointed should Iran be successful in producing such weapons of mass destruction. Israel's one, common declaration amidst all of the political infighting remains the core of its defense. "Never again!"

The following summary of atrocities to the Jewish race presents compelling evidence why "Never again!" must be their passionate declaration, backed by nuclear strength.

> Due to [Israel's] disobedience the Jews have suffered terribly. They were ruled by Rome in Christ's day but rebelled in AD 70 and 250,000 were killed. They rebelled again in AD 135 and again Rome smashed them, killing even more and scattering them throughout the empire. Since then they have been bitterly persecuted. [They were] forcibly expelled from England in 1290 and from France 1306. In 1298 more than 100,000 were killed in Europe. From 1648 to 1658 some 400,000 were massacred. From 1939–45 Hitler's Nazis killed more than 4 million.... In its history Egyptian pharaohs, Assyrian kings, Babylonian rulers, Persian satraps, Greek Hellenists, Roman Caesars, Holy Roman emperors, Roman Catholic pontiffs, Medieval monarchs, Christian crusaders, Spanish inquisitors, Nazi dictators, Communist commissars, Arab sheiks and United Nation delegates have all turned against the Jew yet they still survive.[113]

SEPTEMBER 2011

The Jewish people of Israel declare they will never again let themselves be enslaved within regimes that want them erased from the earth. Never again will they allow the genocide they have suffered through the centuries. Their national vow is backed by the ominous "Samson Option." This last-ditch military imperative is not lost on the leaders of the international community, which is headed by the G-8 nations.

These leaders of this enlightened age might not believe the Bible is the word of God, but, they know the story of Samson and what happened when he was finally put in a predicament in which he could no longer be free. The world's diplomats—at least those of the Western world—have no doubt that the Israeli Defense Force will bring the house down around them, if it comes to that as Israel's only viable option. The international community—once termed "the New World Order"—has developed a systemic neurosis involving the bleak outlook for the future of the Israeli-Palestinian conflict. The "Roadmap to Peace" seems to be the nerve-soothing therapeutic course of action upon which the powers-that-be have chosen to eliminate the possibility of nuclear conflict being triggered over earth's most coveted city.

World leaders are obsessed with Jerusalem. They consider Jerusalem the trigger to Armageddon; they will do whatever it takes to defuse that trigger.

September 12, 2011
Togarmah Turbulence Stirring in Mideast

Current turmoil over last year's Israeli Defense Force naval commandos' interception and action against a ship carrying pro-Palestinian operatives intent on running an Israeli blockade brings to the surface of Mideast tensions a reminder of Turkey's future connection with the Gog-Magog prophecy.

Present-day Turkey sits geographically on much of the territory known in ancient times as Togarmah, whose inhabitants are predicted to be among the peoples that will attack Israel. The prophesied assault is termed the battle of Gog-Magog. The nations listed to invade from Israel's north are given in Ezekiel 38:3–6. Turkey was governed by a secular government more or less friendly to Israel for many years. For the past several years, however, that country has turned toward religionists of the Islamist persuasion to govern, and Turkey has moved away from the ties that once held the two states together in a nonconfrontational, even cooperative, disposition.

The most recent wedge issue further alienating the countries is Turkey's determination to bring Israel before the United Nations to seek UN judgment against IDF actions that resulted in nine Turkish citizens being killed. Turkey is seeking the action through the International Court of Justice (ICJ). Based in the Hague, the ICJ is a permanent UN court set up to rule on state-to-state disputes. The primary judgment being sought is against Israel's blockade of Gaza.

The nine pro-Palestinian Turkish citizens killed were on board the Turkish-flagged ship, Mavi Marmara, at the time the Israeli navy intercepted it on May 31, 2010, while it sailed toward Gaza's coast. The pro-Palestinian activists on board at the time of the interception and boarding said the commandos started shooting as soon as they hit the deck. But the Israeli military said its commandos fired live rounds only after being attacked with clubs, knives, and guns. IDF reports said its troops faced significant, violent, organized resistance from a group of passengers upon boarding the vessel. They were therefore required to use force equal to the resistance in order to protect themselves.

International pressure is mounting against the Israeli government over the ongoing controversy. Like in so many areas of the Jewish state's interaction with other nations, a readily discernible anti-Israel bias is developing. This is seen, in particular, by the actions of almost every nation within the UN, which seem in collusion to bring into being the Palestinian state by majority vote, bypassing the UN Security Council input and excluding Israel from having any say in the matter.

UN Secretary General Ban Ki-moon has stated that he, along with most others in the UN, considers Israel occupiers in Jerusalem. Demands are being made that the Israeli government apologize for the action taken in blockading Gaza, and for every other trumped-up atrocity the haters of Israel can think of in accusing the Jewish state.

Israel's Prime Minister Benjamin Netanyahu, however isn't biting into that poison apple.

> Prime Minister Binyamin Netanyahu vowed on Sunday that Israel will not apologize to Turkey over the events of the Mavi Marmara raid, in light of the recommendations put forward by the Palmer report on the incident:
>
> "We don't need to apologize for our soldiers who protected themselves against violent attacks by IHH [short for the Foundation for Human Rights and Freedoms and Humanitarian Relief] activists and we don't need to apologize for working to stop weapons being smuggled to the terror group Hamas," he said at the beginning of the

weekly cabinet meeting. "Israel expresses regret that lives were lost, and I hope that we will find a way to improve relations with Turkey," Netanyahu added. "We need not apologize for the fact that naval commandos defended their lives against an assault by violent IHH activists. We need not apologize for the fact that we acted to stop the smuggling of weapons to Hamas, a terrorist organization that has already fired over ten thousand missiles, rockets and mortar rounds at our civilians. We need not apologize for the fact that we act to defend our people, our children and our communities. To the naval commandos, I would like to say that just as you and the rest of the IDF defend us, we will defend you everywhere and in every forum. I reiterate that the State of Israel expresses regret over the loss of life. I also hope that a way will be found to overcome the disagreement with Turkey. Israel has never wanted a deterioration in its relations with Turkey; neither is Israel interested in such a deterioration now."[114]

While the prophet Zechariah's prophecy that the whole world of nations will come against God's chosen nation (Zechariah 12:1–3) is manifest in this generation, the prophet Ezekiel's Gog-Magog prophecy as it involves Turkey is in view upon the geopolitical horizon.

September 19, 2011
Fascinating Prophetic Details: Part 1

We have been observing prophetic developments in these commentaries for years. So, why present an article on prophetic matters in an overall sense as if it was covering something new?

Last-Days Diary

SEPTEMBER 2011

I hope, in this multi-part essay, to do something significantly different. Rather than look in a broad, general way at the major issues we cover so often, I want to take a look at the fascinating, specific way these prophecies have been brought into focus at a time I believe is the very end of this dispensation, the Age of Grace (Church Age). That is, I want to look at some of the more intricate details of the dynamics and circumstances that have shaped each of the major prophecies for this very hour.

Geopolitical Details

Modern Israel, as we consistently say, is the number-one signal of where this generation stands on God's prophetic timeline. That nation is, therefore, the best example in the geopolitical arena to use for focusing on details of issues and events setting the stage for Bible prophecy fulfillment. The student who watches Bible prophecy develop from the premillennial, pretribulational viewpoint has, with clarity others can't see, seen Israel come back into its own land with its ancient national language restored. It did so following a miraculous rebirth into modernity on a single day, just as prophesied (Isaiah 66:6–9). The intricate details of the amazing rebirth are there to be gleaned by the hundreds, if not thousands.

Pressured in AD 135 through genocidal action by Roman Emperor Hadrian to leave their homeland given them by God, the Jews scattered into many nations of the world. God's chosen people never truly found peace; rather, they mostly encountered persecution and death during the intervening centuries leading to coming back in large numbers following the Balfour Declaration of 1917.

SEPTEMBER 2011

Hitler's perpetration of genocide upon the Jews during the time leading up to and through World War II, culminating in the Holocaust, shamed the world into allowing a Jewish state to be reborn. What Satan meant for evil in trying to thwart God's promise to Israel being fulfilled, God turned into good. However, demonic rage by the false religion of Islam continued to fester, breaking into all-out warfare against Israel on numerous occasions. God gave Israel the victory in every instance that nation was attacked.

Now, to look at the clearly observable, detailed kinds of prophetic movement wrought by recent events involving the modern Jewish state. Zechariah the prophet declared the whole world will turn against Israel and Jerusalem, in particular, at the end of human history. Israel's refusal to give in to demands by the Palestinian Authority—merely the proxy entity for all of Israel's Islamist Arab and Iranian antagonists—has brought condemnation of practically every nation on earth.

We've all watched the anger spew from UN Secretary General Ban Ki-moon and from the leadership of practically every nation represented in the UN General Assembly. They threaten to grant the PA its request for nationhood, using much of Israel's land, including East Jerusalem, in which to establish the new country's capital. The U.S. presidential administration has thus far, in my estimation, shown little more than token interest in opposing this assault on Israel's sovereignty.

Israel's only true friends left on the planet consist mostly of evangelical Christians, particularly those who see with the clarity mentioned above through the premillennial, pretribulational prism. When the church is called out of this fallen planet, Israel will be alone, or so it will seem.

But, not so.

At that moment when all seems lost, Michael the archangel will stand for that chosen people (Daniel 12:1). God Himself will deal with and for His chosen people and the city He equates to the apple of His eye. All is shaping into the prophetic picture, with details filling in moment by moment the matters involved in getting to the total fulfillment of every jot and tittle that is foretold. The intricacies of the peace process provide details that fascinate the student of Bible prophecy, for example.

The development of the atomic bomb (an invention of Jewish scientists, incidentally) and the hydrogen bomb, for that matter, has caused a worldwide furor stemming from the Middle East. Israel is at the center of the controversy, of course. Israel has nuclear weaponry and is threatened with extinction—as the Jews always are. They have vowed, "Never again!" Never again will they be subjected to genocide without fighting to the death with those who want every Jew on the planet dead.

Israel is, as of a year ago or so, completely surrounded on all but the Mediterranean side by those whose avowed intention is just that—to eradicate the Jews, thus the nation of Israel.

The world knows that the end of the human race through nuclear war could easily begin at Jerusalem. Thus, that city is ground zero for the entire world's attention, just as Zechariah and other prophets foretold. Isaiah prophesied that a peace covenant will be made over this very city. It will be a covenant that will, in fact, be made with "death, and with hell." It will bring the wrath of God down on the whole world for forcing such an agreement upon His chosen people and upon His most beloved city. (Read Isaiah 28:15, 18.)

America is at the heart of just such a covenant-producing process. The "Roadmap to Peace" has been a part of world diplomatic jargon for more than a decade now. Jerusalem, with the strong-arming of the diplomatic world to make Israel stop building in that city and with the PA (the Islamist world) demanding that Jerusalem be given over to them, is at the epicenter of the coming earthquake of wrath as foretold by God Almighty through His prophet, Zechariah.

> And this shall be the plague with which the LORD will smite all the peoples that have fought against Jerusalem: their flesh shall consume away while they stand upon their feet, and their eyes shall consume away in their holes, and their tongue shall consume away in their mouth. (Zechariah 14:12)

God willing, we will continue to look next time at the fascinating details that are filling in more and more of the end-of-the-age prophetic puzzle.

September 26, 2011
Fascinating Prophetic Details: Part 2

Every examination of prophecy about the very end of the Church Age that deals with the nations and their individual and collective fates must begin and end with Israel. Therefore, we continue looking at details of modern Israel as juxtaposed against all nations—thus to determine how the minute elements of ongoing developments in geopolitics are setting the prophetic stage for Christ's return.

Previously, we looked at how Israel and Jerusalem are at ground zero for the diplomatic world. The international community correctly sees this as the place on earth most likely to be the ignition point for World War III. It is intriguing to dissect with the scalpel of Bible prophecy each layer of development in the geopolitical issues and events of our time that involve the modern Jewish state. Iran is a most fascinating case in point.

Persia, as we have looked at many times, is listed as a key player that assaults Israel in the Ezekiel 38–39 Gog-Magog prophecy. Modern Iran is at the center of what was ancient Persia, as we know.

With Iranian Shah Mohammad Rezā Pahlavi being in power through most of the 1970s, Israel didn't have to be overly concerned about neighbors to that section of its north. One reason was because America's military, particularly the U.S. Air Force, worked closely with the shah's air force in training and maintenance missions. I can report this from more-or-less personal secondhand information, because my own father-in-law was in charge of all aircraft maintenance for American-made military aircraft in Iran's arsenal through 1976. The shah was America's friend, even if sometimes being beastly in treatment of his own people, and looking down his nose at Israel to his south.

Point is, Bible prophecy students were hard pressed to see how the Gog-Magog force could ever be formed with this arrangement in place. We know what happened, as we think on how quickly things have fallen in place one event after the other since the shah's fall in 1979.

America, under the Carter administration, was run out of town, literally, with the coming of the Iranian Revolution, as the Islamists came to power under the Ayatollah Ruhollah Khomeini. Iran became increasingly bellicose against the West, and, of course, became bloodlust determined to erase Israel and every Jew off the map.

SEPTEMBER 2011

Russia and the present Iranian regime have become working partners at many levels, the most troubling at the nuclear level. The Gog-Magog nucleus has formed between Russia, Iran (Persia), and Turkey (Togarmah) within less than two years.

It's also amazing to watch a most-asked question in the process of being answered by the flood of developing issues and events: "Why is America not mentioned in Bible prophecy? It is the most powerful nation ever to exist." Again, it is intriguing to consider that America was instrumental in all of these developments—as one would expect the most powerful nation ever to exist to be, I suppose.

America "defeated" the "Soviet Union" through tactics involving cold war attrition—and the heart of that antagonist became again "Russia." This territorial rearrangement aligns almost precisely with the ancient geographical area called "Rosh," the leader of which the prophet Ezekiel foretold will be "Gog" of the Gog-Magog war against Israel.

The United States has slipped from its ultimate superpower status since that time of the Reagan-led peaceful defeat of the Soviet Union. Under the Obama administration, America's economic standing, thus its fiscal hegemony over the other nations of the world, has declined, some say precipitously. Prophecy students of the premillennial, pretribulational perspective can point with a certain amount of credibility to the fact that America's slippage coincides closely with this nation's bringing pressure on the Israeli government to give in to demands that they give up land for peace with their Islamist neighbors.

At the same time, China, the chief nation that will make up the "kings of the East" force that will one day kill one-third of the world's population, is draining U.S. economic power while buying up American assets. America is, in effect, funding the development of the awesome military force predicted in Revelation 9:16. This would have been flabbergasting to even consider during those Reagan years, and that hasn't been that many years ago. China! Of all nations on earth, China has answered the question about why America is not mentioned in Bible prophecy. The United States can also be seen as instrumental in the details of developing Bible prophecy regarding the region that is foretold to spawn the world's most despicable dictator.

Daniel the prophet said that this "prince that shall come" will emerge from the people that "destroy the city and sanctuary." This means that Antichrist will come from the area of Rome—from Europe, in general—as the Romans destroyed Jerusalem and the Jewish Temple in AD 70. The premillennial, pretribulational viewpoint of these matters is important to recognize because it provides logical placement, thus explanation, of what we have watched develop in world headlines, especially since Israel became a nation again May 14, 1948.

America's influence has been absolutely profound in bringing the modern Jewish state into prominence. My book entitled *The American Apocalypse: Is the United States in Bible Prophecy?* details the intricacies of America's part in that rebirth. The United States' influence in bringing modern Europe into prophetic configuration is only slightly less profound. Next time, Lord willing, we will continue looking at the many facets of those and other developments toward fulfillment of the final prophecies leading up to Christ's Second Advent.

OCTOBER 2011

Profound Prophetic Perspective

October 3, 2011
Fascinating Prophetic Details: Conclusion

Those of us who look at world conditions through the lens of the premillennial, pretribulational scope of things to come believe ours is the correct view of Bible prophecy. We reach that understanding, in part, when considering that: 1) Israel must be at the center of world controversy at the very end of the age; and 2) Antichrist can't be revealed as the man of sin until believers of the Church Age are removed from planet earth.

Now, the details of developments on the geopolitical last-days' landscape grow ultra fascinating. We have shown that Israel has become the center of controversy, exactly like Zechariah the prophet foretold that nation will be at the end of the age. We have looked at how this has eventuated, with America's alliance with and influence upon Israel bringing the Jewish state to the center of the end-times spotlight.

At the same time, we've delved into how the United States of America has gone into decline like the deteriorating visage of a terminally ill cancer patient. Why is the U.S. not mentioned in Bible prophecy? Perhaps we are learning why, as previously dissected, with America's wealth currently being siphoned by the geopolitical power that will one day have a military force that will kill one-third of all peoples on earth at the time China and others of East Asia rampage into the occidental world across the dried-up Euphrates River.

American tax dollars are paying for the equipping of that future juggernaut, it appears. America's decline seems related to the country's movement away from friendship with and close support of God's chosen nation. Again, America looks to be key when thinking about what's going on with the area out of which history's final and most despotic tyrant will emerge. Antichrist's launching pad will be Europe—the area of ancient Rome, according to the prophet Daniel (Daniel 9:26–27).

Europe spawned World Wars I and II, and was in near total shambles following the Allied victory over Germany, Japan, and Italy. The Marshall Plan—conceived, implemented, and paid for by the United States—rebuilt that prophetically destined continent.

The European Common Market came into being in 1957, engendered by the Treaty of Rome. This followed a number of European nations agreeing to form the European Coal and Steel Community (ECSC) in 1951, which was implemented in 1952. Other agreements moved European nations closer, like the treaties establishing the European Atomic Energy Community (Euratom). The formation of the European Economic Community (EEC) brought Europe to the point of coming into the prophetic picture as what will one day form the revived Roman Empire. The point is, none of these developments would have happened as they did if not for U.S. rescue of Europe from the ravages of World War II. This isn't meant to give America undue accolades. The U.S. would, itself, never have existed if not for the God of Heaven's divinely appointed purpose for the American republic in end-times development.

The intricate linkages with the U.S. economy have kept Europe—and the Western world, for that matter—at an elevated economic level never attained in history. The interlinkages of America and its dollar with all of these nations mentioned in Bible prophecy are nothing short of miraculous. America's loss of economic power is presently having a deleterious impact on most every nation on the planet—except, perhaps, China, which, again, looks to be the entity assigned by destiny to be the chief agent for siphoning wealth and power from the most materially blessed nation to ever exist.

The ominous bubble of economic catastrophe is building hourly for America and all nations of the earth. There is almost certainly no human way to prevent it from eventually bursting. It becomes more obvious by the day to those who see prophetic developments from a premillennial, pretribulational viewpoint that it is only God's staying hand that prevents the explosion that will collapse the global economy.

I believe that it will be the Rapture of the church that will burst that explosive bubble.

All stage-setting factors are in place, in detail, for the coming to power of Antichrist and his regime of murderous tyranny. It will be an economically driven dictatorship of absolute control over buying and selling, as Revelation 13:16–18 clearly presents.

That "prince that shall come" (Daniel 9:26) can't appear on the world stage (2 Thessalonians 2:3) until the church is removed to

Heaven when Jesus Christ calls all believers to be with Him (John 14:1–3; 1 Thessalonians 4:16–17; Revelation 4:1). It is upon the Rapture that this world's immense bubble of false security based upon Satan's lies will burst and the humanistic structures of false hope will come crashing to dust.

The singular, most fascinating detail out of all of prophecy to remember is the following:

> And it shall come to pass, that whosoever shall call on the name of the Lord shall be saved. (Acts 2:21)

His name is Jesus!

October 10, 2011
Isolating Israel

Israel continues to be made the hold-up to peace in the Middle East, thus the stumbling block to peace for the whole world. That nation's isolation is being maneuvered and manipulated by pressures from every direction.

The Islamist nations of the region hate the Jewish state—while at the same time refusing to acknowledge it even exists. They surround Israel on all sides except the Mediterranean side. Submarines of Israel's enemies even lurk in those waters, awaiting the right time to strike. The countries within the United Nations, led by the Secretary General Ban Ki-moon, are for the most part overwhelmingly opposed to Israel in every vote taken that involves Israel's right to exist and thrive in that land the UN antagonists proclaim belongs to the Palestinians.

The European Union consistently comes down on the side of

the Palestinian Authority's demands that Israel give up whatever territory necessary to accommodate the two-state solution—thus to construct a homeland for the Palestinian refugees. This is demanded, although the refugees are from the surrounding Arab states, nations that prefer to keep the hapless refugees in geographical limbo so hatred of the Jews and accusations that the Jews are cruel occupiers can continue to spew forth.

At the same time, Israel has absorbed thousands upon thousands of those refugees under legal emigration practices. Those émigrés are among the most content people in the Middle East because they are treated fairly and allowed to prosper by the Israeli government and the Jewish citizenry.

The entire world comes against Israel in the form of the Quartet (the U.S., the UN, the EU, and Russia) who, while putting up a façade that the group of powerful nations wants fairness and peace for all people of the Mideast region, in actuality works through deceit and subterfuge to force Israel to give up land in every negotiation that comes up in the "Roadmap to Peace" process.

Most troubling is that the United States is at the forefront of the arm-twisting in dealing with Israeli leadership. This is plainly demonstrated despite peripheral niceties by U.S. administration officials. The following recent report is a case in point:

> TEL AVIV, Israel—Israel must find a way to resume negotiations with the Palestinians and has a responsibility to try to ease tensions with its neighbors in the region, Israeli Defense Minister Ehud Barak said Monday amid prodding from the United States to return to peace talks.

> Standing next to Defense Secretary Leon Panetta, Barak pushed back a bit on the Pentagon chief's warning that Israel is becoming increasingly isolated in the region, threatening its security. And he offered no new thoughts on the thorny issues that have stymied the peace talks, including the proposed timetable and the contested settlements in the West Bank and East Jerusalem.
>
> Making his first trip to Israel as defense secretary, Panetta has pressed the Obama administration's view that the two sides must restart the long-stalled peace talks. And during a news conference with Barak, Panetta said it's time for bold action by both sides to move toward a negotiated two-state solution.
>
> The visit comes amid new international pressure to reach a peace deal by the end of next year, fueled by Palestinian President Mahmoud Abbas' move two weeks ago asking the UN Security Council to recognize an independent Palestinian state in the West Bank, east Jerusalem, and Gaza Strip.[115]

The U.S. State Department operatives and the Quartet negotiators are concerned about Palestine President Mahmoud Abbas' asking the UN Security Council a couple of weeks ago to acknowledge the presence of an independent Palestinian state in the West Bank, East Jerusalem, and the Gaza Strip. They want to avoid a vote on granting this, and prefer that both parties sit down and negotiate Israel's acquiescence in giving up land for peace. Regardless of the façade of wanting a peaceful solution, the international community, like Abbas—like all of the Jew-hating

Islamists—won't relent until Israel gives them what they want. The deadly, humanistic peace plan stems from a satanic rage long ago prophesied to come to a climax at the end of the age, just before Christ's return.

It is an infection that grows more virulent. Anti-Semitism is on the rise around the world. American universities are among the most receptive hosts of the infection. Professors inculcate students with the venom of luciferic hatred for the Jewish state. Israel is increasingly made the root cause of all that is wrong within the Middle Eastern cauldron. Like in the days of Hitler's rise in the mid 1930s, the Jew is made to look like the troublemaker of the world in politics and in business. From the imploding economy to the threatened war over the Palestinian refugees, Israel is the focus of attention.

Israel and the Jewish people are being isolated, just as the prophets of the Old and New testaments foretold.

October 17, 2011
Jesus, Jeffress, and Romney

Mainstream news media got their chance to paint evangelical Christianity as bigotry, and they were quick to do so. Dallas First Baptist pastor, Dr. Robert Jeffress, told reporters that Mormonism is not Christianity, but a cult. He made the statement after introducing Texas governor Rick Perry to the audience Tuesday, October 7, at the Value Voters Summit at Washington D.C.

The eventual topic emerging to the forefront spun off of reporters, following his introduction of Perry, questioning Jeffress about whether the Christian Right would support a Mormon.

Several questions led to asking why Christians objected to the Mormon religion, at which point the Dallas First Baptist pastor gave the answer that Mormonism is a cult, not true Christianity. The Associated Press also reported that he said: "[Mitt Romney] is a good moral man, but those of us who are born-again followers of Christ should prefer a competent Christian."

The national mainstream press went into a gleeful feeding frenzy over what they perceived to be and continue to insinuate is a clear indication that the Tea Party, as it is called, is influenced and manipulated by the Christian hard-line right. That is no surprise. What is a surprise to some is that the Republican Party elite, who detest the Tea Party, also were quick to point to Jeffress—and all of the religious right—as being bigots of the most despicable order.

Up front, it is obvious to state, perhaps, that both the mainstream news media and the GOP elite want the same thing in this presidential election. They want Mitt Romney to be the Republican nominee for the office of president of the United States—even if for differing reasons.

The mainstream press wants Romney as the GOP candidate because it collectively thinks—as does its chosen party, the Democrats—will be easier to run against and defeat than a Republican conservative. The GOP elitists—those who have long wielded controlling influence within the Grand Old Party, and who are Washington-inside-the-Beltway power brokers—want the Tea Party and Christian conservatives discredited because those Beltway insiders fear loss of control if a truly conservative Republican president is elected.

That happened more or less with the election of Ronald

Reagan in 1980, and they watched their control sputter and pop to a large extent throughout the eight Reagan years.

Bill Bennett, one of those GOP insiders, was quick to remind the crowd at the Values Voter Summit of that GOP ruling elite view—which, of course, those in attendance should follow to the T, as opposed to things advocated by the Tea Party.

Bennett said, in reference to Dr. Jeffress:

> You stepped on and obscured the words of Perry and [former Sen. Rick] Santorum and [businessman Herman] Cain and [Rep. Michele] Bachmann and everyone else who has spoken here. You did Rick Perry no good, sir, in what you had to say.[116]

So, to take this dispute from the realm of the political and into where things really matter—God's realm of His interaction with humanity—the question must be raised: What did Dr. Jeffress say, in fact, that was off base so far as speaking the truth is concerned?

He has been called a bigot so many times since his comments that the term has probably begun to take on a different definition within the American lexicon. Those wanting to make him the central focus of their hatred for Tea Party types are unrelenting. Yet the truth is on the Dallas pastor's side, not on the side of his attackers.

My good friend Jack Kinsella stated it as succinctly as could be stated:

> It is not bigotry to say that a faith that denies the most basic of all Christian doctrines according to all the main-

> stream canons of Christianity qualifies as a non-Christian cult. That isn't bigotry. It is theology.[117]

Regarding facts wrapped up in Robert Jeffress' comments as relates to truth about Jesus Christ, Mitt Romney, and his Mormon religion, there is absolutely nothing whatever to be found that shows there is error in the preacher's words. Mormonism is not the Christian religion, but a cult.

The Mormon religion denies the Bible's truth about who Jesus is, and bases its diversion from Christianity upon a book authored by a man—Joseph Smith, who is the cult figure Mormons follow within their belief system.

Even one of Mormonism's own central, contemporary cult members confirms the fact as stated by Dr. Jeffress:

> Michael Otterson, a spokesman for the Church of Jesus Christ of Latter-day Saints—as the Mormons prefer to be known—and one of a stable of bloggers for the Washington Post On Faith site, is well versed on refuting the "cult" slur.
>
> "Lest anyone think I am unduly thin-skinned, it's the insult implicit in the word 'cult' that I am objecting to, not the reasonable point that some Christians are indeed uncomfortable with aspects of Latter-day Saint theology. Of course they are. I am equally uncomfortable with some aspects of traditional, orthodox Christianity, which was the very issue that gave rise to The Church of Jesus Christ of Latter-day Saints in the first place.... It is perfectly true that Mormons do not embrace many of the orthodoxies of mainstream Christianity, including the nature of the Trinity."[118]

Jeffress is right, even according to Romney's fellow elite Mormon cultist. The question then becomes: Why is it wrong in America, in the longstanding political process, to simply state facts when recommending to people of like mind one candidate or another, based upon whether those candidates fit or not within our views and beliefs?

Jeffress didn't speak from a pulpit in recommending Perry. He didn't speak from behind his Dallas pulpit—or any other pulpit—when answering the reporters in a frank way.

It is essential to remember here that the same mainstream news media didn't pursue the Rev. Jeremiah Wright—presidential candidate Obama's pastor of twenty years—when he, from his pulpit in Chicago, called on God to damn America for U.S. actions in a political context. He was allowed to speak in a way that made it obvious he hates this nation and most everything to do with it. Never did the mainstream press hold any of his political rhetoric, again, spewed from his church's pulpit, against him or his long-sitting parishioner, then-candidate Barack Hussein Obama.

Mormonism is a religious cult. It denies the very Christ of the Bible as being the everlasting God, making Him instead the created equal of the one they say is Jesus' brother—Lucifer. Mormons base this, among other things, on the Book of Mormon and the writings of their long-dead cult guru, Joseph Smith.

If you wish to vote for Mr. Romney because of his ability, in your view, to lead this country out of the critically damaged condition in which we find ourselves, then it's your call, of course. But, don't do so thinking that Mitt Romney is a Christian. He is not.

I leave you with a proof text of the matters just presented:

> But though we, or an angel from heaven, preach any other gospel unto you than that which we have preached unto you, let him be accursed.
>
> As we said before, so say I now again, If any man preach any other gospel unto you than that ye have received, let him be accursed. (Galatians 1:8–9)

The Mormon cult claims its members are Christians. They are saying that Jesus is their Christ. But, the Mormon Christ is not the Christ of God's Holy Word, because the Mormons say He is a created being—an angel, not the Eternal Son of the Living God. As a matter of fact, the Bible—Jesus, Himself—claimed that He is God, the Second Godhead Member of the Holy Trinity—which the Mormon cult denies.

Jesus—the REAL Jesus—foretold that the time just before His Second Coming would be an era of great deception. At the center of that deception will be those who come claiming that He is Christ, but are saying at the same time that they are Christ. This, in my view, is most profound, considering what we are seeing today with regard to our own presidential election process.

> And they asked him, saying, Master, but when shall these things be? and what sign will there be when these things shall come to pass?
>
> And he said, Take heed that ye be not deceived; for many shall come in my name, saying, I am Christ; and the time draweth near. Go ye not, therefore, after them. (Luke 21:7–8)

October 2011

October 24, 2011
Invasion of the Mind Snatchers

A science fiction film of 1956 called *Invasion of the Body Snatchers* riveted me as a kid of fourteen or so. Sinister, unseen—even unknowable—diabolical entities were taking over the personhood, bodies and all, of earthlings. The protagonist, a physician, was frightened and frustrated as to how to deal with the situation, and was unable for most of the movie to convince those around him that something disastrous was being set up to destroy humanity.

Almost the whole town was replaced by the invaders before… well, you will have to see the movie—I don't want to spoil it for you.

The storyline was a grand scheme of delusion and deception. You wanted to shout at the big screen for the people to recognize what was going on: "You are being set up for falling victim to the body snatchers!" But, the course of the storyline could not be changed. It was inevitable that the otherworldly beings would soon take over, as they say, lock, stock, and barrel.

I find the movie and what is happening today in real life to be analogous in several troubling respects. I've given this commentary the title "Invasion of the Mind Snatchers" because it has become evident that the thought processes of people of this generation are being set up for the most profound deception ever perpetrated—well, that is, except for the original deception, when the serpent beguiled Eve in the Garden of Eden.

Jesus had told His followers He would be going away from them, but would return. He answered His disciples' questions about when things He was prophesying would come to pass.

They wanted to know when the end of the age would be, and when He would return.

He began His lengthy and in-depth answer with the words:

> Take heed that no man deceive you. For many shall come in my name, saying, I am Christ; and shall deceive many. (Matthew 24:4–5)

So began what has become known as the Olivet Discourse. This section of Scripture is considered perhaps the most important of all prophecies in the Bible because it is from the mouth of God in the flesh. And, the very first thing Jesus said was that deceivers would mark the very end of the age. Great deception would characterize the time just before He comes back. Jesus forewarned that His disciples must be on high alert for this particular societal condition.

The invasion by the mind snatchers is here. No matter which way we look, we see the delusion settling upon the thinking processes of men, women, and children. It has completely changed the character of our nation.

In America, it is relatively easy to look back and see that the entertainment industry has been a tool used by the master deceiver to pollute the common sensibility of the people. Hollywood has caused the suspension of disbelief to such an extent that the lines between fiction and fact have been catastrophically blurred. Morality guided by biblical principles has gone by the wayside in our society and culture.

The film industry, for example, has propagandized us to accept that it is okay to sleep around with other than one's legally sanctioned spouse. As a matter of fact, the very term "sleeping with" is an entertainment industry-spawned term invented to help avoid the stigma attached to the sinful activity of having sex outside the God-ordained union of wedlock.

Deception is the progenitor of delusion—a mental illness that robs one of the ability to discern what is moral and what is not. Values clarification and situational ethics, through incessant inculcation, especially by the political, judicial, and educational progressives (liberals) since the 1960s, have declared that there are no moral absolutes (the Bible is irrelevant). The supreme evidence of how this has deleteriously affected life in the United States is seen in our political process and the results the lack of discernment has produced.

Socioeconomically, geopolitically, and every other way, deception has invaded and taken the minds of humanity farther and farther from God, thus from sanity. No element of this deceptive assault has been more deadly than has the false teachers and preachers of this Laodicean age. Strange winds of doctrine have joined forces with the humanist agenda to blow away every semblance of true spiritual discernment. These satanic, psycho-babble concepts have constituted the ingredients for deception that has brought much of society to the point that it is now ready for suffering the great delusion of Bible prophecy yet future.

That prophesied delusion is outlined in 2 Thessalonians, as the apostle Paul writes:

> For the mystery of iniquity doth already work; only he who now letteth will let until he be taken out of the way. And then shall that wicked one be revealed, whom the Lord shall consume with the spirit of his mouth, and shall destroy with the brightness of his coming,

Even him, whose coming is after the working of Satan with all power and signs and lying wonders,

And with all deceivableness of unrighteousness in them that perish, because they received not the love of the truth, that they might be saved.

And for this cause God shall send them strong delusion, that they should believe a lie,

That they all might be damned who believed not the truth, but had pleasure in unrighteousness.

(2 Thessalonians 2:7–11)

Like disease that causes dementia to progress within the human brain, the deceptive tendrils of willful godlessness are pushing this generation toward the strong delusion prophesied for the Tribulation hour.

October 31, 2011
The Ultimate Bestiality

It constitutes a real-life Halloween story. The bestiality of which I write is in the courtship stage. The consummation waits just ahead in the murkiness of history yet future, but one can sense its nearness.

Although it all appears benign—even a union to be desired for the good of humanity—it will result in a relationship of the most debased sort, more horrendous in its evil than sexual acts between human and animal. The courtship took a major step along its biblically prophesied pathway just this week. The mating call for this monstrous union revolves around another biblically prophesied matter—the end-time cry for peace. We will try to understand the nature of these things that are foreshadowing the quickly approaching Tribulation hour. We begin by looking at news that has developed over the past week.

> Pope Benedict XVI called three hundred religious leaders to a gathering in Assisi, Italy, for the purpose of dealing with the violence perpetrated "in the name of God," fueled by "fundamentalists" across the world. The event, termed the "Day of Interreligious Council," held Thursday, October 27, in the town where St. Francis of Assisi was born, was meant to be a "journey of reflection, dialog and prayer for peace and justice in the world," according to the Vatican. More than fifty Islamist representatives from a number of countries were scheduled to attend the talks, including those from Saudi Arabia and from Iran....
>
> They will be joined by rabbis, Hindus, Buddhists, Jains, Sikhs, a Zoroastrian, a Bahai, and representatives of Taoism and Confucianism as well as of other traditional religions from Africa and America....
>
> For the first time, four atheists will also attend the meeting, which is traditionally organised so as not to coincide with the Muslim day of prayer on Friday, the Jewish one on Saturday, or the Christian one on Sunday....
>
> At the end of the day of talks, the main participants will renew their commitment to peace in the square in front of St. Francis' Basilica.
>
> A burning torch will be symbolically presented to the delegations in the hope that they will take the message back with them to their communities.[119]

Although Pope John Paul II was instrumental in getting the ecumenical agglomerate organized initially, this pope and his Vatican power base have moved things forward in a portentous way. When considering his strongly asserted efforts this past week to influence another area of prophetic import—the global economy—the lateness of the hour shouldn't be missed by the student of Bible prophecy.

> The Vatican called Monday for radical reform of the world's financial systems, including the creation of a global political authority to manage the economy.
>
> A proposal by the Pontifical Council for Justice and Peace calls for a new world economic order based on ethics and the "achievement of a universal common good." It follows Pope Benedict XVI's 2009 economic encyclical that denounced a profit-at-all-cost mentality as responsible for the global financial meltdown.
>
> The proposal acknowledges, however, that a "long road still needs to be traveled before arriving at the creation of a public authority with universal jurisdiction" and suggests the reform process begin with the United Nations as a point of reference.[120]

What we are witnessing just within the past week, I believe, is the woman putting on her seductive clothing and harlot makeup for her prophetic date with the "kings of the earth," who are represented by the composite beast of Revelation 13 and 17. The prophecy is one that we have covered many times in these commentaries. But, never has the timing of developments seemed more profoundly relevant than at present. The ultimate act of bestiality is about to take place.

> And there came one of the seven angels which had the seven vials, and talked with me, saying unto me, Come here; I will show unto thee the judgment of the great whore that sitteth upon many waters;
>
> With whom the kings of the earth have committed fornication, and the inhabitants of the earth have been made drunk with the wine of her fornication.
>
> So he carried me away in the Spirit into the wilderness and I saw a woman sit upon a scarlet colored beast, full of names of blasphemy, having seven heads and ten horns.
>
> And the woman was arrayed in purple and scarlet color, and decked with gold and precious stones and pearls, having a golden cup in her hand, full of abominations and filthiness of her fornication;
>
> And upon her forehead was a name written, MYSTERY, BABYLON THE GREAT, THE MOTHER OF HARLOTS AND ABOMINATIONS OF THE EARTH.
>
> And I saw the woman drunken with the blood of the saints, and with the blood of the martyrs of Jesus; and when I saw her, I wondered with great admiration.
>
> And the angel said unto me, Why didst thou marvel? I will tell thee the mystery of the woman, and of the beast that carrieth her, which hath the seven heads and ten horns.
>
> The beast that thou sawest was, and is not; and shall ascend out of the bottomless pit, and go into perdition;

and they that dwell on the earth shall wonder, whose names were not written in the book of life from the foundation of the world, when they behold the beast that was, and is not, and yet is.

And here is the mind which hath wisdom. The seven heads are seven mountains, on which the woman sitteth. (Revelation 17:1–9)

November 2011

Christ: Center of All History

November 7, 2011
History's Most Important Q & A

Many ministries and other forums send me their newsletters/information during the course of any given day. Yesterday I received such an information piece. Its contents hammered home that a profound disconnect exists in the minds of mankind brought on by the original sin in the Garden of Eden. Sin disrupted understanding between God and man to such an extent that it took God coming to dwell among humanity as a flesh-and-blood Person to restore the relationship that was torn when Adam disobeyed and brought sin and death into the world.

The item illustrated the problem of denial of Heaven's plan for restitution of the God-man relationship. The words of an e-mailer to the information forum demonstrate the disconnect wrought by the disruption in Eden.

> Isn't it time to let that poor guy Jesus alone? He lived, he died and he hasn't been heard from since. He gave his thirty-three years and just let him rest in peace. Good grief, why try to rebirth him into this crazy world? He

would be overwhelmed. He was a poor, illiterate carpenter for heaven sakes. He never traveled more than fifty miles from his home in the desert. He espoused simple truths that anyone and many have also espoused. He didn't have the only patent on spiritual truths.

Let's move toward a new spiritual understanding that humans are responsible for their own actions and that they cannot rely on mythical characters or real characters that have been made into perfect myths. The major religions are all desert religions by some very backward and illiterate tribes. For instance, I am from Sweden. I should bow down to Thor as my god because that's my tribe. Instead, I think for myself and I stand as a beacon of spiritual energy for my own life. Thor had his time and I've got mine.

Now we come to the purpose of this commentary. The title, "History's Most Important Q & A," encapsulates the problem and the solution manifested in the above-quoted thoughts about Jesus, the God-Man sent from Heaven to be the sacrificial Lamb that takes away the sin of the world. The question, the most important ever asked, and its answer are found in the account of the Lord Jesus Christ and His disciples as they engaged in a Q & A while traveling in ministry.

When Jesus came into the coasts of Caesarea Philippi, he asked his disciples, saying, Whom do men say that I the Son of man am?

And they said, Some say that thou art John the Baptist; some, Elijah; and others, Jeremiah, or one of the prophets.

Terry James

NOVEMBER 2011

> He saith unto them, But who say ye that I am?
>
> And Simon Peter answered and said, Thou art the Christ, the Son of the living God.
>
> And Jesus answered and said unto him, Blessed art thou, Simon Barjona; for flesh and blood hath not revealed it unto thee, but my Father, who is in heaven.
>
> And I say also unto thee, That thou art Peter, and upon this rock I will build my church, and the gates of hell shall not prevail against it. (Matthew 16:13–18)

Jesus first asked His immediate followers who people in general said He was. They answered that people had various opinions about who this miracle-working, itinerate preacher might be. Jesus then asked the question of the ages: "Who do you say that I am?"

Peter, the burly fisherman who was always quick to assert his thoughts into any situation, for once spoke up with the most profound answer ever given and won the total approval of the Lord: "You are the Christ, the Son of the Living God!"

The big, rough-hewn fisherman had breached the gap that had formed when Adam disobeyed in the Garden of Eden. God, the Father, had Himself given Peter that understanding. Jesus is the very Son of the Living God!

It seems that at no time in human history has that disconnect been more front and center than today. Jesus Christ is blatantly misunderstood, and that is bad enough. But it is the fact that His Holy Name is dragged through the muck of this fallen cesspool of a world that stabs most painfully the spiritual heart of the true follower of Christ.

Today I was listening to Glenn Beck as he chatted with his radio partner and his audience. I've listened many times to the famous Mormon talk-show host use the name of Jesus to claim his being a Christian. I've recently covered the points of difference between what God's Word says about Jesus and Mormonism's view of Jesus. In brief, that cult holds Jesus to be the created brother of Lucifer. Yes, the same Lucifer (the serpent) who brought about the disconnect between God and man through seducing Eve and tempting Adam to disobey God.

Mr. Beck was intimating how Jesus had no interest in "rapturing" His "people" from this world; rather, He wants His people to make this world a wonderful place of freedom–a heaven on earth.

That is Mormonism. The Mormon Church will be the final authority in any such "New World Order," according to its eschatology. Beck, in his usual way, became increasingly sarcastic and chiding while he mocked the Rapture. He talked about how if the rapturists wanted to really make a statement, they should, rather than set dates for the Rapture, simply state that they are leaving, go to some spot, and let their clothes drop to the ground as if they had been taken. Then they should stay out of the picture so the world would perceive they were gone. Thus, Beck implied slyly that those who believe in such nonsense would get out of the way so "real" religionists—the Mormons—could bring about utopia.

This, as much as anything, proves two things. First, it shows that Beck has no thought of Jesus being the same Jesus in whom I believe and who I follow. Second, it reaffirms that the Rapture is very close because of Beck and others like him mockingly fulfilling a most relevant prophecy for these troubling yet exciting times. Appropriately, it is the same Peter who gave the following prophecy who gave the most important answer to Christ's all-important question of history:

NOVEMBER 2011

> Knowing this first, that there shall come in the last days scoffers, walking after their own lusts,
>
> And saying, Where is the promise of his coming? For since the fathers fell asleep, all things continue as they were from the beginning of the creation. (2 Peter 3:3–4)

My Jesus is God, who cannot lie. My Jesus says He, not the Mormon Church, will establish a glorious millennial reign. My Jesus keeps His promises, and He promises this:

> Let not your heart be troubled; ye believe in God, believe also in me.
>
> In my Father's house are many mansions; if it were not so, I would have told you. I go to prepare a place for you.
>
> And if I go and prepare a place for you, I will come again, and receive you unto myself; that where I am, there ye may be also. (John 14:1–3)

The question that is the most important in all of human history is posed by the Lord Jesus Himself. It is asked directly to you who are reading these words. Who is Jesus to you? Who do you say He is?

Glenn Beck, like so many others, believes Jesus is something other than who the Bible says He is. The Bible, through the words of Peter, whom Jesus said gave the God-inspired answer, said Jesus is the Christ, the Son of the Living God.

Jesus is not a created being. He is God, who came to planet earth in the flesh to save you and me from sin that has all of lost mankind headed down the broad way to the lake of fire (Revelation 20:12–15).

November 2011

Jesus said He came "to seek and to save that which was lost" (Luke 19:10). He asks you: "Who do you say that I am?" How you answer this most important question of history will determine whether you go to Heaven or to Hell for all of eternity.

Answer wisely.

November 14, 2011
Liars' Club and Prophetic Truth

French President Nicolas Sarkozy didn't know the microphones were switched on when he spoke in hushed tones to President Barack Obama. "I cannot bear Netanyahu, he's a liar," he said.

The American president, equally unaware that he was being recorded, responded: "You're fed up with him, but I have to deal with him even more often than you."[121]

The technical gaffe took place week before last at the G20 Summit in Cannes, France, when the microphones were activated prematurely in the process of allowing reporters in separate locations to listen in to translations of the meetings. The "accidental" broadcast is almost as interesting as that so-called Stuxnet worm computer virus that disrupted Iran from bringing its nuclear program online. By that, I mean the revealed thoughts of the two men who are at the center of wanting to prevent Israel from militarily attacking Iran's budding nuclear facilities show the truth about the enemies Israel faces in this end-of-the-age time frame. It seems that worms are being introduced and switches are being manipulated in high places.

If Benjamin Netanyahu is a liar, then he has joined the "Liars' Club" that has been a part of the diplomatic world for many years, and one that has been lying to him and the world in recent times—particularly since he again became Israel's leader. Practically every leader of any significance in Europe has in these last several years held up Israel as the sticking point to Mideast and world peace. Certainly, this U.S. administration has played surreptitious games with the Israeli prime minister, and has done its best to make him look and feel like a second-class world citizen.

Remember, for example, the American president's treatment of the prime minister when Netanyahu came to the White House early on in this administration? The meeting was set as an important time of talks on the Middle East situation and was to be a photo opportunity to show solidarity between the two nations and their leaders. Instead, Obama abruptly stopped the meeting, summarily dismissing the Israeli. The president said he had to go to dinner with Mrs. Obama, or some such excuse.

Even the mainstream news media was stunned at the snub, but quickly let it drop from the ongoing reportage. Most of us would never have learned of the insulting behavior of our president if not for all of the alternative news forums through Internet and the cable news outlets.

All the while the diplomatic speak—the language of lies as it has come to be—was telling us that the president was as strong an ally to the nation Israel as any in the history of relations between the countries. But, behind the scenes and more and more often in the glare of the spotlight of unfolding news coverage, the Europeans and the U.S. State Department, under Hillary Clinton's leadership, did their worst to make the back-door deals that would pressure Netanyahu to cave to demands made by the international community. Always, the pressure involved–as it still does—demands that Israel allow the powers that be to bring about the two-state solution to Mideast turmoil based upon the boundaries they stipulate. These lines are much the same in configuration as Israel's Islamist enemies in the region demand.

And now comes to the surface of the diplomatic subterfuge the short, but telling, conversation of the leaders of two of the most central nations in the "Roadmap to Peace." While they smile and claim to have Israel's interest at heart, they show utter disdain for the leader of the Jewish state. They call him a liar, and I infer that much deeper detestation rages just below the surface of that accidental broadcast.

In our childhood days—and maybe even in our adulthood—we've used the get-back-at-'em old adage: "It takes one to know one."

Sarkozy and Obama, like most of the international community's rulers-elite, are liars of the first magnitude, thus it angers them when they know they are being lied to. They know the routine so very well. Their very existence and power-grabbing prowess depend upon being able to lie.

Truth is, they are right. Benjamin Netanyahu is now lying to them. He smiles and nods agreement to their deadlines and their pressures to negotiate a settlement in East Jerusalem and all the rest. But, those sit-downs and negotiations that would give away Israel's territory of vital importance to Israel's security never eventuate. Like solutions to the world's woes, the proverbial can always seems to get kicked farther down the road in the peace process. Netanyahu seems as slippery…well…as slippery as the Arab leadership of Israel's enemy neighbors have always been in failing to live up to any agreement to negotiate peace. These have always spoken to the news cameras and microphones, promising to negotiate in good faith with the hated Israel. Remember Yasser Arafat, as one example?

NOVEMBER 2011

To state it as plainly as I know how, Benjamin Netanyahu is now playing by their rules, and is beating them at their own game. The Arabs and the international community see nothing wrong with lying, if it achieves what they want: complete control over how the Middle East, particularly Israel, is divided. Arab leadership takes its orders from Allah—from the Koran. Lying to get what you want—of what serves Allah—is perfectly acceptable, even preferable, in efforts to conquer the world in as little or as large portions as the resistance allows.

This Israeli prime minister's repertoire of resistance now includes lies and subterfuge, exactly like that so long exhibited by Israel's enemies. It's driving them all completely nuts. Sarkozy's words and Obama's response demonstrate the frustration. How dare Netanyahu lie to them!

Benjamin Netanyahu is doing the right thing by smiling before the cameras and saying Israel will participate in the peace process—a process that God's Word says will one day be lethal to the Jewish people. But, for now at least, the prime minister plays by their cunning rules, beating them at their own game, while facing perhaps the most challenging situation for the Jewish state to date.

The one situation on the minds of many around the world at present is: Will Israel attack Iran's nuclear program facilities?

Netanyahu and his government openly applaud the international community—and the Obama administration talking about applying "lethal" sanctions against Iran's economy in order to get them to back away from producing an atomic bomb, then weaponizing it (engineering one small enough to attach to a missile). But, one just knows that the hawks within the Israeli government—and they are in the majority these days—know that the threat by the leadership of the international community to lethally sanction Iran through collapsing Iran's Central Bank, for example, is all smoke and mirrors. It is a lie.

The following gives a very brief thumbnail overview of the Netanyahu government's thinking:

> Israeli Defense Minister Ehud Barak told Israel Radio that since Russia and China are unlikely to back "lethal" sanctions on Iran, it would be unwise "to take any option off the table," meaning that military strikes should be considered. He also said a naval blockade to cut off Iran's oil exports might be a good idea.[122]

Sarkozy and Obama are frustrated—as are all of those of the international diplomatic Liars Club. They know Israeli leadership is onto them. BiBi Netanyahu is the most current form of the Stuxnet worm in the humanistic plan to divide God's land. The powers that be know he is lying to them—that he could, indeed, applaud their "lethal sanctions" sophistry while planning strategic strikes of the deadly military sort.

How long kicking the can down the road of diplomatic flim-flam, false peacemaking will last before it all comes to a head is anyone's guess. But, the One who knows the end has given us prophetic truth regarding where it's all heading:

> I will also gather all nations, and will bring them down into the valley of Jehoshaphat, and will plead with them there for my people and for my heritage, Israel, whom they have scattered among the nations, and parted my land. (Joel 3:2)

NOVEMBER 2011

November 21, 2011
Rapture and Sudden Destruction

Every week I find in my e-mail inbox a number of predictions for this or for that concerning Bible prophecy. Many involve the writer's prediction of the time of the Rapture, based upon a specific formula he or she has figured out, or has adopted from someone else's thoughts.

Some, such as one particular writer, send out a dozen or more Rapture timing predictions each year, including to Todd and me. This one writer's predictions usually revolve around traditional Jewish holy days. Although every prediction has thus far failed, the writer is persistent, becoming more adamant about the validity of his date-setting with each succeeding "forth telling."

I've come to sort of look forward to unwrapping these missives to peek at what we might have—kind of like opening a surprise package. One thing is sure: It's never a disappointing exercise. He always has something new and unusual to spring upon the recipient. If he remains so persistent—based upon the way world events are shaping up—he is bound to be at least nearly right about the timing of the Rapture at some point.

The week just past, his e-mail offering was a little less absolute in its predictive tenor, but nonetheless given with confidence, as usual. At any rate, this one struck a chord and prompted me to think again on the words of Jesus that have burned in my spirit since I wrote a ten-part series entitled "Scanning a Fearful Future" (see commentaries for November 22, 2010–January 24, 2011). But more about that momentarily.

The e-mailer wrote:

DOES THE BIBLE GIVE US THE DAY OF THE YEAR FOR WWII (Ezekiel 38–39)? I have written much over the past three years about my biblical studies that show World War III (the sudden destruction) and the Rapture to be the very same day. If the start of the Great Tribulation is going to take place in the next five months, and I am totally convinced that it is, then we need to take a very close look at this BIBLICAL day (it is in the very near future, still in 2011). In light of current events all around the world, especially involving a very possible imminent attack involving Israel and Iran and/or Syria, this rapidly-approaching BIBLICAL day takes on a very urgent and ominous meaning for 2011. The Bride of Christ may have already celebrated its last Christmas on this earth.

Yes, well…I guess he was a bit more adamant about things than I remembered at first reading. Still, the prognostication was mild in comparison to many of his previous declarations about the Rapture and its timing. Just so you won't be wondering—if I read it correctly—I believe that the date to which he refers is April 11, 2012.

I give this article the title "Rapture and Sudden Destruction" because I believe the persistent e-mailer is right in this instance. He is not correct on the date, because it is, again, based upon Jewish traditional holy days—and all of those have failed to produce the Rapture. Besides, no man knows the day, we are told by the Lord. There is no relationship anyone has been able to show, so far as I can tell, between any Jewish traditional holy day and that "twinkling-of-an-eye" moment prophesied in 1 Corinthians

15, 1 Thessalonians 4, and, I believe, by Jesus Himself as recorded in John 14:1–3, and given by John in Revelation 4:1–2. The Rapture of the church will be sudden, unannounced, and unanticipated by most of the world's population.

Paul the apostle, who, of course, was chosen by God to prophesy the Rapture, foretells much about that coming time when millions of believers will go to be with Christ in one *atomos* of time (an increment of time so brief that it cannot be divided). Paul writes further about the time immediately surrounding the moment of the Rapture:

> But of the times and the seasons, brethren, ye have no need that I write unto you.
>
> For yourselves know perfectly that the day of the Lord so cometh as a thief in the night.
>
> For when they shall say, Peace and safety; then sudden destruction cometh upon them, as travail upon a woman with child; and they shall not escape.
>
> But ye, brethren, are not in darkness, that that day should overtake you as a thief.
>
> Ye are all the children of light, and the children of the day: we are not of the night, nor of darkness.
>
> Therefore let us not sleep, as do others; but let us watch and be sober. (1 Thessalonians 5:1–6)

Paul tells Christians to be ever alert to the times that surround them. He exhorts them to "watch." Jesus said the same thing as recorded in Mark 13:37: "What I say unto one, I say unto all; watch."

Jesus and Paul were referring to watching the events and issues of the times in which they will be living. There is no specific signal of the Rapture, but all of the signs of societal conditions will indicate that the time of Christ's coming in the Rapture is very near, even at the door. The day of God's judgment beginning to fall upon rebellious mankind, the apostle Paul wrote, would begin like a thief breaking into a home at night. Jesus had likened His coming to a thief in the night in Matthew 24.

While writing the "Scanning a Fearful Future" series of articles (see November 22, 2010–January 24, 2011), I sensed the Lord impressing upon my spirit that Jesus' words were all important in foretelling exactly when all of His impending judgment would break loose upon a world that has shown its hatred for His Son, who came to die for the sins of mankind. There will be no world-rending things, like all-out war or total economic collapse at that time. Even though portentous signs of the times will be prevalent, it will still be, relatively speaking, business as usual when Christ breaks in upon a world ripe for judgment. The persistent e-mailer is on the right prophetic page in this instance. It will be the Rapture that brings the awesome judgment of God upon this fallen planet.

Again, Jesus foretold:

> And as it was in the days of Noah, so shall it be also in the days of the Son of man.
>
> They did eat, they drank, they married wives, they were given in marriage, until the day that Noah entered into the ark, and the flood came, and destroyed them all.

Also as it was in the days of Lot; they did eat, they drank, they bought, they sold, they planted, they built;

But the same day that Lot went out of Sodom, it rained fire and brimstone from heaven, and destroyed them all.

Even thus shall it be in the day when the Son of man is revealed. (Luke 17:26–30)

November 28, 2011
"Distress...with Perplexity"

I wrote the following for *Nearing Midnight* on March 7 of this year, under the title, "End Times—The Bottom Line":

> Global economic chaos is driving the distress and perplexity of the nations of planet earth. The words of the greatest of all prophets, Jesus Christ, echo in cavernous reverberation with each succeeding news report from the capitals of earth's monetary centers. "And there shall be… upon the earth distress of nations, with perplexity; the sea and the waves roaring" (Luke 21:25b).

Jesus' Olivet Discourse spoke to conditions exponentially moved beyond norms. In other words, the "distress" and "perplexity" that nations will be experiencing as His Second Coming nears will be beyond any ever known. And, in biblical terms, "seas and waves" refer to the masses of peoples. Jesus said that because there will be unprecedented distress and perplexity among the nations, the peoples populating those nations will be "roaring."

"Distress of nations, with perplexity" has ratcheted up…

well...exponentially, since that date. The bottom line more than ever projects that America and the other nations have moved beyond critical mass, as far as the point of economic implosion is concerned. Only the staying hand of God prevents that inevitable collapse.

Yet, distinctive cracks are developing in the global economic structures. Those cracks are harbingers of things to come. The governmental heads of Greece and Italy have been symbolically lopped off by the European Union leadership, who are themselves largely unelected by Europe's peoples. And, those peoples are becoming like "the seas and the waves roaring." The results of the incentive-crippling, socialistic economic model that most governments of Europe have for decades employed have come home to roost.

The inability due to Italy's Prime Minister Silvio Berlusconi and Greece's Prime Minister George Papandreou to stick to strict austerity agendas brought the wrath of the economic powers elite down on them. The European bankers' inner circle is blamed or credited—depending upon one's view—for engineering the *coup d'etat.* The action has thrown the whole of Europe into uncertainty as to what comes next. It is "distress...with perplexity" of the first order. Even Germany, the most stable of the European states, is feeling the pressures of the budding EU dictatorship—the banking money powers—in their demand that all of Europe conforms to their emerging new economic order.

America moves headlong down the same pathway as Europe. Economic cataclysm hangs like the sword of Damocles over the heads of U.S. and state governments and those of the banking industry. While America's people are for the most part still law-abiding and want to restore economic tranquility in a peaceful manner, leftist elements are doing all within their power to bring the seas and waves to a roaring state of self-destructiveness. The mainstream media seems determined to do all within its power to assist in the movement to rev up anarchy in this nation.

While forces here are determined to bring the United States into a new economic order just as forces in Europe are doing the same over there, it is vital to notice the difference between the two forces at work. It was the leftist-socialistic governance that operated in Europe for decades that drove it to bankruptcy. Now, it is a rightist movement that is demanding austerity and an almost fascist form of governance determined to save Europe.

In America, we are witnessing a Marxist-Leninist-style attempt from the political left to bring new economic order in the form of the current presidential administration as it strives to bring about socialism to this country. The effort has succeeded on a level beyond even that which destroyed the USSR. By that, I mean it has succeeded more profoundly than the dynamics that destroyed the former Soviet Union, because we are now more than $15 trillion in debt—an amount the Soviets could not have imagined.

Two political ideologies working at changing the world in their parts of the globe move toward each other from opposite directions. It is an amazing thing to behold! The so-called super committee, appointed to find creative new ways to cut trillions of dollars from federal spending in the U.S., dramatically presents the degree of "distress, with perplexity" that is front and center on today's prophetic landscape. They failed miserably, as if by design. No cuts were agreed to by anyone.

"The seas and the waves" (the malcontents who are uprising against any suggestion of cutting social programs) threaten to desert and/or vote out politicians who cut off their handout lifestyles. More than this, threatened anarchy and destruction of inner cities simmers at the fear centers of our political leaders' thinking.

Those leaders thus help generate and incubate the "distress, with perplexity" of these troubling times. They choose to placate their political power bases rather than to transcend selfish ambition. They choose the path of least resistance—the one to destruction—rather than working toward securing the blessings of liberty and promoting the general welfare of their nation, which each has pledged to do.

As disheartening as the "distress, with perplexity" is, Jesus' words have never resonated more clearly:

> And when these things begin to come to pass, then look up, and lift up your heads; for your redemption draweth nigh. (Luke 21:28)

Terry James

December 2011

Raging Rumors of War; Be Rapture Ready

December 5, 2011
Rumors of War Rampant

Nearing Midnight commentaries have for months been devoted in large measure to examining the building economic bubble that threatens to bring about worldwide cataclysm. We have written on, for example, things like the crisis this past week involving the collapsing euro, which is feared to be creating irreparable cracks in global financial structures.

Todd and I pretty much agree: 1) We are amazed that the bubble hasn't burst; 2) We believe that the longer the crises build, the greater will be the explosion; 3) We maintain that only the staying hand of God has thus far prevented it from bursting; and 4) We are of the opinion that it will likely be the Rapture of the church that will pop that bubble.

I, at least, was under the illusion that second only to Israel's position at the center of world controversy; the impending global economic catastrophe has to be the next most profound signal of how near the end of the age this generation finds us. Jesus, of course, didn't first specifically mention either Israel or the global economy as being the most significant signs of His return when His disciples asked Him directly. He did, however, mention the subject of this commentary:

> And as he sat upon the Mount of Olives, the disciples came unto him privately, saying,
>
> Tell us, when shall these things be? And what shall be the sign of thy coming, and of the end of the world? (Matthew 24:3)

The Lord described a number of things that would be on the world scene at the time He would return to the earth—or at least to above the earth. Among the first signals He mentioned are in the following:

> And ye shall hear of wars and rumors of wars; see that ye be not troubled; for all these things must come to pass, but the end is not yet.
>
> For nation shall rise against nation, and kingdom against kingdom. (Matthew 24:6–7a)

As prophetically stunning as Israel being at center stage is the global economic cataclysm looming above this rebellious, judgment-bound planet. The sudden proliferation of potentially world-rending military conflicts on the prophetic horizon is equally astonishing. "Rumors of war" are literally in every direction we look. We will have brief looks at a number of the "rumors of war" that are presently front and center in the news:

Afghanistan to Back Pakistan against U.S.

ISLAMABAD, October 23—After being critical of Pakistan over its links with Taliban militants, Afghan President Hamid Karzai has now said his country would stand by Islamabad in the event of hostilities with any nation, including the United States or India.

"God forbid, if at any time there is a war between Pakistan and America, then we will be with Pakistan," Karzai said in an interview with Pakistan's Geo News, excerpts of which were aired by the channel.[123]

Iran Threatens to Bomb Turkey if U.S. or Israel Attacks

Iran will bomb Turkey if the U.S. or Israel tries to destroy its nuclear installations, a senior military commander warned today. General Amir Ali Hajizadeh, head of the aerospace division of the powerful Revolutionary Guard, threatened to target NATO's missile defence shield in the neighbouring country. The system, which Turkey only agreed to install in September, is designed to prevent Iranian missile attacks on Israel. The warning is part of a new strategy devised by the Supreme Leader Ayatollah Ali Khamenei that consists of responding "to threats with threats."

General Hajizadeh said: "Should we be threatened, we will target NATO's missile defense shield in Turkey and then hit the next targets."[124]

Russia's Military Chief Warns that Heightened Risks of Conflict Near Borders May Turn Nuclear

MOSCOW—Russia is facing a heightened risk of being drawn into conflicts at its borders that have the potential of turning nuclear, the nation's top military officer said Thursday.

Gen. Nikolai Makarov, chief of the General Staff of the Russian armed forces, cautioned over NATO's expansion eastward and warned that the risks for Russia to be pulled into local conflicts have "risen sharply." Makarov added, according to Russian news agencies, that "under certain conditions local and regional conflicts may develop into a full-scale war involving nuclear weapons."[125]

N. Korea Threatens S. Korean Leader's Office over Drills

SEOUL, South Korea—North Korea threatened Thursday to turn Seoul's presidential office into a "sea of fire," one day after South Korea conducted large-scale military drills near a front-line island attacked by North Korea last year. The exercises marked the first anniversary of North Korea's artillery attack on the South Korean island of Yeonpyeong that killed two marines and two civilians. The North's military warned in a statement Thursday that "a similar sea of fire" may engulf Seoul's presidential Blue House if South Korean forces ever fire a single shot into North Korea's territory. The warning was carried by North Korean state media.[126]

Egypt's El Baradei Threatens War with Israel

Troubling signs are beginning to emerge from post-Hosni Mubarak Egypt: The prime minister is making new overtures to Iran—and a leading presidential candidate is threatening war with Israel. Mohamed El Baradei, the former director of the International Atomic Energy Agency who has announced his candidacy for president in Egypt, said on Monday that "if Israel attacked Gaza we would declare war against the Zionist regime."

The *Digital Journal* observed: "In the world's first glimpse of the policies that may emerge from the results of the upcoming Egyptian presidential election, one candidate for president outlined his insistence on protecting Palestinians in Gaza from Israeli military assaults. Mohamed El Baradei's position on the matter is clear: An Israeli military strike against Gaza would result in a declaration of war from Egypt."[127]

Iran Threatens Israel with Missile Barrage if Attacked

Iran continues to threaten Israel, this time hinting it will hit it with up to 150,000 missiles if its nuclear facilities are attacked. In a continuation of its statements from the past several days, Iran on Sunday threatened Israel with a barrage of missiles, if the Jewish state attacks its nuclear facilities.

Iran's Defense Minister Brigadier General Ahmad Vahidi told the Farsnews agency that Israel will not have a minimal chance of survival after attacking Iran.[128]

China vs. Taiwan

> Despite showing goodwill and friendliness in its economic and cultural exchanges with Taiwan, China has never ceased its military exercises simulating attacks on the nation, former deputy defense minister Lin Chong-pin said yesterday. Lin made the remarks after the US Department of Defense released its annual report on military and security developments in China, saying that Beijing has not slowed its efforts to expand its military options to deny any outside intervention in the Taiwan Strait, despite improvements in cross-strait ties in recent years.
>
> While briefing reporters on the Pentagon report to be delivered to the US Congress, Michael Schiffer, U.S. deputy assistant secretary of defense for East Asia, said that over the past year, China has continued to beef up its naval and aerial combat arsenal, including extending the range of its jet fighters and updating its submarines and surface warships, as well as conducting sea trials of its first aircraft carrier.[129]

Rumors of war are indeed rampant upon today's prophetic horizon. With the impending threats and military preparations, it becomes clear the coming "sudden destruction" of Paul's forewarning (1 Thessalonians 5:3) cannot be far distant in time. Jesus' words foretelling what this world faces when the Rapture occurs are starkly in view at this very moment.

> And as it was in the days of Noe, so shall it be also in the days of the Son of man.

December 2011

They did eat, they drank, they married wives, they were given in marriage, until the day that Noah entered into the ark, and the flood came, and destroyed them all.

Also as it was in the days of Lot; they did eat, they drank, they bought, they sold, they planted, they built; But the same day that Lot went out of Sodom, it rained fire and brimstone from heaven, and destroyed them all. (Luke 17:26–29)

December 12, 2011
Prince of Persia on the Loose

Those of us who examine world issues and events of our time from a pretribulational viewpoint consistently pronounce that the uprisings that began months ago in the Middle East would result in an expansion of Islamist control over the region. Mainstream news pundits proclaimed it a great day for democracy's spreading among the tyrant-laden nations of the Middle East. Mainstream religionists, at the same time—including, sadly, many of the neo-evangelical sort such as Saddleback's Rick Warren—declared it a new day for all faiths to come together in peace and understanding. The Arab Spring, as it has come to be called, was to bring in a kind of Mideast utopia, it was gleefully expected by the uprising's cheerleaders.

Soon Egypt's president-dictator, Hosni Mubarak, was forced out as the nations surrounding Israel on three sides fell one by one into the hands of peoples that are under the control of…well… that's another matter into which we will have a look. No matter what news network or outlet, the talk has centered on something peaceful and good coming out of the so-called Arab Spring. The movement is a supposedly righteous rebellion to oust dictators that will bring the installation of democracy to most if not all of the nations in the region that has been the most volatile on earth since Israel was reborn in 1948.

But a funny thing happened on the way to all of that promised freedom to choose. The following news item provides enlightenment:

> Egypt's military rulers say that the next parliament will not be representative enough to independently oversee the drafting of a constitution, and that they will appoint a council to check the influence of religious extremists on the process.
>
> The announcement followed a surprisingly strong showing by Islamist groups who took the overwhelming majority in the first round of parliamentary elections. The outcome caused concern among the liberals who drove Egypt's uprising and the military, which took power from ousted leader Hosni Mubarak....
>
> Liberal groups and the military—a secular institution that has traditionally controlled access of Islamists to its ranks—are concerned that religious extremists will exert too much influence and could try to enshrine strict Islamic law, or Shariah, as the only guiding principle for state policies.
>
> Voters chose both parties and individuals in the complex electoral system. The Muslim Brotherhood, an Islamic fundamentalist group that was the best known and organized party, and the more radical Al-Nour party—

> ultraconservative Islamists known as Salafis—took about 60 percent of the vote for parties together, according to official results....
>
> The result was a devastating blow for the mostly secular and liberal youth who drove the uprising.[130]

We have watched and reported on the unrest that began many months ago and continued until the time of the Egyptian elections just reported. Since December 18, 2010, there have been revolutions in Tunisia and Egypt; a civil war in Libya; and civil uprisings in Bahrain, Syria, and Yemen. Major protests have been launched in Algeria, Iraq, Jordan, Morocco, and Oman, as well as on the borders of Israel. There have been minor protests in Kuwait, Lebanon, Mauritania, Saudi Arabia, Sudan, and Western Sahara.

Moammar Gadhafi of Libya has met his fate, and Bashar al-Assad faces the same in Syria, as the Islamist uprisings build toward a fever pitch in that tyrant's kingdom. It is interesting that Satan has trouble controlling his own diabolist minions within the Mideast madness, even as some rebellious leaders infesting Christianity fight against the good the God of Heaven wants to get done during this dispensation. Of course, this shouldn't surprise. The fomenter of both incendiary actions is one and the same.

In the case of things going on in the Israel-hating nations that surround the tiny Jewish state, the fingerprints are obvious. The same satanic general that instigated and carried out warfare in high places during the prophet Daniel's time has been turned loose today to stir the boiling Middle East cauldron. His most visible involvement is evidenced within the Islamist fury that rages under the guise of democracy on the move. The most overt evidence of the immediate danger this general poses is the nuclear threat Iran presents against Israel.

The prince of Persia (Daniel 10:20) is on the loose in these last of the last days.

December 19, 2011
On Being Rapture Ready: Part 1

Being prepared to meet Jesus Christ face to face—as far as trying to make that my constant state of mind is concerned—has been part of my every waking moment since Good Friday of this year. I don't wish to go over it in a public forum like this one ad nauseum. Nonetheless, I've been considering the relationship between my near-death moments of April 22 and being Rapture ready, as is the thought wrapped up in our website's name. So, here goes yet again...

This is intended to be an exhortation for all of us who name Christ as our Lord—urging us individually and collectively to hold Him close to our spiritual hearts during this Christmas season. It is not meant to dwell upon my personal experience as an overriding point of focus. Many who read this column on a regular basis know some of the details of my heart event on Good Friday of this year. I'm often corrected by my wife, Margaret, for not calling it a "heart attack." For some reason that description just doesn't register within my aging gray matter. Others have heart attacks, not me.

I remember thinking at the time it was occurring that this wasn't possible. The EMT working on me told the hospital dispatcher that he had a "coronary in progress." It didn't register then, either. There I was, however, being rushed toward Saline Memorial Hospital, gasping for breath, the pain behind my sternum feeling as if it would explode my chest at any second.

I remember arriving and the gurney being tugged toward the ER outer doors. Then, there was the computer-like *blip* and I was suddenly before a large heavenly throng of young, beautiful, cheering men and women. The ambience of my surroundings was dazzling, and I wanted to join them. There was no recollection whatsoever of where I had been—no memories of this planetary existence.

I was, the doctor later told Margaret, dead on arrival.

They hit me with the defibrillation paddles—yes, just like you've seen in the shows where they say "Clear!" and then apply the paddles, making the body nearly jump off the table.

I felt nothing, but the action did cause me to leave the place I never wanted to leave. I remembered thinking, "I want to stay here forever in this perfect place." But, everything turned dark and I awoke in total darkness on the gurney. This is because I'm blind due to a retinal disease, as many know. The pain behind the sternum grew worse and I heard the *blip* twice more. Each time I was before that cheering, enthusiastic throng of vibrant, young people. The sights were astonishing, colors of every description emanating from somewhere I could neither determine, nor cared to investigate. The third time I was among them, we were all racing, or being drawn by some powerful energy toward a destination I would never know. I was again in the hospital, this time on the cardiac unit's procedure table. I had again been hit with the paddles.

I had survived the widow maker, an artery blockage that I was told only 5 percent of victims live through. I was clinically dead three times, my heart having stopped each time. I had been given a journey and a return trip that few are privileged to experience—and I say that meaning it as humbly as it is possible to express.

The reasons for and meanings of this experience have been confirmed and affirmed in my spiritual understanding. I've dealt briefly with those impressions from the Holy Spirit in a previous article. God willing, there will be a more in-depth presentation on these matters in a book we have planned for release in 2012, entitled *HeavenVision: Glimpses into Glory.*

I continue to be given insight into what it all means. As stated at the beginning of this commentary, my thoughts have been turned toward being ever ready to meet the Lord Jesus Christ face to face since that Good Friday when my heart ceased to beat those three times. One of the things constantly on my mind is that my heart could fail again at any moment.

My rehabilitation has been an absolutely amazing success story. And, in that regard, I thank so many of you whose prayers were obviously heard in the throne room of Heaven. I honestly haven't experienced one moment's problem, in any way, with my heart or anything else of consequence regarding my health. In fact, I was given the "Arkansas Cardiologist Association's Patient of the Year Award for 2011" on November 18. I was asked to speak to their convention and I told them that I don't know why I should be honored. All I did was survive. My Lord, Jesus Christ, deserves top honors, because He holds the keys to death and Hell. I then said that they, the wonderful medical professionals, also deserve honors for being the ones God chose to put me back into this race.

The only problem has been cracked teeth and one crowned tooth broken completely off that resulted from being hit with the paddles those three times. Nonetheless, the thought is there that one's last heartbeat can occur at any moment.

Each time my heart stopped, I stood not before Jesus Christ, but in front of a cheering cloud of witnesses as given in Hebrews 12:1–3. This simply means, I've been assured in my spiritual understanding, that this wasn't really death. It was a preview I was given for reasons the Lord has determined. But, I will, when God's timing has come to fullness for my life, stand before my Lord and Savior. It will happen just as instantaneously as did my near-death trip to the fringes of glory. I am ready for that moment, because Jesus saved my soul with His work of redemption on the cross at Calvary nearly two thousand years ago. When my heart beats that final time, I will, in the twinkling of an eye (see 1 Corinthians 15: 52), stand before Him, and will be with Him for all of eternity.

But, my heart has not stopped for that final time. When Christ calls all believers, living and dead, to Himself, I will, if still alive, stand instantaneously before Him just as I stood instantaneously before that cheering cloud of witnesses on Good Friday, April 22, 2011.

Being Rapture ready is being ready, period. It means you are prepared to meet the Lord at any moment—at all times. Every believer has the same promise—to be present with the Lord when life on earth is over.

> Therefore, we are always confident, knowing that, while we are at home in the body, we are absent from the Lord (For we walk by faith, not by sight);
>
> We are confident, I say, and willing rather to be absent from the body, and to be present with the Lord. (2 Corinthians 5:6–8)

Next week we will go in-depth, examining details about what it means to be Rapture ready.

December 26, 2011
On Being Rapture Ready: Part 2

There is no specific signal that presages the Rapture of believers in the Scriptures. That calling by Christ to those who know Him as Savior will be unannounced and instantaneous. Paul the apostle's words inform us of that stunning event:

> Behold, I show you a mystery; We shall not all sleep, but we shall all be changed,
>
> In a moment, in the twinkling of an eye, at the last trump; for the trumpet shall sound, and the dead shall be raised incorruptible, and we shall be changed. (1 Corinthians 15:51–52)

Paul says further:

> For the Lord himself shall descend from heaven with a shout, with the voice of the archangel, and with the trump of God; and the dead in Christ shall rise first;
>
> Then we who are alive and remain shall be caught up together with them in the clouds, to meet the Lord in the air: and so shall we ever be with the Lord.
>
> (1 Thessalonians 4:16–17)

The website Todd Strandberg began in 1987, before the Internet was making an impact to any extent on life in America and throughout the world, encompasses what Christ expects every born-again believer to become. Todd gave it the name "Rapture Ready," defining a spiritual condition eternally crucial to every individual.

All who have died during this Church Age are now beyond getting "Rapture ready." They are either "Rapture ready" or not. People alive at the present time, if they don't know Christ as Savior, still have the opportunity to get Rapture ready. All who know Jesus as their Savior are Rapture ready in one sense, but might not be Rapture ready in another. We will try to clarify these matters. It is most important that we do so.

I testified in my commentary last week of instantaneously standing before a throng of heavenly witnesses (see Hebrews 12:1–3) the moment my heart stopped beating. This happened three separate times. Each time my heart ceased to beat, I was somewhere in eternity. God the Holy Spirit's assurance of where I was and who the beautiful, cheering young people were becomes more strongly burned into my own spirit by the day.

The only action I have taken in my life to warrant being instantly transported to that heavenly realm was to accept Christ as my Savior. There is no other action I could take while in this physical life to assure my instant transport into those stunning surroundings. While my near-death experience wasn't the Rapture, of course, I believe with all that is within my spiritual understanding that it was a type of what awaits the generation of Christians alive at the time of that great event, as described by the apostle Paul's prophetic words above. At that future moment of Rapture, all who have died during the Church Age or who are living at the time will stand not before a throng of witnesses as I did, but before the Lord Jesus Himself!

> Beloved, now are we the sons of God, and it doth not yet appear what we shall be: but we know that, when he shall appear, we shall be like him; for we shall see him as he is. (1 John 3:2)

All who are living today who do not know Jesus Christ as Savior stand in mortal danger. When their hearts beat the final time, they will find themselves in the same, unimaginably horrid place as the rich man described by Jesus in the story of the rich man and Lazarus (read Luke 16:19–31). Likewise, the moment Christ says at the Rapture: "Come up here" (Revelation 4:1), the person who hasn't accepted Christ will be left behind on earth to face a time in human history of which the Lord Jesus Himself said:

> For then shall be great tribulation, such as was not since the beginning of the world to this time, no, nor ever shall be.
>
> And except those days should be shortened, there should no flesh be saved. (Matthew 24:21–22a)

Being Rapture Ready

So, it is imperative to make clear what it means to be Rapture ready. Our eternal souls hang in the balance of God's impending judgment. The Lord of Heaven must judge sin, because He cannot abide sin in His holy presence. No sin can enter the gates of Heaven. And this is where God's magnificent love comes to the forefront of how He deals with each of us sinners.

He loves us so much that He sent His Son—God in the flesh, Jesus Christ—to come to earth to be the perfect sin sacrifice, the

Lamb slain from the foundation of the world, whose blood takes away the sin of the world. To be Rapture ready, you and I must be "saved" from our sins and made pure in the righteousness found only in Christ. When we believe God and accept Christ as Savior, we become Rapture ready in the eternal sense. We will go to Heaven upon our death, or will be raptured when Jesus steps out on the clouds of glory and shouts: "Come up here!"

But, there is another meaning of being Rapture ready. Each Christian is responsible for being Rapture ready in this sense. To be Rapture ready as a child of God means we are to be living in a way pleasing to God. We are to lift the name of Jesus so that men, women, and children will be drawn to Him for salvation. We are to be watching for His any-moment return in the Rapture.

Let me make it clear. I believe the Word of God tells us that every person who is saved through the redemptive blood of Jesus Christ will go to be with Him at the moment of Rapture, no matter the state of one's fellowship with the Lord. We will ALL stand before Him, Paul tells us.

However, to be truly Rapture ready as a Christian means that we are living life in such a biblically prescribed way that when Jesus calls us we will not be ashamed to look Him in His omniscient eyes. We should desire above all else to hear Him say:

> Well done, good and faithful servant; thou hast been faithful over a few things, I will make thee ruler over many things. Enter thou into the joy of thy lord.
> (Matthew 25:23b)

End-times world conditions today are unmistakable. That face-to-face meeting could take place at any moment!

Notes

1. Agence France-Presse, "U.S. Seeks to Relaunch Mideast Peace Talks," Ynetnews, 12/28/09, http://www.ynetnews.com/articles/0,7340,L-3826326,00.html.
2. Ibid.
3. David Sessions, "Brit Hume: Tiger Woods Should 'Turn to the Christian Faith,' Politics Daily, 1/4/10, http://www.politicsdaily.com/2010/01/04/brit-hume-tiger-woods-should-turn-to-the-christian-faith/.
4. Matthew Hay Brown, "Hume Doubles Down on Tiger Comments," In Good Faith, 1/5/10, http://weblogs.baltimoresun.com/news/faith/2010/01/brit_hume_tiger_woods.html.
5. "Obama Admin Threatens to Withhold Aid to Israel," *Israel Today,* 1/10/10, www.israeltoday.co.il.
6. Natasha Mozgovaya, "State Dept.: U.S. Not Planning to Withhold Israel Loan Guarantees," *Haaretz,* 11/1/10, http://www.haaretz.com/news/state-dept-u-s-not-planning-to-withhold-israel-loan-guarantees-1.261254.
7. "Obama Admin Threatens to Withhold Aid to Israel."
8. "Senators Won't Let Obama Freeze Aid to Israel," Ghana Word, 1/11/10, http://ghanaword.com/index.php?option=com_content&view=article&id=6784%3Asenators-wont-let-obama-freeze-aid-to-israel&catid=31&Itemid=46.
9. Leigh Phillips, "EU Unclear about Next Move on Iran," EUobserver, 1/26/10, http://euobserver.com/13/29339.
10. Caroline Glick, "Column One: Keeping Zionism's Promise," *Jerusalem Post,* 1/29/10, http://www.jpost.com/Opinion/Columnists/Article.aspx?id=167185.

11. Aron Heller, "Berlusconi: Bring Israel into the EU," *Miami Herald,* 1/2/10, www.MiamiHerald.com.
12. "Prospective Resources off Israel's Coast Could Be up to 6 Trillion Cubic Feet," *Jerusalem Post,* 2/2/10, http://www.jpost.com/Israel/Article.aspx?id=167585.
13. Stephen Castle, "European Debt Issues Top Agenda for Meeting," *New York Times,* 2/9/10, http://www.nytimes.com/2010/02/10/world/europe/10union.html.
14. Robert Burns, "Saudi Official Questions New Sanctions on Iran," Associated Press, 2/16/10.
15. Ibid.
16. Ibid.
17. Nick Pope, "If the Cosmic Phone Rings…Don't Answer," *Sun,* 1/28/10, http://www.thesun.co.uk/sol/homepage/news/ufos/2828017/Should-we-be-offering-hand-of-friendship-to-ET.html.
18. Chelsea Schilling, "Life with Big Brother: Killer Way to Slay the Google Beast!" World Net Daily, 1/27/10, http://www.wnd.com/2010/01/123391/.
19. Ibid.
20. Laura Meckler, "ID Card for Workers Is at Center of Immigration Plan," *Wall Street Journal,* 3/8/10, http://online.wsj.com/article/SB10001424052748703954904575110124037066854.html.
21. Ibid.
22. Aluf Benn, "Netanyahu Must Choose between Ideology and U.S. Support," *Haaretz,* 3/14/10, http://www.haaretz.com/print-edition/news/netanyahu-must-choose-between-ideology-and-u-s-support-1.266496. Thanks to John Stettin for providing articles excerpted in this commentary.
23. Associated Press, "U.S. Wants Israel to Cancel Building Plan," Newsmax, 3/16/10, http://www.newsmax.com/InsideCover/ML-Israel-Palestinians/2010/03/15/id/352694.
24. "In the News," *Arkansas Democrat-Gazette,* 3/26/10, 1.
25. "China, DPRK Armed Forces Vow to Further Cooperation," *China Daily,* 3/30/10, http://www.chinadaily.com.cn/china/2010-03/30/content_9664572.htm.
26. Hillel Fendel, "Jerusalem Construction and Demolition Back in the News," 4/13/10, http://www.israelnationalnews.com/News/News.aspx/136990#.Tw4D76U7Xko.

27 Ed Koch, "A Dangerous Silence," Huffington Post, 4/13/10, http://www.huffingtonpost.com/ed-koch/a-dangerous-silence_b_534809.html.
28. Major Brian L. Stuckert, "Strategic Implications of American Millennialism," emphasis added; quoted in Chuck Baldwin, "Army Report Says Christians Threaten U.S. Foreign Policy," Chuck Baldwin Live, 4/14/10, http://chuckbaldwinlive.com/home/?p=1192.
29. Ibid.
30. Leigh Phillips, "Citigroup Says Only 'United States of Europe' Will Save Euro," EU Observer, http://euobserver.com/19/29905, 4/21/10.
31. Associated Press, "Chicago Lawmakers: Call In the National Guard," Fox News, 4/26/10, http://www.foxnews.com/us/2010/04/26/lawmakers-military-quell-chicago-violence/.
32. Steve Kingstone, "Times Square Bomb Suspect Arrested in New York," BBC News, 5/4/10, http://news.bbc.co.uk/2/hi/8658888.stm.
33. Neal Armstrong, "Unconventional ECB Measures to Weigh on Currency," Reuters, 5/11/10, http://us.mobile.reuters.com/article/wtMostRead/idUSLDE64A0IJ20100511?ca=rdt. Thanks to John Stettin and John Rolls.
34. Leo Cendrowicz, "The EU's $950 Billion Rescue: Just the Beginning," *Time,* 5/10/10, http://www.time.com/time/business/article/0,8599,1988216,00.html. My thanks to Dana Neel.
35. Andrew Walker and Nicholas Farrelly, "The End of Democracy in Thailand?" ABC News, 5/18/10, http://www.abc.net.au/unleashed/34518.html.
36. Honor Mahoney, "Van Rompuy Wants Clearer 'Hierarchy' to Deal with Future Crises," EU Observer, 5/26/10, http://euobserver.com/18/30132.
37. Israel Ministry of Foreign Affairs, "IDF Forces Met with Pre-Planned Violence when Attempting to Board Flotilla," 5/31/10, http://www.mfa.gov.il/MFA/Government/Communiques/2010/Israel_Navy_warns_flotilla_31-May-2010.htm.
38. Wilfred Hahn, "European Union: Is the Revived Roman Empire Finished?" Rapture Ready, http://www.raptureready.com/featured/hahn/h39.html.
39. Ibid.
40. Associated Press, "Many Americans Expect Jesus' Return by 2050," Ynet News, 6/23/10, http://www.ynetnews.com/articles/0,7340,L-3909431,00.html.

41. I omit the source because its credibility is in question, in my view.
42. Wyre Davies, "Analysis: Little Room to Manoeuvre," BBC News, 7/6/10, http://www.bbc.co.uk/news/10515377.
43. Associated Press, "Obama, Netanyahu Deny Israel-U.S. Problem Exist," News One, 7/7/10, http://newsone.com/obama/associated-press/obama-netanyahu-deny-israel-u-s-problems-exist/.
44. Geert Wilders, "America as the Last Man Standing," Snopes, 5/09, http://www.snopes.com/politics/soapbox/wilders.asp.
45. Leigh Phillips, "EU to Hold Atheist and Freemason Summit," EU Observer, 7/19/10, http://euobserver.com/851/30506. Thanks to Denise Styka.
46. Sudhin Thanawala, Associated Press,"Gay Lutheran Pastors to Join Church Roster," *Boston Globe,* 7/24/10, http://www.boston.com/news/nation/articles/2010/07/24/gay_lutheran_pastors_to_join_church_roster/.
47. Tom Topousis, "Landmark Vote Opens Door to Ground Zero Mosque," *New York Post,* 8/3/10, http://www.nypost.com/p/news/local/manhattan/landmark_vote_opens_door_to_ground_bglyGZSizoS6TzMo944NRJ.
48. Myra Adams, "Building the 9-11 Mosque Will Not Breed Tolerance," *Daily Caller,* 8/5/10, http://dailycaller.com/2010/08/05/building-the-9-11-mosque-will-not-breed-tolerance/.
49. Nathalie Boschat and David Pearson, "Sarkozy Outlines G-20 Priorities," *Wall Street Journal,* 8/26/10, http://online.wsj.com/article/SB10001424052748703632304575451820235798674.html?mod=WSJEUROPE_hps_LEFTTopStories.
50. Ari Shavit, "Barak to Haaretz: Israel Ready to Cede Parts of Jerusalem in Peace Deal," *Haaretz,* 9/1/10, http://www.haaretz.com/print-edition/news/barak-to-haaretz-israel-ready-to-cede-parts-of-jerusalem-in-peace-deal-1.311356. Thanks to John Stettin.
51. AFP, "Ashton Unable to Attend Mideast Peace Talks,"Google News, 8/28/10, http://www.google.com/hostednews/afp/article/ALeqM5gVij5PjtdbWbjtGmLoJpLLiUCngg.
52. Newscore, "Mideast Peace Envoy Announces Second Round of Peace Talks," *New York Post,* 9/2/10, http://www.nypost.com/p/news/national/secretary_clinton_opens_renewed_S6UqNXObSz0Ywdng1TivzI. Thanks to Christopher Mangan.

53. Paul Taylor, "Analysis: Sarkozy to Press Currencies Role for G-20," Reuters, 9/6/10, www.reuters.com.
54. "New Interface Could Increase Contactless Processing Speed," Squid, 9/7/10, http://www.squidcard.com/corporate/emoneynews/international/new-interface-could-increase-contactless-processing-speed502.html.
55. Alan Franklin, "Big Brother is Here," *The Departure: God's Next Catastrophic Intervention into Earth's History*, (Crane: Defender, 2010).
56. The book was released in 2010 by Defender Publishing and is available at www.amazon.com (http://www.amazon.com/Departure-Catastrophic-Intervention-Earths-History/dp/0984061169), as well as through other booksellers.
57. Baarak Ravid, "Lieberman Presents Plans for Population Exchange at UN," *Haaretz*, 9/28/10, http://www.haaretz.com/news/diplomacy-defense/lieberman-presents-plans-for-population-exchange-at-un-1.316197.
58. Natasha Mozgovaya and Barak Ravid, "Bibi: Israel, Palestinians Can Reach Agreement within a Year," Jewish Daily Forward, 9/28/10, http://forward.com/articles/131676/.
59. Thomas Erdbrink and Ellen Nakashima, "Iran Struggling to Contain 'Foreign-Made' Computer Worm," *Washington Post*, 9/27/10, http://www.washingtonpost.com/wp-dyn/content/article/2010/09/27/AR2010092706606.html.
60. "Skyline Movie," Teaser Trailer, http://teaser-trailer.com/skyline-movie/.
61. "San Francisco Riots Follow Giants World Series Victory," AOL News, 11/2/10, http://www.aolnews.com/2010/11/02/san-francisco-riots-follow-giants-world-series-victory/.
62. Associated Press, "Unemployment Offices to Add Armed Guards," The Indy Channel, 10/27/10, http://www.theindychannel.com/news/25539273/detail.html.
63. "Report: EU Leaders Pushing U.S. away from Israel 'and closer to the Arabs,'" World Tribune, 11/8/10, http://www.worldtribune.com/worldtribune/WTARC/2010/ss_israel1102_11_08.asp.
64. Barak Ravid, "Obama: East Jerusalem Building Plans 'Unhelpful'to Peace Efforts," *Haaretz*, 9/11/10, http://www.haaretz.com/news/diplomacy-defense/obama-east-jerusalem-building-plans-unhelpful-to-peace-efforts-1.323794.

65. Ibid.
66. Ibid.
67. "Canada 'Bruised' for Pro-Israel Stand?" Ynet News, 11/10/10, http://www.ynetnews.com/articles/0,7340,L-3981757,00.html.
68. "Obama Acknowledges decline of U.S. Dominance, *Times of India,* 11/8/10, http://articles.timesofindia.indiatimes.com/2010-11-08/india/28228910_1_largest-economy-globalisation-unemployment-rate.
69. "Beck Talks Faith in Rally Coinciding with Anniversary of King's Speech," CNN, 8/28/10, http://articles.cnn.com/2010-08-28/politics/glenn.beck.rally_1_glenn-beck-political-rally-lincoln-memorial?_s=PM:POLITICS.
70. Ibid.
71. James Herron, "Iraqi Gas Discovery Boosts EU Hopes of Gas Independence," *Wall Street Journal,* 1/26/11, http://blogs.wsj.com/source/2011/01/26/iraqi-gas-discovery-boosts-eu-hopes-of-gas-independence/.
72. "Russia, Turkey Sign Strategic Cooperation Protocol," People's Daily Online, 1/26/11, http://english.peopledaily.com.cn/90001/90777/90853/7268195.html.
73. Charles Levinson, "Israel to Launch State Fund Within a Year," *Wall Street Journal,* 1/26/11, http://online.wsj.com/article/SB10001424052748703293204576105830038749802.html.
74. A note of thanks to Jonathan Stettin for providing articles on these matters.
75. Gil Ronen, "Digging on Temple Mount 'to Erase Traces of Jewish Altar,'" Israel National News, 2/7/11, www.israelnationalnews.com/News/News.aspx/142187#.TwijTDU7Xko.
76. For a full copy of the report, visit http://www.imf.org/external/np/pp/eng/2011/010711.pdf.
77. Nicole Horrelt, "Union for the Mediterranean: Revives to Meet the Challenges of a New Middle East," Examiner, 3/7/11, http://www.examiner.com/canada-bible-prophecy-in-canada/union-for-the-mediterranean-revives-to-meet-the-challenges-of-a-new-middle-east. Thanks to Jonathan Stettin for help with information.
78. "World Bank Supports Palestinian State," PressTV, 4/7/11, http://www.presstv.ir/detail/173511.html.
79. Associated Press, "Palestinian Leader: There Will Be No New Uprising," Ynetnews, 4/20/11, http://www.ynetnews.com/articles/1,7340,L-4058986,00.html.

80. "Quartet May Recognize Palestinian State," Ynetnews, 4/20/11, http://www.ynetnews.com/articles/0,7340,L-4058472,00.html.
81. Editor's note: Mr. Hitchens passed away on December 15, 2011, at age 62.
82. Mick Brown, "Godless in Tumourville," *Telegraph,* 3/25/11, http://www.telegraph.co.uk/culture/books/8388695/Godless-in-Tumourville-Christopher-Hitchens-interview.html.
83. "Hamas Accepts 1967 Borders," *Haaretz,* 5/11/11, http://www.haaretz.com/news/diplomacy-defense/hamas-accepts-1967-borders-but-will-never-recognize-israel-top-official-says-1.361072.
84. Ibid.
85. Ibid.
86. See note 86.
87. "Atheist Hitchens Skips His Prayer Day," Drudge Report, 9/21/10, http://www.drudgereportarchive.com/drudge-report-topic/prayer%20day/.
88. Nia Williams, Paul Casciato, ed., "Heaven Is a Fairy Story for People Afraid of the Dark," Reuters, 5/16/11, http://in.reuters.com/article/2011/05/16/idINIndia-57043620110516, 5/.
89. "Israel's Netanyahu Keeping Mum about Obama's Virtual Arms Embargo," *World Tribune,* 2/10/11, http://www.worldtribune.com/worldtribune/WTARC/2010/me_israel0104_02_10.asp. Thanks to Jonathan Stettin.
90. Heather Haddon and Doublas Montero, "Doomsayer Confused as World Doesn't End," *New York Post,* 5/22/11, http://www.nypost.com/p/news/local/what_the_hell_ICUDxj5woqe2eg03U1voSK. Thanks to Chris Mangan.
91. Drudge Report, 5/31/11. Note: This article has been removed and is no longer in the website's archives.
92. Ibid.
93. Ibid.
94. Emily Kaiser, "China Warns U.S. Debt-Default Idea Is 'Playing with Fire,'" Reuters, 7/7/11, http://in.reuters.com/article/2011/06/08/idINIndia-57573120110608.
95. Ibid.
96. Associated Press, "China Overtakes U.S. as Top Energy Consumer," Salon, 6/8/11, http://www.salon.com/2011/06/08/eu_world_energy/.
97. Drew Zahn, "Police State, USA: Government Demands Keys to Your Kingdom," World Net Daily, 6/13/11, www.WorldNetDaily.com.

98. "Army-sponsored Report Suggests New 'Police Force' Domestic Agents Could Be Used in 'Shaping an Environment Before a Conflict,'" WorldNetDaily, 1/20/10, http://www.wnd.com/index.php?fa=PAGE.view&pageId=122533.
99. Ibid.
100. Jewel Samad, "Hackers Breach U.S. Senate Website," Yahoo! News Network, 6/14/11, http://ph.news.yahoo.com/hackers-claim-breach-us-senate-website-214520588.html.
101. Barak Ravid, "EU Pushing Peace Plan Based on Obama's '1967 Borders' Speech," *Haaretz,* 6/14/11, http://www.haaretz.com/print-edition/news/eu-pushing-peace-plan-based-on-obama-s-1967-borders-speech-1.367512.
102. Europe Union Times, "Obama Wants to Jail Americans with New Law," Gold Coast Chronicle, 1/15/11, http://www.goldcoastchronicle.com/politics/obama-wants-to-jail-americans-with-new-law/. Thanks to Jonathan Stettin.
103. Joel Richardson, "Turkey to Double Size of Its Army," WorldNetDaily, 7/5/11, http://www.wnd.com/index.php?fa=PAGE.view&pageId=318757. Thanks to Mike Hile.
104. Amiel Ungar, "Sovereign Debt Crisis Menaces Italy as Securities Tumble," Israel National News, 7/11/11, http://www.israelnationalnews.com/News/News.aspx/145604#.TwyQZzU7Xko, 7/11/11.
105. Tzvi Ben Gedalyahu, "Biblical Jewish Roots Irrelevant, Says PA Activist," Israel National News, 7/24/11, http://www.israelnationalnews.com/News/News.aspx/146005#.TwyU-jU7Xko.
106. Nasouh Nazzal, "Israel Seriously Considering Voiding the Oslo Accords," *Gulf News,* 7/25/11, http://gulfnews.com/news/region/palestinian-territories/israel-seriously-considering-voiding-the-oslo-accords-1.842734.
107. Declan McCullagh, "House Panel Approves Broadened ISP Snooping Bill," CNET News, 8/1/11, http://news.cnet.com/8301-31921_3-20084939-281/house-panel-approves-broadened-isp-snooping-bill/.
108. "Arab Spring," Wikipedia, http://en.wikipedia.org/wiki/Arab_Spring.
109. Robert Hutton, Ben Edwards, and David Goodman, "Cameron Recalls Commons as 525 Held After Three Nights of Riots," *Bloomberg Businessweek,* 8/9/11, http://www.businessweek.com/news/2011-08-09/police-deploy-in-force-to-stop-u-k-riots-commons-recalled.html. Thanks to Jonathan Stettin.

110. Martyn Brown, "Europe 'On Course to Become One Country,'" Express, 8/16/11, http://www.express. co.uk/posts/view/265048/Europe-on-course-to-become-one-country.
111. "Tea Party Europe: Sarkozy, Merkel Call for Balanced Budget Laws," Newsmax, 8/16/11, http://www.newsmax.com/Headline/merkel-sarkozy-balanced-budget/2011/08/16/id/407586.
112. Tzvi Ben Gedalyahu, "Blair's Sister-in-Law Incites Muslims to 'Liberate' Jerusalem," Israel National News, 9/28/11, http://www.israelnationalnews.com/News/News.aspx/147264#.TlukeV3h98F.
113. Charles L. Monk, Sugar Land Bible Church, "A Look at Bible Covenants and Their Meanings," Believer's Web, 2/22/03, http://www.believersweb.org/view.cfm?ID=29.
114. Herb Keinon and staff, "PM: Still Won't Apologize to Turkey over 'Marmara' Raid," *Jerusalem Post,* 9/4/11, http://www.jpost.com/DiplomacyAndPolitics/Article.aspx?id=236604. My thanks to Jonathan Stettin.
115. Lolita C. Baldor, Associated Press, "Barak: Israel-Palestinians Must Find Path to Talks," *Guardian,* 10/3/11, http://www.guardian.co.uk/world/feedarticle/9876752.
116. Michael Falcone and Emily Friedman, "Mitt Romney on Mormon Critic: 'Poisonous Language Doesn't Advance Our Cause,'" ABC News, 10/8/11, http://abcnews.go.com/blogs/politics/2011/10/mitt-romney-on-mormon-critic-poisonous-language-doesnt-advance-our-cause/.
117. *The Omega Letter Intelligence Digest,* Vol. 121, Issue 11, 10/11/11.
118. Cathy Lynn Grossman, "Will Romney, Perry Race Be Christian vs. Christian?" *USA Today,* 10/10/11, http://content.usatoday.com/communities/Religion/post/2011/10/mormon-romney-perry-cult-christian-/1.
119. Agence France Presse,"Pope to Promote Peace in Talks with World Religious Leaders," Capital FM News, 10/25/11, http://www.capitalfm.co.ke/news/2011/10/pope-to-promote-peace-in-talks-with-world-religious-leaders/.
120. Associated Press, "Vatican Calls for New World Economic Order," Fox News, 10/24/11, http://www.foxnews.com/world/2011/10/24/vatican-calls-for-new-world-economic-order/.
121. Yann Le Guernigou,"Sarkozy Tells Obama Netanyaho Is a 'Liar,'" Reuters, 11/8/11, http://www.reuters.com/article/2011/11/08/us-mideast-netanyahu-sarkozy-idUSTRE7A720120111108.

122. Dan Murphy, "Plenty of Apocalyptic Talk," *Christian Science Monitor,* 11/8/11, http://www.csmonitor.com/World/Backchannels/2011/1108/Ahead-of-Iran-nuclear-report-plenty-of-apocalyptic-talk. Thanks to Jonathan Stettin for information used throughout this entry.
123. *One India News,* 10/23/11, http://news.oneindia.in/2011/10/23/wouldstand-by-pakistan-if-it-is-attacked-by-anyonekarzai.html.
124. *Daily Mail,* 11/28/11, http://www.dailymail.co.uk/news/article-2066959/Iran-threatens-bomb-Turkey-U-S-Israel-attack-nuclear-installations.html.
125. Associated Press, *Washington Post,* 11/7/11, http://www.washingtonpost.com/world/europe/russias-military-chief-potential-conflicts-near-russian-borders-may-grow-into-nuclear-war/2011/11/17/gIQAWQTJUN_story.html.
126. Associated Press, *USA Today,* 11/24/11, http://www.usatoday.com/news/world/story/2011-11-23/North-Korea-South-Korea-military/51377434/1.
127. Jim Meyers, Newsmax, 4/5/11, http://www.newsmax.com/Newsfront/ElBaradei-Israel-War-Gaza/2011/04/05/id/391829.
128. Elad Benari, Israel National News, 11/28/11, http://www.israelnationalnews.com/News/News.aspx/150159#.TtPgJWPNltM.
129. "China Still a Threat, Former Official Says," *Taipei Times,* 8/27/11, http://www.taipeitimes.com/News/taiwan/archives/2011/08/27/2003511779.
130. "Egypt's Military Leaders to Appoint Council to Oversee Drafting of New Constitution," *Telegraph,* 12/8/11, http://www.telegraph.co.uk/news/worldnews/africaandindianocean/egypt/8942166/Egypts-military-leaders-to-appoint-council-to-oversee-drafting-of-new-constitution.html.